HOLIDAYS OF THE REVOLUTION

HOLIDAYS OF THE REVOLUTION

Communist Identity in Israel, 1919–1965

Amir Locker-Biletzki

SUNY PRESS

Cover image: Tamar and Yorm Gozansky. Palestinian and Jewish Banki members strike a heroic pose, Acra, 1951. Reprinted with permission.

Published by State University of New York Press, Albany

Printed in the United States of America

For information, contact State University of New York Press, Albany, NY
www.sunypress.edu

Library of Congress Cataloging-in-Publication Data

Name: Locker-Biletzki, Amir, 1973– author.
Title: Holidays of the revolution : communist identity in Israel, 1919–1965 / Amir Locker-Biletzki.
Description: Albany : State University of New York Press, [2020] | Includes bibliographical references and index.
Identifiers: LCCN 2020018352 | ISBN 9781438480855 (hardcover : alk. paper) | ISBN 9781438480855 (pbk. : alk. paper) | ISBN 9781438480879 (ebook)
Subjects: LCSH: Communists—Israel—History—20th century. | Jewish communists—Israel—History—20th century. | Communism and Judaism—Israel—History—20th century. | Nationalism—Israel—History—20th century. | Holidays—Israel—History—20th century. | Israel—Social life and customs.
Classification: LCC HX378.5.A6 L53 2020 | DDC 335.43095694/09041—dc23
LC record available at https://lccn.loc.gov/2020018352

10 9 8 7 6 5 4 3 2 1

Contents

Illustrations

Acknowledgments

The men and women of Israeli Communism, their struggles, achievements, failures, and flaws, have been the center of my intellectual life for sixteen years. My thanks go to those who opened their homes and memories to me and helped me understand the holidays of the revolution. I am also beholden to those who shaped my intellectual curiosity and encouraged my continued interest in the history, culture, and identity of the Communists in Palestine/Israel. Avner Ben-Amos, Alan McDougall, Meir Amor, and Anat Biletzki challenged and expanded my thought, making my work and this book better for it. Special recognition goes to Jasmin Habib, a teacher, a mentor, and a friend. Our ongoing passionate debates about the Communist Party—infused with her and my intimate knowledge and love for the men and women of the party—are reflected in *Holidays of the Revolution*.

Thanks are due to Csaba Nikolenyi for his encouragement and advice, which were vital for me to start writing this book. He, together with the infallible Jennifer Solomon, gave me the space, during my 2016–2017 year of fellowship in the Azrieli Institute of Israel Studies at Concordia University, to begin the road that ended in this book. I also owe a debt of gratitude to Rafael Chaiken, my editor, for steadfast support and patience that made this book possible. He and the staff of State University of New York Press deserve singular appreciation.

I want to thank Yael, my partner and the bedrock upon which my life stands. Without her help and love this book may well have not been written. Our children Eyal and Illy are and forever will be the love of my life. Underlying this book are the ideals of social justice and internationalist solidarity. I hope these values will be theirs as much as they are my own. My father did not live to see me publish this book and I am certain that it would have been a source of great pride for him. This book is dedicated to him.

Introduction

On a beautiful noon in May of 2009, a crowd of about 1,000 to 1,500 congregated at a Jerusalem mountain overlooking the ancient village of Abu Ghosh. Beside the stone monument in the foreground, overlooking the wooded valley below, stood a small podium decorated with a photographic image taken by Yevgeny Khaldei of a Soviet soldier waving the flag over the Reichstag. Behind it, in anachronistic defiance of post-1991 reality, the Israeli flag flew alongside the Soviet flag. The ceremony at the foot of the monument was simple, made up of speeches in Hebrew, Russian, and Arabic and the laying of wreaths. The audience consisted mainly of young Palestinians, many of them adorned in red and bearing the image of Che Guevara; Communist youth members in white shirts and red scarves intermingling with older party members; Arabs and Jews; and the representatives of the Russian delegation in Tel Aviv. At the end of the ceremony, the participants held a mass picnic, with the youth singing revolutionary songs in Arabic while engaged in barbecuing. This mixture of ritual and mass picnic commemorating the Soviet victory in World War II is organized by the Israeli Communist Party and its affiliated organizations, and it has taken place every year since 1950. This cultural practice and others like it lie at the heart of this book, which deals with the rites of the Jewish Communist subculture of the 1920s to the mid-1960s.

The basic premise of this book is twofold. First, I argue that the Jewish Communists developed a unique subculture of their own in the years 1919 to 1965. This subculture was formed in a process of negation and absorption vis-à-vis two local political cultures: the dominant Socialist-Zionist culture of pre-1948 Palestine, to the point that the Communists participated in the political culture around them as a dissident stance in Socialist-Zionist discourse, and the statist culture of the post-1948 State of Israel. Another influence that shaped the Jewish Israeli Communist subculture was the Soviet and East German cultures and the traditions of the European Left. Through its cultural practices, rituals, myths, and symbols, the Jewish Communist subculture disseminated its values among the members of the Communist Party and its youth movement. Second, I claim here that the cultural practices of the Jewish Communists were used to create a distinct Jewish-Israeli Communist identity, made up of Jewish traditional, Israeli local, and Soviet and left-wing European elements. This identity was created within the confines of the Communist subculture and outside the mechanisms that created a Jewish-Israeli native culture in Palestine/Israel.

The merger, in 1954, of MAKI (Israeli Communist Party) and Banki (Israeli Young Communist League) with the Socialist Left Party[1] led by Moshe Sneh was a watershed in both the political and cultural history of post-1948 Israeli Communism. I contend that this event upset the equilibrium between the local and universal elements in MAKI and Banki. In an attempt to give the party and its youth movement an Israeli character (in effect transforming it into a Zionist movement), the "Left Men" accelerated the adaptation of local Israeli elements at the expense of the Communist ones, thus contributing not just to the political but also to the cultural disintegration of MAKI.

Historiography of Israeli Communism

Communism in Palestine/Israel has drawn relatively thin scholarly attention, although scholars of different stripes have debated its history and created a small body of works about its different aspects. The Israeli Communist movement has been the subject of scholarly attention since 1948, beginning with the article "Communist Tactics in Palestine" by Martin Ebon.[2] The historiography of Communism in Israel can be differentiated into three groups: Zionist-Jewish historians; cultural historians, some of them post-Zionist and others not identified as such; and Palestinian historians. The main paradigm dominating the field is the question concerning the relation between Palestinians and Jews within the party. Historians of Communism in Palestine/Israel depict the Communist Party as having been perpetually torn between the national orientations of its members. Zionist historians argue that Communism inevitably clashed with Zionism and that the Arabization of the party after the 1929 riots prevented the party from becoming truly binational, that is, Palestinian and Jewish.[3]

By contrast, the Palestinian historians researching Communist history in pre-1948 Palestine claim that there was an ever-growing compatibility between Palestinian nationalism and the party. Driven by a desire to locate the Palestinian national movement's origins in progressive Marxism, they argue that the Arabization of the party gained it its first Palestinian followers. This process reached its peak in the 1943 split-up of the party when the Palestinian Communists set up their own faction, in fact integrating Communism and Palestinian nationalism.[4] Cultural historians for their part look at Palestinians and Jews as part of the same discourse, one that, despite the conflicts between Palestinians and Jews, featured cultural concepts that drew both sides together.[5]

Banki, the party's youth movement, has rarely been researched. This disregard reflects the emphasis that researchers of the Israeli youth movements place on the Socialist-Zionist movements, to the neglect of a movement like Banki, which existed outside the political consensus. There is one exception, the work by Jacob Markovizky, *White Shirt and Red Tie*. Markovizky's book is the first history of Banki and, though unpublished, is to be considered the foundation for future research.

In many ways, Markovizky shares the basic assumptions of Zionist writers on Israeli Communism. Though he recognizes the contribution made by Palestinian historians, he says that "it can be argued that the weight of those [Palestinian nationalists] was negligible in comparison to the inner Jewish process in the consolidation of the Communist Party in Eretz-Israel."[6] Despite its Zionist bent, his summary of Communist history is devoid of the virulent anti-Communism that some Zionist scholars indulge in.

Three main themes emerge from the detailed narrative of Banki's history constructed by Markovizky. The first is the attempt by ex-members of the Left party, mainly from the mid-1950s, to endow Banki with an Israeli character that would make the movement part of mainstream Israeli society.[7] A second point follows from this basic point, namely, the incompatibility between the national and the international. Markovizky portrays Banki as a movement torn between the growing desire of its Jewish members to be part of the national body, the international and socialist values that were an integral part of party ideology, and the growing national feelings of the Palestinian members. When it came time to choose between these value systems, most of the Jewish members awoke from the internationalist dream and preferred a growing affinity with Jewish nationalism. The third theme is the breakdown of the system of Palestinian-Jewish cooperation within the ranks of Banki and MAKI, making "the national conflict the main obstacle . . . in the development of the movement and its chances of surviving."[8] In that sense, Markovizky positions himself in the mainstream of this field. Markovizky's pioneering work marks the first time the full extent of Banki's history and activity has been explored. Nonetheless, the nature of his work, which presents an overview of the movement, precludes going into the details of the unique Communist subculture developed in Banki and MAKI. Another flaw in Markovizky's work that compels more research of Banki is his Zionist slant. In his introduction, he admits that "Rakah members who split from MAKI were reluctant to talk. Those who did talk were close-minded or developed a one-sided approach that sought to justify their historical and movement activity."[9] By the same token, it can be argued that those who remained in the Jewish MAKI developed their own justifications for their historical actions.

On the contrary, this book argues that MAKI and Banki had achieved an equilibrium between forms of a non-Zionist Jewish-Israeli identity that accommodated, to an extent, internationalist Socialism. It was the drive of these elements in Banki and MAKI that came from the Left party to—in effect—Zionize the Communist movement that contributed to the destruction of Banki and its mother party.

The History of Communism in Palestine/Israel

The identity formation process of the Jewish Communists with its rites, symbols, and myths took place as part of the history of the Communist Party—with its complicated and at times strenuous relations between Arabs and Jews. The history of the Communist Party in Palestine/Israel can be divided into five periods. The first, 1919–1924, witnessed the formation of an anti-Zionist Communist Party out of the far left of labor Zionism. The second, 1924–1929, was a period of attempts to create an Arab-Jewish Communist Party, while trying to form an effective ideology and political practice suitable for Palestine. The third stage of party history, 1929–1936, was characterized by the Comintern-ordered Arabization of the party. The fourth phase of party history, 1936–1943, presents one of the most politically unstable times in Communist history, when time after time tensions erupted between Palestinian and Jewish Communists. Unable to contain their differences, the Communists split twice in the 1930s and 1940s. This period of instability ended with the dramatic events of the 1948 War that opened the fifth period of party history; the era of the Arab-Jewish MAKI that ended with the 1965 split of the Communist Party.

The Rise of Communism in Palestine

The roots of Communism in Palestine can be traced to the contradiction between internationalist ideals, brought by the first Eastern European Jewish settlers, and the practices of Zionist Socialism, as seen when some members of the first Marxist party in Palestine, Po'aley Zion (Workers of Zion), voiced their concerns about the exclusion of Palestinian workers from the evolving movement.[10] To these local factors were added the repercussions of the 1917 October Revolution. The example of the Bolsheviks inspired those in the left-wing of Po'aley Zion to split the united party abroad between right and left:

> The official starting point for the Party can be traced back to 1919, when a small group of Jewish communists led by Yitzhak Meirson, M. Khalidi, and Gershon Dau, some of whom had arrived in the Second *Aliyah*, or wave of migration (lit. ascent), broke away from the *Po'aley Zion* (Workers of Zion) movement and founded the *Mifleget Poalim Sozialistit*, or MPS.[11]

Renamed for the 1921 Histadrut (the all-inclusive union that organized most of the Jewish workers) founding conference the Hebrew Socialist Workers Party (MPSA), it sent six delegates to the meeting.[12] In the convention the MPSA presented radical demands. It called for the separation of the union's economic enterprises from its trade union ones and for opening the union to Palestinian workers.

Still, the brief stint of MPSA as a legal organization was over that same year. In a tragic coincidence, MPSA's May Day parade clashed with its political opponents just as a Palestinian mob murdered Jews in Jaffa.[13] The British authorities reacted by blaming what came to be known as the 1921 Riots on MPSA, arresting and deporting many of its activists. The wave of repression resulted in the termination of the party as a coherent political body. Palestinian Communism was fractured into small squabbling factions. The action against MPSA also heralded the pattern of relations between the Communists and the British colonial state for the next twenty years. The Communist Party was pronounced illegal and became an underground persecuted organization. The relations between the Zionist Yishuv (Hebrew: "Settlement," the pre-1948 Jewish Zionist community in Palestine) and the Communists were set a year earlier. In January 1920 members of the Zionist-Socialist Ahdut HaAvoda (Labour Unity) had stormed the MPSA Workers Club in Haifa. In mid-February a group of students from Hertzeliya Hebrew Gymnasium violently upended a Yiddish play of MPSA's "club Borochov." The Communists became a pariah group, outcast from the formative institutions of Zionist settler society in Palestine.

The years 1921–1923 were marked by the emergence of a fully anti-Zionist Communist Party and its admittance to the Comintern. MPSA was still in many ways linked to its Marxist-Zionist roots in Po'aley Zion. The Jewish Communists viewed themselves as "part of Zionism, members of the Jewish national movement, and they did not see a way for building Eretz-Israel and Aliyah but through the social revolution."[14] MPSA did not depart from its "Palestinian centered self-image,"[15] endeavoring to create a Zionist-Socialist proletarian culture apart from the bourgeoisie one. However, the Comintern demanded that Jewish leftists flocking to its gates shed their Zionist garb in order to be recognized. By 1922 the two main Communist groupings in Palestine, the KPP (Communist Party of Palestine) and the PKP (Palestinian Communist Party) had started that process. In the PKP congress held in 1922, the party still adhered to some Zionist-Socialist principles—mainly Aliyah. But by 1923, at the second party congress—where the two main groupings of Palestinian Communism united—the unified PKP turned decidedly against Zionism. The program of the new party had "seen in the Arab national movement one of the main factors in the struggle against British Imperialism . . . it was also proclaimed that Zionism is a movement of the Jewish bourgeoisie that linked its fortunes with British Imperialism. This movement seeks new markets while exploiting romantic nationalism for its own economic gains."[16] This was enough to persuade the Comintern, and in 1924 the PKP became its Palestinian section.

In Search of an Arab-Jewish Party

When the PKP was recognized as a section of the Comintern, it was overwhelmingly Jewish. Many of its activists were former Zionists who had turned against Zionism both theoretically and politically.[17] The party's recognition by Moscow meant that it started to recruit Palestinians and tried to integrate with their anticolonial struggle. The most notable incident signaling the break with the Yishuv was the Afula Affair, where the PKP "had a central role in supporting Arab *fellahin* resistance"[18] to Zionist land purchases. This action brought on the expulsion of the Communists from the Histadrut, greatly diminishing its ability to approach Jewish workers.

The mid- to late 1920s were characterized by a continued effort by the PKP to recruit Palestinian membership. The acceptance of the PKP to the Comintern was conditioned on the Arabization of the party—meaning the enlistment of an Arab cadre that would reflect the demographic majority in Palestine. Nonetheless, the process was met with opposition within the party and with the limited response of Palestinians to the slogans of the Communists. The party did maintain some links to some considered by the Communists to be anti-imperialist and progressive Palestinian leaders. The party also planted the seeds of Communism in Lebanon and Syria as its delegates tried to recruit local support. However, the attempts to implement the Comintern policies of cooperation with bourgeoisie nationalists against imperialism had only moderate success.[19] By 1925 the proportion of Palestinian members in the PKP had moved to between 5 and 8 percent.[20]

As for the Yishuv, the PKP advanced the theory of Yishuvism. Developed between 1924 and 1928 by the foremost leader of the party in the 1920s, Wolf Averbuch, it was "basically 'pro-Palestinian' covered with extreme anti-Zionism."[21] Yishuvism rejected Zionism not only for being a bourgeoisie movement allied with imperialism, but because it was a hindrance to the economic development of Palestine. Immigration of Jews to Palestine was perceived as a deterministic process, an "objective necessity, the result of the political and economic conditions under which the Jewish masses in Eastern Europe live."[22] Affluent as well as poor Jews arrived in Palestine, creating a Marxist process of class differentiation and capital accumulation. This capitalist project was hindered by Zionism as a result of two contradictions. One was the fact that Zionism needed "feudalism, which enables it to purchase lands and create a separate Jewish economy."[23] But the emigration of Jews and the creation of the Yishuv "instigates an economic development that destroys the feudal conditions."[24] At the same time, Zionism aligned with the British colonial ruler—wishing to make Palestine into a colonial market for British goods, enacting heavy tariffs and taxes in order to inhibit the development of local manufacturing—and stifled the development of Jewish industry. Therefore the Jewish Yishuv should abandon the Zionist nationalist project. It is to join hands with the Arabs of Palestine in an anti-imperialist and anti-Zionist struggle for political and economic independence. This ideological dividing line between the Jews of Palestine and Zionism enabled the PKP to remain active in the Yishuv's elected bodies and among Jewish workers. While Yishuvism was officially condemned by the Comintern in the late 1920s, it reemerged, in different forms, among the Jewish Communists in years to come.

Arabization

The end of the 1920s was a watershed moment in the history of Communism in Palestine. The weeklong 1929 Riots in late August of that year shook the PKP to its core. At first the party's Central Committee issued a pamphlet that deplored the violence. It viewed the disturbances as a way for the Arab and Jewish ruling classes to divert the masses from the real enemy—imperialism.[25] Still, by October 1929, the Comintern rejected this view, describing the riots as part of a Palestinian anti-imperialist struggle—one that the PKP failed to recognize because it miscarried the Arabization of the Communist Party. In the wake of the 1929 Riots, the Jewish leadership of the PKP was mostly recalled to Moscow—where most of them would perish in Stalin's 1930s purges—and was replaced by a Moscow-trained leadership made up of Palestinian and Jewish native cadres. In 1930 the PKP Conference enshrined the Arabization in the party's platform. The Party Central Committee—by Comintern directive—had an Arab majority and the PKP vowed to redouble its efforts among Palestine's Arabs. These acts ended the first formative stage of Communism in Palestine, when the party had been comprised mostly of Jews and led by Jews.

The intensified pace of Arabization can also be attributed to a change of policy of the Comintern. In the wake of the 1920 Second Comintern Conference that ordered cooperation between Communists in the colonial world and non-Communist nationalists, the PKP attempted to contact those Palestinian nationalists it deemed progressive. As Stalin took over the Comintern—as part of his drive for absolute power—the organization directed the Communist parties outside Europe to undergo a process of indigenization. As a result, colonial Communists were to relinquish their ties to local nationalists. Palestine was no exception.

The formative era of Communism saw the official founding of a Communist youth movement in Palestine. Early in 1925 a plan was laid for a Communist youth section of the party by a young activist named Haim Davidovich. The young Communists were mostly preoccupied with attempting to radicalize members of Zionist-Socialist youth movements. The Communist Youth, as will be detailed later, attacked the attempts to create a Zionist secular culture, offering to replace Zionism with Marxist class theories. However, given the conditions of an underground organization, large-scale activities of Communist Youth were impossible. Only in the wake of World War II and the legalization of the party did a coherent and active youth movement appear.

The first half of the 1930s were marked with an increased surveillance and arrests of Communists. The British viewed the activity of the Communist Party as part of Soviet preparations for war against Britain. Palestine, with its strategic location on the road to the Persian Gulf and India, was an extremely valuable part of the empire. For these reasons, the British increased their repression of the PKP. In 1932, for instance, they arrested 210 suspects for Communist activity.[26] While Communism in Palestine was being repressed, the Soviets plunged into the bloody upheaval of Collectivization, the Five Year Plan, and the Moscow Trials. The PKP, for its part, continued to commend the "Socialist construction" in the USSR. The Soviets, in contrast, while controlling the affairs of the PKP, were not pleased at what they saw as the failure of the party to implement the Comintern's directives. The continued pressures on the party resulted in its political ineffectiveness. In fact, it failed to play a significant part in the 1933 wave of Palestinian protest. Some measure of stability was reachieved with the 1934 appointment of the first Palestinian general secretary of the party, the Moscow-trained Radwan al-Hillou, known by his nom de guerre Musa. Yet a new wave of arrests that included the new party leader furthered internal party volatility. Still, despite all the turmoil, the PKP started to make inroads into the then still small Palestinian working class, recruiting new members and penetrating the fledgling Palestinian labor movement.

The Breakdown of the Arab-Jewish PKP

The Arab Revolt (1936–1939), the largest anticolonial rebellion in the history of Palestine, raised, again, the tensions within the party. Since the forced Arabization of the late 1920s and early 1930s, tensions between the Jewish and Palestinian comrades had simmered beneath the surface. For instance, one Palestinian party member, Amin Aref, approached the Comintern in March 1935, asking to expel the Jewish members from the party. He argued that some of the Jewish leaders had "said that the Arab masses did not attain a sufficient consciousness in order to retain revolutionary ideas."[27] The outbreak of rebellion in Palestine was accompanied by yet another change in Soviet policy. Alarmed by the rise of Fascism in Europe, the 1935 Seventh Congress of the Comintern ordered the Western Communist parties to form Popular Fronts with Social Democrats and Liberals. In the colonial world, the Communists were directed to resume collaboration with nationalist forces. In Palestine that meant the Palestinian national movement.

At first the PKP sided with the Palestinian rebels, considering them anti-imperialist and progressive. The Jewish members—although some had indulged in sporadic acts of violence[28]—were directed by the Central Committee to assume political work in order to weaken Zionism. The Palestinian Communists participated in armed actions against the British. The increasingly radical views of the party alienated some of the Jewish Communists. A few retired altogether from political activity, others were expelled from the party. Another group of Jewish Communists traveled to Spain—away from the political and ideological complexities of home—to fight on the Loyalist side. Still, a number of Jewish Communists organized in 1937 into the Jewish section of the PKP. This group, known as the Emet (Hebrew: truth) group (for its newspaper), had by 1940 split from the party's Central Committee. This Jewish section developed some ideas that had reverberated among Jewish Communists since the 1920s. It argued that the Jews of Palestine had developed, as a product of capitalist socioeconomic changes, a national character. This new national group therefore deserved national rights within a unified Arab-Jewish Palestine. The Communists' immediate political task was to cooperate with some progressive groups within the Yishuv.

As the differences between Jewish and Palestinian Communists started to manifest themselves, the British Peel Commission offered the first of many partition plans for Palestine. The Communist Party rejected partition—oddly making common cause with the Revisionist Right and parts of the Zionist Labour movement—arguing that only reconciliation would solve the Palestine problem. The end of the Arab Rebellion consequently found the party fractured along national lines. Conversely however, the sorry state of the PKP changed when World War II started. At the outbreak of the war, the Communists blindly followed the Moscow line. In the wake of the Molotov–Ribbentrop Pact the PKP defined the war as an imperialist one—a war between two predatory imperialist groupings. The party's opposition to the war naturally unleashed on it the full fury of the

British, who were mainly concerned with the Communist efforts to disrupt recruitment to the British Army. This position was shared by the Haganah (Hebrew: defense), the main underground Jewish military organization in Palestine. Thus, to British suppression were added the Yishuv's own forms of exclusion, as "beatings and firings became day to day occurrences."[29]

The desperate state of Communism in Palestine/Israel changed dramatically on June 22, 1941. The Nazi attack on the USSR signaled the legalization of the Communist Party by the British—for the first time in twenty years the Communists emerged into the open. With the onset of legalization the Jewish section and the Central Committee patched up their differences. Consequently, from 1942 until 1943, Arab and Jewish Communists were part of the same organization.

The war brought with it far-reaching economic and social changes to Palestine. The needs of the British Army fighting in the Mediterranean theater of war stimulated an immense growth of Palestine's industry. The needs for foodstuffs and industrial goods heralded the industrial revolution in both the Palestinian and Jewish sectors of the economy.[30] Palestinian peasants became factory workers, giving the Palestinian Communists an opportunity to work among them in unions and cultural clubs. In addition, the growing prowess of the Red Army on the battlefield attracted a new wave of Palestinian activists, mostly Christian-Orthodox intellectuals. The Jewish comrades, on their part, turned to intensive activity in support of the war effort and the Soviet forces.

However, the legalization of the PKP and the reunification with the Jewish section did not end the tensions between Palestinian and Jewish Communists. In May 1943 they burst again into the open when the Palestinian members refused to support a strike of the workers in the British Army camps. The Arab members argued that the strike was announced by the Histadrut—a Zionist organization—and was therefore not to be supported. The issue came to a head on May 29, 1943, at the party's conference. Radwan al-Hillou ordered the dissolution of the PKP branches in Haifa and Tel Aviv that supported the strike, but weakened by the dissolution of the Comintern, leaving him with no real political base, he could not impose his will on the party. This move—part of the Soviets' efforts to placate their Western allies—deprived him of the organizational clout that had enabled his leadership. It also allowed Communist parties outside the USSR and Eastern Europe to accentuate their national character.[31] Despite attempts at reconciliation, a leaflet circulated in Haifa in the name of the Central Committee of the Palestinian Communist Party, asserting that "the Palestinian Communist Party is an Arab national party that includes within its ranks those Jews that agree with its national program"[32] and making the break final.

For the next five years Communism in Palestine was split between two national Communist parties. The Palestinian section formed the National Liberation League (Usbat al-Taharur al-Watani, NLL). The organization grew out of the involvement of the Palestinian Communists in cultural clubs and the Palestinian trade unions. While in its founding manifesto the NLL was not outright declared a Communist organization, its structural characteristics and reliance on urban workers and intelligentsia pointed to its orientation. The NLL positioned itself at the left-wing of Palestinian nationalism. Like the Arab Higher Committee (AHC), it objected to Jewish immigration to Palestine and the establishment of a Jewish state. Instead, it demanded an Arab national state in Palestine. However, in sharp difference to most Palestinian nationalists, the NLL insisted that the Jews of Palestine would have full civil rights. In contrast, the AHC maintained that all Jews who arrived in the country after 1918 should leave it. But the NLL was never entirely incorporated into the Palestinian political class. The leftist intellectuals with their workers constituency never entirely fit in with the traditional notable leadership. Part of the problem apparently lay in the demands of the NLL for democratization of Palestinian political life, directly criticizing the traditional autocratic ways of Palestinian leaders in patriarchal families that controlled Palestinian politics as heads of clientele and clannish networks.

The Jewish Communists reformed the PKP along the ideological lines of the Jewish section. The Jewish Communists recognized that the Jews of Palestine were developing into a nation with national rights. They called for the fulfillment of these rights in an Arab-Jewish democratic state. Still, the politics of the PKP showed an increased co-optation of the Communists into Yishuv institutions. In 1944 the party was readmitted into the Histadrut, after the organization lifted the ban on acceptance of individual Communists. The Communist Party participated in the elections to the Yishuv's elected bodies, becoming an integral part of the political scene. Naturally, also, the news of the Holocaust—personally touching many of the Jewish Communists, most of whom were from Eastern Europe—aroused national feelings among many of them.

As the Communist Party emerged out of illegality, a Communist youth movement was reestablished. In February 1942, at a conference in "Napoleon's Hill" in Ramat Gan, the Communist Youth was reestablished in a militantly anti-Zionist atmosphere.[33] The anti-Zionist zeal of the young Communists was not the only prevailing trend in the Communist Youth. Out of the youth movement's seniors emerged groups that even wished to harmonize Communism and nationalism. The most notable of these groups was officially named the Educational Communist Association in Eretz-Israel, or by its unofficial name, the Hebrew Communists.[34] It was established in 1945 by young Hebrew-speaking Palestine-born youth from the PKP. This was the first case where young Israeli Communists led a process of nationalization of Communism—which, as later events showed, led to a split from the Communist Party.

The Rise and Fall of MAKI

For five years—from 1943 to 1948—Communism in Palestine was divided along national lines. However, the escalating conflict between Palestinians and Jews brought another historical change: both Palestinian and Jewish Communists objected to the establishment of a Jewish state. However, this long-standing position changed in November 1947. At the United Nations General Assembly the Soviet delegate, Andrei Gromyko, supported partition if a unitary state could not be established in Palestine. The new Soviet attitude was further clarified by the Soviet consul in Washington, Semyon Zerfkin, who unequivocally supported the UN Partition Plan. The change in Soviet policy was adopted by the Jewish PKP that had already developed an ideological affinity with the Yishuv's national aspirations. The NLL, on its part, was torn between a majority that accepted the Soviet position and a minority that objected to it. In December 1947, in a dramatic meeting of the NLL secretariat in Nazareth, it recognized the UN Partition Plan. Those who opposed partition "were deposed from the Party and formed a more militant organization 'The National Liberation League, Northern District.'"[35] The official acknowledgment of partition by the Palestinian Communists led to reunification with the Jewish Communists approximately a year later.

As Palestine descended into wide-scale conflict, the Jewish Communists aided the Yishuv's war effort, using their connections in Eastern Europe. The Palestinian Communists turned to oppose the invasion of Palestine by the armies of the neighboring Arab states. But the war left the NLL in shambles. The mass deportation of Palestinians left it without many of its followers, its newspaper had been closed by the British at the outset of the war, and its activists were arrested by the Arab armies and later by the IDF (Israel Defense Forces), leaving it with only one choice. In October 1948, the NLL and PKP formed MAKI.

The unified party enjoyed some sympathy as a result of Soviet and Eastern Bloc support for Israel. However, with the worsening of Soviet-Israeli relations MAKI lost many supporters. In its eleventh conference in 1949 MAKI's platform combined a limited loyalty to the State of Israel and "support for the right of Arab refugees to return to the country and the right for self-determination of the Palestinian People."[36] Loyalty to the Soviet Union was reaffirmed when MAKI—in a move that eroded much of its support among Jews—uncritically followed the Moscow line regarding the Prague Trials and the 1953 Doctors Trial. Domestically, MAKI was concerned with supporting workers' struggles for the betterment of their work conditions in the context of the emergence of Israel's state capitalist system. Other campaigns the Communist Party was involved in were against the military government imposed on the Palestinians in Israel. By doing so the party became the lone voice that expressed the suppressed national yearnings of Palestinians in Israel. Yet when the party adopted the Soviet misgivings about Gamal Abdel Nasser's Pan-Arab nationalism, its Palestinian voters turned against it in the 1959 elections. Not until Soviet-Egyptian relations improved, in 1961, did MAKI regain and even increase its Palestinian electorate.

The reintegration of the Palestinian Communists into the Arab-Jewish Party did not mean that the recurring tension between the two groups was gone. Even though after the eleventh party conference the divergences between Jewish and Arab Communists were muted, they still existed. MAKI seemed to construct a consensus that enabled it to reflect the national feelings of both Arabs and Jews—advocating Palestinian nationhood and loyalty to the Israeli state with objection to Zionism. Nevertheless, a chain of events, regional and global, shook this agreement, shattering it to the point where the party could not contain the two nationalisms.

The first seeds of the division of Israeli Communism were sowed as early as the October 1948 unification. The Palestinian leaders had to undergo self-criticism repudiating the ideological doctrines of the NLL. This process was most harshly applied to Emile Touma, one of the most gifted Palestinian intellectuals of MAKI. Due to his objection to the partition plan, he was obliged to perform a humiliating self-criticism. In it he strongly renounced his prior principles and was removed from leadership positions within the party until the 1960s. Such events no doubt left their mark on future relations between Arab and Jewish Communists.

MAKI unity started to explicitly unravel after the mid-1950s, precipitated by a number of events. First were the shockwaves created by Khrushchev's speech and the resultant Destalinization leading to the 1956 Hungarian Revolution; its suppression by the Soviets brought about crises in all the Western Communist parties. Second was the growing split of World Communism between the Chinese and the Soviets, dividing Communist parties into Maoist and pro-Soviet ones, mainly in the developing world. Although both factions of MAKI remained loyal to the Soviet Union, the cracks in the Communist political and ideological monolith also enabled the cracks in Israeli Communism.

Nonetheless, local reasons played the more prominent part in the breakdown of MAKI. Moshe Sneh and his men joined the party in 1954. While numerically his followers were not many, they came from the cultural and political core of Zionist Socialism. As such, they arrived with symbolic capital that captivated many Jewish Communists. While they all ideologically rejected Zionism, their cultural and political inclinations remained in their original hearth. In their eleven years in the Communist Party, they tried to mold the party, and mainly Banki, the youth movement, in their own image. This attempt—in fact the Zionization of Communism—shook MAKI's core values, nationalizing it to the point that it lost its anti-Zionist uniqueness.

Next was the awakening of national feelings among the Palestinian Communists. Here regional events played an important part. The 1956 Sinai War ended with the political victory of Egypt and its president, Nasser. The wave of Arab Pan-nationalism that swept the region, culminating in the unification of Egypt and Syria in the 1958 UAR (United Arab Republic), effected the Palestinians in Israel. The growing nationalization of the Palestinian Communists and the growing inability of the party to embrace it was first indicated in the thirteenth party congress in 1957. The Palestinian leaders of the party pushed for a resolution recommending "that Israel will retreat to the 1947 Partition borders."[37] Under pressure from the Jewish leadership, a more moderate resolution was adopted where MAKI recognized the Palestinians' right of self-determination to the point of separation from Israel. The party also recognized the right of the refugees to return to their homes. To balance these radical demands, the Communist Party insisted on the Arab states' recognition of Israel and on a peaceful solution to all pending issues between them.[38]

The compromise achieved in 1957 did not put an end to the revival of a more assertive Palestinian national identity and the Zionization of the Jewish comrades. An incident in 1958 demonstrates this process. In a meeting of the Palestinian Communists at the veteran NLL leader Emile Habibi's house—recorded by Israel's Security Agency and presented to the Jewish leaders—the participants supposedly discussed an Algerian-style guerilla war. They also attacked the Jewish leaders personally.[39] Considering the fact that Jewish leaders were made aware about the meeting by an organization that kept surveillance on them and was adamantly anti-Communist, that Palestinians in Israel never attempted massed armed resistance, gives credence to the assertion that the alleged contents of the meeting is fabricated. At the same time, the whole affair points to the increased tensions that fragmented MAKI. While the 1961 MAKI fourteenth conference presented a more moderate platform and the party did well at the polls that year, the changes in Israeli politics in the 1960s accelerated the rift in the party. In 1963 David Ben-Gurion resigned as prime minister, to be replaced by Levi Eshkol. The departure of the staunchly anti-Communist Ben-Gurion was perceived as an opportunity by Sneh, who assumed that alliances with the Zionist left would increase the party's power. The Palestinian Communists, in contrast, held that the electoral future of the party lay with Arab voters, which meant a more pronounced anti-Zionist line. The mounting disagreements became an open division in 1964, when the party's general secretary Shmuel Mikunis tried to publish an article criticizing the speech of Algerian president Ahmed Ben Bella. In the speech—given when Ben Bella was awarded the Lenin Peace Prize—he called for the destruction of Israel. When *Al-Ittihad* (The Union), the Arabic newspaper of the party, refused to print the article, the divisions in MAKI became public.[40]

By the summer of 1965, the rift in MAKI had grown into an abyss that prevented the convening of a united fifteenth party congress and the two factions of Israeli Communism held separate conferences. The Jewish faction assumed the name MAKI while the Arab-Jewish section became Rakah (New Communist List). The Jewish MAKI drifted toward the Zionist mainstream, dissolving into the Zionist left by the mid-1970s. Rakah in its different manifestations is rooted in Israel's Palestinian electorate. The party remains the main far-left party in Israeli politics today.

Along with MAKI's rise and demise, we can also note the Communist youth movement that emerged after the 1941 legalization of the PKP and was reorganized after 1948. In contrast to the blue-shirted movements of labor Zionism, whose membership ended at the age of eighteen, Banki members remained in the organization until their student days, wearing white shirts and red ties. The movement was organized into seven districts, each with a regional committee elected by the district's conference. The district was subdivided into individual branches, each headed by a committee elected by the members of each chapter.[41] The highest institutions of the Communist Youth were the national convention, which elected the central committee every three to four years; the central committee ran the day-to-day activities of the movement. Importantly, all of Banki's institutions were elected democratically—in stark contrast to the Labour Zionist youth movements.

Differing also from the Zionist-Socialist youth movements, who set the ultimate goal of their members to establish a new kibbutz or to become members of an existing one—Banki concentrated on the plight of the downtrodden and of working youth, new immigrant youth, and Palestinians. The movement was unique in being an educational organization of Arabs and Jews. While most branches were not mixed, the interaction of Jewish Banki members with their Palestinian comrades was unprecedented. The internationalist ideology and practice of the young Communists were most evident in the struggle against the military government (1948–1966). Banki members were the first to oppose this travesty and pioneer a struggle that, by the mid-1960s, swept many on both the left and the right. Still another important area of activism for the young Communists was the ever closer relationship between West Germany and Israel. Banki members led the Communists' protest against the reparations scheme in 1952, up to the arrival of the first West German ambassador in 1965.

Obviously though, the Communist youth movement was not impervious to the tensions that split MAKI. The attempt at what was in fact the Zionization of Banki by Sneh's men, headed by his protégé Yair Tzaban, was a contributing factor to the demise of Banki. Out of the unified Banki two Communist youth movements emerged: one linked with the Jewish MAKI, the other with Rakah.

Written and Oral Histories of Israeli Communism

One of the problems that bedevil the scholarship concerned with Communism in Israel is the absence of primary documents that can reveal the inner workings of MAKI and Banki. Particularly lacking are those from the governing bodies of Communism, as well as local branches.

The deficiency of primary sources has been noticed by Markovizky. He noted that some party members were not interested in their party's history, so they did not take care of preserving it. Others "were used to underground conspiratorial types of activity."[42] Therefore they kept quiet about their activities, even destroying records. Another reason for the scarcity of primary sources is the result of the historical reality in which the party operated. Hence, "the persecution of the authorities . . . the arrests of activists"[43] disrupted any attempt to keep ordered accounts of the party. Furthermore, the dearth of archival documents can be traced to MAKI's place in Israeli politics. The Communist Party was a small party that moved from illegal underground to marginalized opposition. Unlike the Zionist Labour movement and its kibbutzim—most of the documents of MAKI and the PKP are located in their archival collections—that were either ruling parties or a part of coalition governments, the Communist Party lacked the resources to build and preserve its written history. In contrast to ruling Communist parties in the Soviet Union and Eastern Europe, the Israeli party lacked the state resources to build its own archive.

Consequently, the primary sources that inform this work originated from a number of sources. First are the archives of the Communist Party. Housed at the Yad Tabenkin archives that hold the documents of the Israel kibbutz movements are MAKI's documents from 1948 until the disappearance of the rump party in the mid-1970s. A second collection is the archives of the Israeli Labor movement located at the Lavon Institute. This archive includes collections of pre-1948 Communism.

With the flaws of the archival record in mind, the archives housing the documents of the PKP, MAKI, and Banki still provided vital sources for my research. Instructors' brochures, written by Banki members, detailing the texts and rites that were used to celebrate the holidays, contributed to my understanding of their roles. Handbills circulated by Communist activists—despite their public nature—gave me a revealing look into the inner beliefs of party members. Wall posters—both imagery and announcements of Communist events—offered profound comprehension of the day-to-day workings of Communist culture.

In order to offset the relative scarcity of archival materials, I approached other sources that added to the textual base of the book. The main subject matter of *Holidays of the Revolution* is the Communist holiday cycle in Palestine/Israel. These events were not private family events. Rather, Communist rite was public both within MAKI and Banki circles and in the public sphere beyond them. As such, they left their mark on the party's press.

Kol Ha'am was the public face, in Hebrew, of Israeli Communism in Palestine/Israel from 1937 to 1965. Its pages are filled with a wealth of information about the rituals of Israeli Communism. The newspaper carries detailed accounts of the public celebrations of the Communists—mainly the anniversary of the October Revolution, the celebration of the Soviet victory over Nazi Germany, and the most public of Communist ceremonials—May Day. An extensive documentary analysis covering all newspaper articles concerned with these holidays was achieved. The details gathered from the study of *Kol Ha'am* became—with the available archival papers—the basis for the reconstruction of the history of November 7, May 9, and May Day. Furthermore, MAKI's official daily did not just carry articles detailing the public holidays of Communism. It also provided important data concerned with the conduct of events that were not at the forefront of Communist political ritual. The attitude toward such Jewish holidays as Passover and Hanukkah was recorded in the culture section of *Kol Ha'am*, giving important insight into the way Communist intellectuals comprehended Judaism and its holidays.

To give more depth to the documents found in archives and the party's press, I turned to the memoirs and accounts written by Israeli Communists. Markovizky has pointed out the problematic nature of such texts. He describes "the first historiographical works about the Communist Party . . . [as] mainly apologetic and subjective. [They were] written by activists and close associates."[44] He notes that the writings of party members were partisan attempts at persuading the reader of the just aptness of the party. In contrast, I do not judge the texts penned by Communists harshly at all. There is no doubt that these texts were written from a subjective, at times misleading, point of view. At the same time, they represent an authentic voice. Marginalized and often persecuted, it was only natural that the Communist writers tried to justify their ideas forcefully. (One could just as well argue that works by Zionists concerned with local Communism were also written from a slanted partisan point of view . . .).

Beyond the written sources, I have endeavored to expand my knowledge of Communist festivity by using personal interviews with former or present members of the Communist Party. Using a snowball sampling, I located and approached several men and women. Their words gave the dry written accounts of rituals a "living tissue," representing themselves and others who took part in these events. They were, indeed, a tool to recreate the day-to-day minutiae of Banki and MAKI members. They described how party ideology, translated into ritual acts, consecrated the values of the

Communist Party in the minds and lives of its members. Most pertinently, these interviewees gave me access to documents absent from the archives. This element is mostly manifested in the chapters dealing with May Day and the celebration of the victory over Germany. With the courtesy of veteran Communists Tamar and Yoram Gozansky, I was also given rarely seen photographs that depicted May Day processions in the late 1940s and 1950s and an exceptional view of the party's victory parade in 1945. This visual evidence, some of which was seen neither in Israel nor outside of it, opens a window into the history described in this book.

Primary and secondary sources originating from archives, written accounts by present and past Communists, the Communist Party's newspapers, and personal interviews together constitute the empirical basis of *Holidays of the Revolution*. Taken together, interpreted, and analyzed, these sources were used to verily reconstruct the world of the Jewish Communists.

Continuity and Innovation in Research of Israeli Communism

One of the few historians to research the history of Communism in pre-1948 Palestine defined it as empty space in the research of Israeli history. There is a hint of exaggeration in this assertion, which deals primarily with the history of Communism in Palestine/Israel. However, the entirety of their efforts pales in comparison to the vast literature on European Communism in Germany and the Soviet Union. It is therefore indicative that in the recent histories of world Communism Israeli and Middle Eastern Communism merit not even a footnote.

This exclusion is unwarranted. After the introduction of Communism to Palestine in the 1920s, Communist parties sprang up in almost every major country of the Middle East. Among Palestinians, before 1948, Palestinian and Jewish Communists modernized and democratized Palestinian politics. After 1948, the Communists forged among the Palestinians left in Israel after the Nakba (Arabic: the Catastrophe; the Palestinian name for the 1948 War) a Palestinian community fighting for its rights within the framework of an exclusive Jewish state. Among Jews, the Communists are the oldest anti-Zionist political body in Israel. In the wake of the March 2020 election, the Communist Party, through its front Hadash (an acronym for the Democratic Front for Peace and Equality), is a vital political force and part of the Joint List (an amalgamation of all the Palestinian parties in Israel, made up of Communists, nationalists, and Islamists), which holds fifteen seats in the Knesset (the 120-member Israeli parliament). Some of the events portrayed in this research, namely, May Day and the Soviet victory celebrations, are still being held, presenting to the historian a living picture of continuity and change. Such an ability to survive and remain a fixture in Israeli politics and society, even to thrive in some small way in a country hostile to Communists, merits a closer look.

I look at the Communists from 1919 to 1965 differently from previous research on Israeli Communism. While I conform to the current tendency to view Israeli Communism from a cultural point of view, this research has as its focal point not Palestinian-Jewish interaction within the party, but the Jewish Communists themselves. The reasons for treating this group separately and as a relatively homogeneous group will be detailed shortly; nonetheless, this focal point is a departure from the Palestinian-Jewish paradigm that has dominated the field. The cultural take on the history of the Jewish Communists enables us to map, for the first time, the Jewish Communist subculture that evolved from the early 1920s to the mid-1960s in Palestine/Israel. With the political and organizational side given less emphasis, a more sophisticated view of Communism as a cultural entity emerges and a whole range of issues in the history of MAKI and Banki are seen in a different light. For instance, the connection to the Soviet Union emerges as not just organizational obedience[45] but as a deep cultural bond. The relation to Palestinians is seen apart from the framing of recruitment levels and politics as a unique way in which the Jewish Communists viewed the Palestinian Other. I place one locale of Israeli Communism in its proper context, on the one hand as part of a global movement that shared the same cultural motifs, and on the other hand as a product of its indigenous Israeli and Jewish roots.

Furthermore, I investigate the identity of the Jewish members of the party, looking at the way MAKI and Banki members became Communists, or more accurately, Jewish-Israeli Communists. This point of view, rarely attempted by scholars analyzing the history of the Communist Party, yields a different understanding of Communism. It and the people that adhered to its principles are viewed here just as much a part of Israeli society, though strongly dissenting against many of its Zionist norms. This kind of analysis gives us a new view of the history of Israel and the people that made it. Instead of the insider outlook of the Socialist-Zionist and even the right-wing Zionist, I present the view from the other side—the side of the anti-Zionist Socialist Jew.

I will argue, contrary to other scholars, that the Jewish Communists did away with the Zionist aspects of their ideology rather quickly; however, as for the rest of their history, they had to confront Zionism. Politically, they negated it completely, as will be explained later, that being a vital principle of party ideology. At the same time, the Jewish Communists did not exist in a void. They were surrounded by the hegemonic Socialist-Zionist culture of the Yishuv, and after 1948 by the cultural practices of the new Israeli state. In a long process that started in the early 1920s, the Jewish Communist subculture was infused with elements from Israeli culture. In that sense, although their political creed set them apart from mainstream Yishuv society, the Jewish Communists were nevertheless part and parcel of it.[46] Their reaction to Zionist culture, defined as a reinvented Jewish tradition with secular nationalist content, in all its modes varied during the long period from 1919 to 1965, from outright rejection, mainly in the initial stages of Communism in Palestine, to greater receptivity. As the Jewish Communists' co-optation of some aspects of Israeli society accelerated, the process of diffusion of Israeli motifs was hastened. At the end of this process in 1965, the equilibrium between the nationalist local and the internationalist Communist elements was disrupted, tearing Israeli Communism asunder.

Socialism and nationalism may have originated in Europe, but they were not confined to European soil. From the late nineteenth and into the twentieth century, the non-European world was penetrated by European ideas. To the Near East the ideas and ideals of Socialism were brought by Eastern European Jews.[47] It took time for Communism to make any headway among Palestinians, and its appeal to Jews, most of them Zionist or Orthodox, was limited. Nonetheless, throughout this history a constant, albeit small, number of ex-Zionists filled the ranks of Israeli Communism, and as the years went by a generation of native Israeli Communists grew up in Banki and MAKI. I show how a European framework of thought, Communism, was reflected in the rites, symbols, and myths of the indigenous and nonnative Israeli Communists. From that argument stems the premise that the second largest influence on the shaping of the Jewish-Israeli Communist subculture was Soviet and European.

Political ritual in the modern world has come down to us from the Middle Ages and the French Revolution. The ideologies of the modern age, like nationalism and Socialism, were disseminated through the use of symbols, myths, and rituals as cultural practices to create nations or call for a radical change in the social order. Within the confines of their own subculture, the emergent and mostly European Jewish Communists in Palestine since the 1920s developed a unique array of political cultural practices. Here I make the claim that those cultural practices were shaped by the two great cultural models toward which the Jewish Communists were inclined: the one local, Jewish, and indigenous, the other Soviet and European.

Borrowing from the tradition of European Socialism, the Bolsheviks shaped a symbolic, ritualistic, and mythical language that became the staple of world Communism. The small band of Jewish Communists adopted this language as part of their subculture from the early 1920s. A detailed history of the development of Soviet ritual culture will follow shortly. Nonetheless, here already it is requisite to note that the Hammer and Sickle, the Red Flag, the Sheaf of Wheat, the profiles of the leaders, the May Day and Revolution military marches all became part of Jewish-Israeli Communist subculture.

As Zionist colonizers arrived in Palestine from the late nineteenth century onward, the Zionist movement and mainly Zionist Socialism developed their own celebrations, symbols, and myths. Working with the traditional Jewish calendar, rich as it was with religious content, the Socialist-Zionists gave it a new-old nationalist slant. Taking holidays previously on the margins of the Jewish cycle, Zionism gave them a prominent place and nationalist secular meaning. Thus Hanukkah, a small and sidelined family celebration, became a public nationalistic rite designed around the myth of the Maccabees. Zionism developed a unique means of transmitting the values of the new nation being built in Palestine through monuments and distinctive theatrical and literary productions. Those and other examples of that cultural transformation will be dealt with later in more detail. Even so, I make the argument here that the Jewish Communists selectively used the cultural means and mechanisms created by the Socialist-Zionists in their own subculture. When, after 1948, new cultural practices evolved centering on the state, the Jewish Communists once again selectively absorbed rituals, symbols, and myths from their surroundings. Thus, the myth of the 1948 War, the Israeli national flag, the myth and celebration of Hanukkah, and many other elements eventually became part of the Jewish Israeli Communist subculture and identity.

"Elik," says one of the most famous lines in the post-1948 Hebrew literature, "was born from the sea."[48] Author Moshe Shamir's brother, who was killed in the 1948 War, became the most recognizable exemplar in the Israeli Jewish culture of the sabra (a desert prickly pear cactus and the name given to native Israeli Jews). The new Jew of the Zionist national revival was to jettison the baggage of Jewish life in Europe; he was to be a tabula rasa with no past. Likened to the Greek gods of antiquity, he would come from the sea.[49]

I deal with another type of Jew who came to Palestine with a distinctively European past. The Jewish Communists intentionally turned away from the Zionist revival project and developed an identity that included local as well as European elements, reflected in their rites, symbols, and myths. That identity was made up of three main layers: the first Jewish, the second Israeli oriented and very local, and the third Communist. This division into distinct layers is made for the sake of convenience, as in reality those identities converged and overlapped with each other. Thus, a Jewish Communist identified with the Holocaust of his brethren in Europe as a Jew, celebrated Israeli independence as an internationalist anti-imperialist, and identified with Soviet victory in a local setting befitting a Zionist Israeli rite.

This book is primarily structured around the main holidays celebrated by the Jewish Communists. Starting with the Jewish traditional holidays, it ends with the way the Jewish members of MAKI and Banki celebrated and symbolized their relations with their Palestinian comrades. The first chapter lays the ground for the rest of the book, analyzing the historical agents underlying the book—MAKI, Banki, and the Jewish Communists. It briefly describes the Soviet, East German, and Zionist ritualistic traditions.

The next chapter examines the ritualistic, symbolic, and mythological aspects of Israeli-Jewish Communist identity—as they relate to the Jewish holidays of Hanukkah and Passover. I claim that by using elements of Jewish tradition deemed progressive, a Communist Jewish identity was developed. From there the book moves, in chapter 3, to an exploration of the Israeli civic calendar, namely, Israel's Independence and Holocaust days, and the way the Communists connected to them. While Israeli independence was framed by the anti-imperialist ideology of MAKI, the Holocaust was understood by the Jewish Communists along the narrative of armed resistance that was prevalent in 1950s Israel.

Chapter 4 investigates the way the Jewish Communists interacted with the developing Jewish working class in Palestine/Israel. I argue that while the Jewish members of the party did not recruit many workers and did not develop a working-class identity, they had a strong identification with the working man. That sympathy was strongly expressed in the Communist May Day rite and symbolism.

In chapter 5 I study the cultural interaction between the Jewish Communists and the USSR. The connection between the superpower and the small MAKI is studied along pseudo-religious lines. I contend that a study of the symbols, ceremonies, and myths around the anniversary of the Russian Revolution and the May 9 victory day over Nazi Germany lays bare the Jewish Communists as believers. The revolution and the Nazi-Soviet war were presented as cosmological events that changed the course of human history—any criticism of the Soviet Union was branded blaspheme.

The sixth chapter departs from the investigation of the holidays of Israeli Communism. It is an exploration of the symbolic, mythic, and ceremonial aspects of the relations between Jewish and Palestinian Communists. In that chapter I maintain that the Jewish comrades developed a positive stereotype of Palestinians, one that describes them as partners in an anti-imperialist and anti-Zionist struggle and subject of a struggle for civil rights—while unwittingly failing to recognize their emerging national identity.

Chapter 1

Basic Concepts and Political Ritual

Basic Concepts

At the heart of this research stand four concepts. The first is the human collective that is the subject of this research, the Jewish Communists; the second is their organizational edifice, MAKI and Banki; the third is Communist anti-Zionism; and the fourth Israeli nationalism.

From 1919 to 1965, the Jewish Communists practiced a defined subculture, made up of Soviet and European as well as Israeli and Jewish elements, which were reflected in their rites, symbols, and myths. In the Israeli historiography and sociological historiography there are few references to the existence of a Communist subculture. Baruch Kimmerling argues that the only autonomous spheres in 1950s Israel were the marginalized Orthodox community in Jerusalem and the "subculture created by the Arab-Jewish Communist Party."[1]

Yet if one gazes into its inner workings, a more complex picture emerges. Beyond the unique and important place that Arab-Jewish fraternity held in it, the Communist subculture existed in constant relation to other cultures. The two major cultural influences on it were the Soviet and Socialist-Zionist. From the time of the revolution in October 1917, the Bolsheviks created symbols, rituals, and myths that became the universal language of World Communism. This system of symbols, codified by the Soviet state, was adopted by the Jewish Communists in Palestine/Israel. Thus their subculture came to include cultural practices such as May Day parades, the myth of the October Revolution, and such symbols as the Hammer and Sickle, among others.

The collective that is the subject of this research is comprised of the Jewish Communists. MAKI and Banki of the 1950s and early 1960s were multicultural organizations. In them emigrant cultures from Bulgaria, Poland, Germany, and Russia mingled with the Palestinian and local Israeli ones. The multiethnic character of the party is supported by the statistics on MAKI. In a 1961 census 54.6 percent of the membership came from Europe, 11.4 percent from Asia, 3.1 percent from Africa, and 1.1 percent from America. That contrasted sharply with the only 29.8 percent of Israel- or Palestine-born Communists, most of them Palestinians.[2] So while they were not the politically dominant group in an organization that self-consciously promoted Palestinian-Jewish equality, they were definitely the largest. Moreover, despite their different cultural tastes, the Jewish members of MAKI and Banki were bound together by party ideology. As will be shown, the Jewish Communists conveyed the same ideological messages about core issues such as Arab-Jewish fraternity, the USSR, and class politics. When analyzing subjects like the Jewish holidays, Zionism, or Israel, they used the ideological terms of Marxism-Leninism. Therefore, despite their cultural differences, the Jewish members of MAKI and Banki shared a common Marxist-Leninist worldview that made them one group.

The Jewish Communists, the subjects of this research, organized in two institutional frameworks from the early 1920s to the mid-1960s, MAKI and its youth movement Banki. One of the points arising from the history of MAKI and Banki is that the Communist mother party had little organizational control over its youth movement. I argue here that notwithstanding the organizational relations between MAKI and Banki, they should be treated as one political, ideological, and above all cultural entity. There was a cultural affinity between them, bonding the elder and younger Communists.

This study deals at great length with the Jewish Communists' relations with Zionist political culture, both during and after the pre-state era. In the pre-state era, one could argue that the Communist Party and its youth movement were both anti-Zionist. When one looks at the Jewish Communist subculture, however, it is hard to avoid the Israeli and Jewish elements that constituted it, especially as regards the way the Jewish European Communists dealt with the 1948 War and the Holocaust. Did the Jewish Communists actually become Zionists in a gradual process from the early 1920s to the mid-1960s? In contrast to such scholars as Johan Franzén and Lea Miron,[3] who have argued that the Communists in Palestine/Israel became increasingly Zionist in all but name, here I claim that the

Communists were anti-Zionist for most of their history. While the content and degree of their anti-Zionism changed, they remained steadfast until the mid-1960s. When nationalism overshadowed their Socialist anti-Zionism, the organizational integrity of the party collapsed.

The Communist Party defined Zionism from the 1920s as a manifestation of the Jewish bourgeoisie and financial capital. In a 1930 letter from the Comintern political secretariat to the PKP, Zionism's link to British imperialism is clearly defined. "The Jewish bourgeoisie is the main agent of British imperialism in Palestine . . . Zionism revealed its true nature as an expression of the Jewish bourgeoisie's desire for exploitation, expansionist nationalism and oppression."[4]

The same basic definition of Zionism was reasserted in 1961 by Samuel Mikunis. In a report to the Fourteenth Party Congress, he stated that "Zionism is the ideological tool of the Jewish bourgeoisie in the era of imperialism and the link between it and imperialist reaction."[5] The same condemnation was extended to Zionist Socialism in all its forms. The party viewed it as no more than a ploy by the Jewish middle class to deceive Jewish workers. As for Marxist Zionism, it had no ideological validity for them. On the whole, they pointed out that the Zionist content of the movement always outweighed any Socialist content.

Zionist Socialism was the hegemonic political faction of the Yishuv era and of the state of Israel until 1977. The Socialist-Zionist movement that had been developing since the early twentieth century in Palestine encompassed the kibbutzim, the workers parties, and youth movements, and it wielded enormous economic power in the hands of the Cooperative Workers' Company that was controlled by the all-inclusive union, the Histadrut. By the early 1930s, Zionist Socialism had become the hegemonic political, cultural, and economic power in Jewish Palestine and the World Zionist movement. In the first decades after 1948, Zionist Socialism preserved its hegemonic position and was the politically dominant power in Israel.

Ideologically, Zionist Socialism was supposed to be a harmonization of Jewish nationalism and Socialism; in fact, however, the two ideological political forces of Labour-Zionism—the one emanating from the unification of the right-wing Ahdut HaAvoda[6] with Hapo'el Hatza'ir (Young Worker), and the other originating in Hashomer Hatza'ir (Youth Guard)—both relegated Socialism to a subordinate role in the aims of political Zionism. In offering this statement, I accept the historical account of Zeev Sternhell[7] regarding the preeminence Zionist Socialism gave to nationalism over Socialism. He argues that from their origins in the second Aliyah,

Labour-Zionists promoted a form of organic nationalism. This type of nationalism, prevalent in nineteenth-century Central and Eastern Europe, perceived the nation in terms of ethnicity and territory. This same organic nationalism was promoted over the Marxist ideology some Zionist Socialists brought with them from Europe. Sternhell's arguments cannot be easily dismissed.[8]

In origin, Hashomer Hatza'ir was heavily influenced by the anarchism of philosopher Martin Buber and Pyotr Kropotkin and the Socialism of Gustav Landauer. However, from 1924 onward it developed a Marxist-Zionist ideology that was formulated by 1927 in the Two Stage Theory. Zionism was defined as "the complete rehabilitation (of the Hebrew People) by the establishment of a Socialist society in Eretz-Israel, which will be realized in two stages: 1) establishment of the Hebrew national home in Eretz-Israel on an independent economic basis; and 2) the Socialist Revolution." The Socialist stage was defined in Marxist terms: "The new Socialist society will be built upon the training and education of the working class toward the seizure of power and the management of the economy and production on the one hand, and the destruction of the existing order on the other hand."[9] Despite the Marxist rhetoric it invoked, the Two Stage Theory was able in reality to indefinitely postpone the realization of the Socialist revolutionary stage. Hashomer Hatza'ir and its settlement movement and successive political parties concentrated on achieving nationalist aims in the 1930s and 1940s, subordinating their Marxism to their Zionism.

MAPAI (Workers of Eretz-Israel Party), which first appeared as a unified party in 1930, went even further in its subordination of Socialism to Zionism. Over the course of the 1930s and 1940s and into the first decades of statehood, MAPAI was the focal point of political and economic power. It was the dominant party in the Histadrut, in the Jewish Agency, and in the world Zionist movement. It was the center of governmental power, heading every Israeli government until 1977. Ideologically, MAPAI developed a form of nationalized Socialism that combined non-Marxist Socialism and Zionism. MAPAI preached the building of workers organizations that would be financed by national funds controlled by the Zionist middle class in Europe. Thus, Zionist Socialism—or, in the ideological jargon of the party, Constructive Socialism—was regarded not as a Socialist vanguard in the class war, but as a national elite meant to rejuvenate the Jewish people. The rejection of Marxist Socialism and the preference for Zionism are evident in the words of MAPAI's historian, Meir Avizohar:

> From the approach of Constructive Socialism, it was concluded that the problem of the Jewish workers in Eretz-Israel was in essence different: capitalism was not the reality they wished to change, but the *galut*. The change was to be accomplished not by revolution and correction, but in exiting. Whoever left the *galut* and came to Eretz-Israel would not find an existing society and economy, which had to be seized, but a largely uninhabited country. Talking about an Eretz-Israeli revolution against the Jewish capitalist class, or against British imperialism, between the wars is *preposterous* empty talk.[10]

These ideological tenets resulted in interclass peace between the labor movement and the bourgeoisie, cooperation with the British, and the exclusion of Palestinians. They constituted the ideological divide that separated Communism from Zionist Socialism from the 1920s to the mid-1960s.

Already in the early twentieth century the contradiction between Zionism and Socialism emerged when the first members of Po'aley Zion arrived in Palestine with their Borochovist ideology. The right wing of the party struggled to shape the politics of its Palestine branch in 1907 in accordance with the tenets that would later form the core of Constructive Socialism. However, not all members of the party agreed with the preference for the nationalist over the Socialist: "How are we to more tightly combine the idea of international proletarian solidarity with the national competition against the Arabs . . . one of the two: if we are 'real' internationalist Socialists, we must not push out foreign workers because we are all brothers and comrades against capital and its rule."[11] When those Po'aley Zion members that opposed the right-wing Ahdut HaAvoda formed the MPS in 1919 to 1920, their preference for internationalist Socialism was declared in a programmatic article:

> Socialist Palestine will be built on a sound economic alliance with the mass of Arab toilers. Our Socialism means one Socialist economy for the whole country and its populace. We do not believe in "Socialism" only for one part of the population. Our demands and slogans must concern all the workers of Palestine. The wall that was erected between Arab and Jewish workers by the bourgeoisie and social-traitor elements must be replaced by a Socialist alliance.[12]

The formation of the PKP and its acceptance as the section of the Comintern in Palestine marked the formulation of its anti-Zionist ideology. Zionist Socialism was defined not only as preferring the nation over the class, but also as a tool in the hands of the bourgeoisie. Thus, Jewish Communist anti-Zionism, which originated from the doubts concerning the compatibility of Zionism with Socialism, became part of a wider Marxist analysis. According to a pamphlet:

> Zionism is a movement that expresses the aspirations of the Jewish bourgeoisie that wants to create its own market, for which purpose it exploits nationalist romanticism. Zionism is linked to British imperialism, and economically to the Zionist colonization project that is based on acute exploitation. All the actions of the Zionist organizations are preparing the ground for capitalist settlement at the expense of the exploited masses. All those parties (like Ahdut HaAvoda and Hapoel Hatzair) that talk about Socialist settlement are making it easy for the Zionist bourgeoisie to achieve its aims.[13]

The 1930s were characterized by the persistence of the basic anti-Zionist tenets that were formulated in the 1920s. The resolutions of the Seventh Party Congress, which accelerated the Arabization of the PKP in the aftermath of the 1929 Riots, give clear expression to the anti-Zionist line of the party. Zionism, according to the Communists, was being used by the Zionist bourgeoisie to transform Palestine's Jews "into a tool for the oppression and control of the Arab workers."[14]

The early 1930s and the first years of the Arab Revolt saw a continuation and radicalization of the strong anti-Zionist ideology formulated since 1924. However, by 1937 the Jewish section of the PKP began a reassessment of the anti-Zionist policy. Driven by what they saw as a growing Palestinian nationalist movement, which was destroying its progressive nature when parts of its leadership sought support in Nazi Germany and Fascist Italy from the late 1930s, the Jewish section argued for a more sophisticated approach to the Yishuv and to Zionism, all the while agreeing to the basic policy of the PKP regarding Zionism. A 1940 document of the Emmet faction, which emerged from the Jewish section and splintered from the party, formulates the Jewish Communists' understanding of Zionism in the latter part of the 1930s. The document deals with Communist activity within various organizations of left-wing and liberal Zionists aimed at Arab-Jewish understanding. In accordance with the PKP line, the Jewish Communists describe Zionism as a tool in the hands of British imperialism used to separate Arabs and Jews and to blur the class war and the liberation struggle of Palestinians and Jews alike. However, on the question of Zionist Socialism, the Jewish Communists softened their approach. For them there could be a distinction between progressive and reactionary forces within Zionism. Thus, it is possible to turn "reactionary Zionism" into "Zionist Socialism," as long as this Zionism remains in the nonnationalist context of Socialism, or, in their words, is a Zionism "that recognizes the cooperation between the peoples as a stipulation for unmitigated class warfare."[15] Despite the contradiction to the more radical line that originated in the 1920s, the Jewish Communists still believed they remained within the boundaries of Communist anti-Zionism. They continued to give preference to Socialism over Zionism, albeit in more moderate form.

The 1940s were marked by further moderation of the Jewish Communists' anti-Zionism. In an article summarizing the party's policies in the aftermath of World War II and before its ninth conference, PKP secretary Shmuel Mikunis presented a new view of Jewish nationalism and Zionism. The PKP now voiced the views first formulated in the late 1930s. The Jewish Communists argued for the recognition of the national rights of the Yishuv within a binational Palestine. They recognized the right of the Jews of Palestine to a National Home, which they viewed as Jewish self-rule in a single Arab-Jewish state. This vision contradicted the Zionist demand for a Jewish state, which became open in the Biltmore Plan of 1942. The Jewish Communists still maintained the link between Zionism and British imperialism, but in contrast to earlier formulations, Mikunis asserts "that lately the British imperialists have not been using the Zionist movement as the *principal tool* [emphasis in the original] to realize their policies in Palestine and the Middle East."[16] In effect, by moderating their approach to Zionism, the Jewish Communists made an ideological adjustment that enabled them to argue in favor of a non-Zionist Jewish nationalism accommodated in a binational state.

This retreat from the anti-Zionist hardline enabled the Jewish Communists to accept the 1947 Partition Plan and join in the Israeli war effort. Despite the growing integration of the Jewish Communists into the Yishuv and their moderation of their anti-Zionism, they never became ardent Zionists. At times, the old analysis of Zionism, most particularly Zionist

Socialism, reasserted itself. On the occasion of the twenty-fifth anniversary of the Histadrut, Mikunis comes back to the basic rift between Socialism and Zionism:

> The workers and the Histadrut were not founded as one. The founders made it into a colonizing tool and decorated it with the right ideology and clung to it until the present time. In a backward colony and under the protection of imperialism, the role of establishing a "new society," of the realization of "Constructive Socialism," and building "The General Commune of the Workers of Eretz-Israel" was presented to "the barefoot and hungry" as the way to solve the Jewish question.

The building of Jewish Palestine was accomplished, Mikunis continues, in order to conquer "a living space for her majesty the bourgeoisie," and all in an effort to "mask the charms of the world revolutionary movement, to twist the struggle of the worker, to prevent the creation of a freedom-loving force, one of proletarian solidarity and fraternity between the peoples for the liberty of the Arab and Jewish masses."[17]

Even as the Jewish Communists recognized the validity of the Jewish nation in a binational Palestine, moderating some aspects of their anti-Zionism, they still clung to the main elements of the 1920s anti-Zionist ideology. The 1950s were marked by continued duality in MAKI's line toward Zionism. In the *Kol Ha'am* trial, Mikunis persisted with the anti-Zionist nationalism formulated by the Jewish Communists since the late 1930s. The ideological commitment to Zionism was replaced by loyalty to the state as the aspiration of the Jewish-Israeli nation. When asked how MAKI related to the state, Mikunis answered: "MAKI's relation to the state is positive. The party fought for Israeli independence."[18] As opposed to the Zionist perception of the Jewish state as a tool for Jewish immigration and of national revival, the Communists saw the independence of the state as its main attribute. When MAKI proposals for the text of the Declaration of Independence were debated, the party demanded that the word "independent" be added in every place where the words "Jewish state" appeared. The independence of the country—in the Communist context, from imperialism—was as important as, if not more important than, the Jewish nature of the state as a basic tenet of Zionism.

This book is, in essence, a historical narrative of the nationalization of the Jewish Communists. In more precise terms, it is the story of the

Israelization of parts of the Communist Party, not an account of the *Zionization* of the Communist Party. Since the late 1930s many of the Jewish Communists had acknowledged the presence of a Jewish national minority in Palestine. While accepting the negative stands of Soviet Communism toward Jewish nationalism,[19] party ideologists in the 1950s used Stalinist concepts—to denationalize World Jewry and nationalize the Jews in Israel.

Stalin qualified the status of a nation only to "a historically constituted, stable community of people, formed on the basis of a common language, territory, economic life, and psychological make-up manifested in a common culture."[20] With Stalin's rise to power in the Soviet Union making him the sole interpreter of Marxism-Leninism, his views became Soviet dogma. Needless to say, the Jews, lacking a shared territory, economy, and language, were disqualified as a nation in the eyes of Stalinists. However, in the hands of Jewish Communists in Israel they became Stalinist markers of a Jewish-Israeli nation, creating an Israeli national identity. One outstanding example of this use is party leader and ideologue Moshe Sneh.[21]

In his 1954 text, written on the eve of his and his followers' entry to MAKI, Sneh refutes Zionism in order to justify a local Israeli national identity detached from Zionism. Right at the outset, he contends that the book will "help to understand, on the one hand, the bourgeois, reactionary nature of Zionist ideology, and on the other hand to understand our affinity to the motherland as Israeli patriots, as the guardians of national independence."[22] He starts with a sweeping survey of the development of the nation in Marxist terms from prehistory to modernity. When he gets to the section titled "The Bourgeois Nation," he follows Stalin's readings. This is clearly evident in the following words: "The nation was historically formed as a result of the territorial, linguistic, economic and cultural association of a stable community of people; as an outcome of capitalist development."[23] In the transition from a feudal to a capitalist system the formation of nations is not yet complete. Mainly in the colonial world, where capitalism is not fully formed, feudal relations still survive.

Moving on from the more theoretical parts of his analysis, Sneh approaches the history and national development of the Jews. After asserting that "Jewish history is like the history of any people: the history of the socioeconomic formations that the people went through during its development,"[24] he proceeds to chart a Marxist history of the Jews. His detailed analysis culminates with a disavowal of the Jewish and Zionist national idea of an extraterritorial eternal nation. Here, again, Sneh uses Stalinist language: "Any talk about all contemporary Jews worldwide as one nation is a mockery of reality, truth and common sense. Historical materialism has proven that only the combination of four shared markers historically formed in a stable community—territory, language, economy and culture—creates the nation."[25] From the arguments about the globalist nature of Jewish nationhood, he turns to the main target of his polemics: Zionism. In a chapter titled "Zionism—The Means of the Jewish, Israeli and Imperialist Bourgeoisie," Sneh uses imperialism as his theoretical weaponry against Zionism. He opens with a class definition of Zionism. It is, he proclaims, "the principal nationalist reactionary ideology of the Jewish bourgeoisie."[26] He then launches into an extensive historical survey of the Zionists' dealings with various powers.

From this basic definition, Sneh goes on to chart a historical narrative of the links between Zionism and imperialism. He argues for links between Zionism and the Ottoman, French, German, Russian, and British empires. In regard to French imperial intentions in the Levant, he claims that the Baron de Rothschild, while in effect turning the Jewish colonies in Palestine into underdeveloped farms and plantations built on cheap labor, actually meant to use them to channel French capital and influence to Eretz-Israel and the Near East. Still, the Zionist movement preferred to link with Britain. Recounting the history of Zionist-British relations, Sneh asserts that "the Zionist movement, from its origins, offered itself as a tool to different imperialist powers, and became at the end of World War I and afterwards a tool in the hands of British imperialism."[27] As British business interests moved into Palestine, the Zionist movement and its leadership became subordinate to British imperialism. When the dependency was no longer possible, the Zionist movement increased its links with American imperialism, subordinating Israel to it after 1948. At the end of this line of argumentation, Sneh manages—in keeping with his ideological preferences—to disavow Zionism and its underlying assumptions as a legitimate national movement. But at the same time that he disavows one form of nationalism, Sneh accords acceptability to another.

In a section titled "Aliya, Settlement, Independence—This Is Not Zionism," he rejects the notion that Zionism is the prime mover behind the Yishuv and Israel. This idea is "a false perception borrowed from idealistic thinking." He sets out to prove that it was "not the Zionist idea [that] 'created' the aliya, settlement, defense, and independence." Rather, it "was formed by the class needs of the haute bourgeoisie."[28] The immigration to Palestine was not ideologically motivated, nor was it an answer to the Jews' plight in the form of the Zionist Ingathering of the Exiles. It is part of the larger sweep of Jewish and global migration, mainly from Europe to the New World. Sneh sees the economic growth of the Jewish presence in Palestine as the result of capitalist development. In this schema Zionism was used to channel British imperialist capital and Jewish private capital to fuel the country's economy, meanwhile exploiting the emerging Jewish working class.

The end product of Sneh's argument is a non-Zionist Israeli local nationalism. This crucial element is evident already earlier in the text when Sneh, while rejecting the extraterritorial nature of Jewish peoplehood, adds: "the Communist movement 'acknowledges' the nation that has been formed in Israel."[29] He further elaborates on the point later in the text. In a piece aptly called "The Struggle for Independence," he outlines concisely how this new nation was formed: "The capitalist development of the Jewish Yishuv in part of Eretz-Israel is the one that caused the development of the nation. The British imperialist rule restricted the development of the forming nation and subjected her to a regime of national oppression and colonial exploitation."[30] Thus, utilizing Stalinist understandings, Sneh denationalizes the Jewish people and nationalizes the Jews in Israel. By using imperialism to disavow Zionism, Sneh creates a local Israeli identity![31]

Interestingly, the Communists' anti-Zionist nationalization project of parts of the Jewish people was not the only such project. The Bund (General Jewish Labor Bund in Lithuania, Poland, and Russia), mainly the Polish section of the party in interwar Poland, created a cultural infrastructure in which a Yiddish-based Jewish nationalism could grow. The cultural practices created by the Bund amalgamated progressive Marxism and Jewish nationalism. Paradoxically, the Bund, with its history of schism from early Bolshevism and hostility to Soviet Communism, presents surprising similarities and dissimilarities with the Jewish Communists in Palestine/Israel. Founded in 1897 in Lithuania, the Bund worked among the Yiddish-speaking Jewish working class of the Western provinces in the Russian Empire.[32] After World War I, when the Russian section of the party was liquidated by the Bolsheviks, the Polish Bund remained active in independent Poland, creating a Yiddish working class culture of the Jewish workers. This included several organizations and institutions, including SKIF (Socialist Children's Union), Tsukunft (the Bundist-oriented youth movement), TSYSHO (Central Jewish School Organization), YAF (Jewish working-class women), the *Kultur lige*, and the Medem Sanatorium.[33] This counter culture was secular Jewish, national, Marxist and anti-Zionist,[34] all conducted in Yiddish.[35] Resembling practices used by the Jewish Communists in Palestine/Israel, Bundist teachers in the

Yiddish educational system TSYSHO linked Jewish antiquity with Bund Marxist ideology. The era of the Second Temple, when Jews encountered Greek and Roman cultures, was likened by the TSYSHO educators "to present Jewish reality in Europe" and the sects of the times were presented as "reflections of contemporary Jewish society."[36]

Like the Jewish Communists—who approached the Jews of the Yishuv and Israel and not a global Jewish nation—the Bundists related to the Yiddish-speaking Jews of Eastern Europe. Ideologically radical Marxists, they tried to work out a national identity based on secularized elements deemed progressive Judaism. Still, the Bund's nationalism was rooted in Yiddish culture and language. Jewish Communists in Palestine/Israel spoke Hebrew. The scale of the cultural enterprises of the Bundists, that included large parts of the Jewish working class in interwar Poland, was unheard of in Palestine/Israel. There, only the small numbers of Communists and their supporters involved with Communist subculture were exposed to such cultural practices.

Political Ritual

Myth, Ritual, and Symbol in the USSR

Four ritualistic traditions originated in Tsarist Russia. There were popular rituals rooted in the pagan past, the Orthodox Church rituals, and the pageantry of the military. The latter projected power and rationality and was geometrically displayed as an impersonal collectivism. Finally there was the revolutionary tradition. Revolutionary ritual was structured mainly around May Day, an importation from Western Europe. The day's main symbolic element was the color red. The demonstration itself was not an elaborate ritual; it consisted of radical songs, a show of red, and speeches. The marchers conducted themselves with an air of militant tension as trespassers into an alien space.[37]

The Russian Bolsheviks developed a ritualistic and symbolic idiom of their own. The early Bolshevik rites mirrored the Tsarist-era ceremonies in which "solemnity and merriment stood side-by-side."[38] These elements became a part of Soviet ritual by late 1918. The early period of Bolshevik ritual was characterized by elaborate and colorfully decorated mass festivals. The first ceremonial occasion of the new regime was the May Day celebration of 1918, which featured a procession-demonstration. There was an innovative, utopian, and carnival side to the early Soviet rite, turning Petrograd into a giant work of art, "a cartoon, a Pleasure Island, a Castle in Spain, and a land of Cockaigne."[39] The anniversary of the revolution in Moscow on November 7, 1918, was a more solemn occasion. In Moscow Lenin was inspired in the design of the celebrations by an unlikely figure, Tommaso Campanella. He "was a fanatical 17th century Catholic, heretic, religio-political rebel of great complexity."[40] In his book *City of the Sun* he envisioned a city-state "which turned religion into science and the urban landscape into a museum and outdoor school."[41] Lenin built on Campanella's ideas, turning Moscow landscape into a giant display. In it sculptures and inscriptions propagating Marxist ideology and the West European and Russian revolutionary traditions were meant to educate the mass about the new regime.

In this early rite the symbols of Communism, the Red Star and the Hammer and Sickle, were first deployed. The focus of the ritual was a march in the Red Square, which was followed by carnival celebrations, including the mass burning of the enemies of the revolution in effigy.

Shaping their own symbolism and rituals, the Bolsheviks connected themselves to ancient rebels like Spartacus, and to regicides like Brutus. Lenin associated the revolution with the French Revolution and European Socialism, from the utopianists to Luxemburg and Libknecht, and with Russian rebels like Sten'ka Razin, the Decembrists, the thinkers of the 1840s and 1860s, the Populists, and Plekhanov.

The end of the civil war and the start of the NEP[42] were characterized by a downsizing of mass spectacles. The task of conducting political rites was assigned to Circles of Artistic Laymen, who were members of Workers' Clubs attached to trade unions. The May Day and November 7th anniversary parades were where the Workers' Clubs could deploy their talents, exhibiting floats of "grotesquely comic representations of imperialism, capitalism, foreign politicians and the enemies at home—nepman, bureaucrat, alcoholic, pope, kulak—made out of wood, papier-mâché, or straw."[43]

The first Five Year Plan was accompanied by a cultural revolution that assaulted the relatively liberal cultural sphere of the 1920s. The May Day and November 7th parades in Moscow became stiffer and more rigid, replacing grassroots and modernist avant-garde artistic innovation with rigidness, standardization, and militarization. The regimentation, standardization, and militarization of Soviet ritual were most evident in the November 7th anniversary. The march encompassed ever greater numbers of military units and marching civilians, all revolving around Stalin. There was still a trace of buffoonery in the ridicule extended to the traditional enemies of the Soviet people. However, the carnival aspect of Soviet ritual culture had been banished to the nonpolitical margins. Mass holidays and ritual activity greatly diminished during World War II—with the notable exception of the November 7, 1941, parade where the soldiers marched from the Red Square to the front.

During the Khrushchev era, the aversion to the massive coercion of the Stalinist era, economic difficulties, and the survival of religious sentiment among Soviet citizens drove the Soviet elites to refashion Soviet rites. The renewal of ritual in the USSR had begun by the end of the 1950s, drawing on three traditions: labor, patriotic, and revolutionary.

Of these three, the most important and sacred was the patriotic-military tradition. The brutal war and the tremendous victory of the Soviet Union over Nazi Germany had aroused patriotic feelings and pride. These feelings were diverted by the Soviet establishment toward love of the Motherland and toward "loyalty to the political unit and its social system, the Soviet Socialist state."[44] Victory Day was first celebrated in 1945 as the "Great Patriotic War" ended. The official celebration took place in the Red Square. There were ceremonies at each town's war monuments, including short speeches, retellings of heroic deeds followed by oaths to replicate them, music, declamation of verse, a minute's silence for the fallen, and the laying of wreaths. The memorial rites were followed by a military march or veterans march through the town's center and the central parade in Moscow.

May Day and the November 7th anniversary were the two mainstays of the revolutionary tradition of Soviet ritual. May Day featured two main forms of ritual, the procession demonstration and the revolutionary rally. The largest procession demonstration marched in the Red Square, with various political and social groups participating. The crowds congregated at the outskirts of each town and marched to the center, holding up banners, slogans, decorated panels, emblems, and so forth. In Moscow, the march passed by Lenin's mausoleum, where state and party leaders stood and watched the parade.

Myth, Ritual, and Symbol in the GDR

German Communism's cultural origins lay in the Weimar Republic. In those early years, the ritual of German Communism developed as "Communists each year celebrated the anniversary of the Bolshevik Revolution and commemorated Lenin's death along with Luxemburg's and Libknecht's in the LLL festivals."[45] In the East German state created after World War II, there were four elements of national myth originating in the Weimar era and the Soviet Zone (SBZ) period: German *Kultur*, the anti-Fascist myth, the myth of the Soviet Union, and the myth of the Socialist Fatherland.

The earliest myth to be propagated during the Soviets' direct rule over the Eastern zone was that of German *Kultur*, which originated in the eighteenth century. It held Goethe, Schiller, Bach, Beethoven, and others to be "*representative* of Germany, rather than, as one might think, absolutely *exceptional*."[46] In the Weimar era, the German Communist Party (KPD) took no part in the discourse of *Kultur*. The profoundly antibourgeois German Communists had little use for what was usually the property of the middle class. However, *Kultur* came to be a part of the arsenal of German Communism at the "Brussels Conference" in 1935, where the KPD called upon its remaining members in Germany to wrest classical German culture away from the Nazis. Under Soviet tutelage, the first celebration of German *Kultur* under the Communists was the National Goethe Celebration in 1949. Goethe was described by SED (German Unity Party) officials as a progressive figure and forerunner of Germany's cultural unity. That event set in motion a process of acculturation of—traditional—German culture by the SED.

The anti-Fascist myth—encompassing German Communist resistance to Nazism from 1933 to 1945—had as one of its pivotal elements the Spanish Civil War and the International Brigades. The war veterans (after the political difficulties some of them experienced during the Slánský trial subsided) became a privileged elite group within East German society, active participants in the memorialization of the war. The Spanish Civil War commemoration inspired a symbolic and ritual language with a military and ideological emphasis and gave rise to its own hero cult. The East German ritual in honor of the International Brigades concentrated mainly on the young and was molded in conformance with the traditional practices of the Free German youth movement: campfire songs and talks with veterans, cross-country marches, all saturated with military indoctrination.

Another facet of the commemoration of the International Brigades was the hero cult celebrating individual German volunteers. The best known and most celebrated on a national scale was Hans Beimler, who was born to a Bavarian working-class family in 1895 and killed in Madrid in 1936. Beimler's legendary status began with his mass funeral in Spain and was intensified by publications in the International Brigades' newspapers, which attributed to him the roles of commissar of the German battalions of the

Eleventh Brigade and member of the KPD's Central Committee. Another way of keeping Beimler's memory alive was his immortalization in Ernst Busch's song "Hans Beimler, Comrade." Beimler was portrayed as an impeccable heroic soldier, a role model to be imitated by the East German youth.[47]

Zionist Myth, Ritual, and Symbol

The ritual and symbolic Zionist language in Palestine/Israel was shaped by elements originating from Jewish history and Zionist ideology, and it constituted the cultural surroundings in which the Jewish Communists shaped their subculture and most notably their identity. Zionist cultural practices originated in the late nineteenth century with the rejection of Jewish culture as it had been created in the *galut* (Hebrew: Diaspora) and the selective adoption of Jewish pre-rabbinic and rabbinic traditions, replacing the religious content of the holidays with nationalist Zionist content. Stemming from the critique of Judaism by the Jewish *haskala* (Hebrew: enlightenment) and the absorption of anti-Semitic motifs into Zionist thinking,[48] *negation of the Diaspora* was meant to create a new Jewish or Hebrew nation in Palestine and a new Jew, the sabra.[49] Other national myths borrowed from antiquity dominated Zionist symbolism, most prominently the myth of Hanukkah and the Maccabees that became important in the Jewish Communist subculture.

Chapter 2

The Creation of a Jewish Progressive Tradition

The Jewish holidays were the subject of an intense process of design and redesign among Jewish Communists. Like others within the cultural discourse of Zionist Socialism, the Communists sought to fill the old vessels of Jewish tradition with new content. But whereas Socialist Zionists sought to infuse nationalistic secular content into the Jewish calendric cycle, the Communists were looking for something different. Rejecting Zionism, while accepting notions of Jewish non-Zionist nationalism, they filled the Jewish holidays with secular progressive content. Their rituals incorporated elements from local Socialist-Zionist cultural practices, Marxist influences, and Jewish traditional rituals. In shaping this tradition, the Jewish Communists created and reflected a unique Jewish progressive identity that, despite being supported by Socialist-Zionist practices, was distinctly Jewish-Israeli Communist.

The high point of this process came in an article written by Moshe Sneh in 1959, on the occasion of the launching of a new school curriculum centered on Judaism. Sneh began by stating that the Communists were not rejecting tradition, though they were conscious of its class content, for "in a society torn by class contrasts and struggles there is no unified spirit and no unified cultural and spiritual work—not in any people and language and not even in our own people."[1] The main impetus for the creation of culture, according to Sneh, would be "the contradiction between the exploiters and the exploited, between the oppressors and the oppressed, between rich and poor."[2] From that basic point, Sneh went on to portray Jewish history from antiquity to the twentieth century as having been driven by a Marxist-style class struggle.

The process of assimilating the Jewish holidays into the Communist subculture alternated between two extremes. The formative period of the party was characterized mostly by rejection of the new Jewish Zionist calendar, which was perceived as a manifestation of Zionist ideology. After the legalization of the party, however, Banki shaped its own rituals and symbols celebrating the Jewish holidays. The movement reinvented in Communist form the rituals of Hanukkah and Passover. In the process, many cultural elements of Zionist Socialism diffused into the Communist subculture. This development escalated with the admittance of the Left Men to Banki and MAKI, which upset the cultural balance between the different identities within the Communist movement.

Admittedly, the 1965 split of MAKI was mainly motivated by political differences regarding MAKI's tactics and ideology concerning the Palestinian-Israeli conflict. However, there was a cultural side to it as well. MAKI could be termed a limited and rudimentary multicultural party. Bound together by Marxist-Leninist discourse, MAKI and Banki partly accommodated the Arab-Jewish culture of Iraqi immigrants, the Eastern European culture of Bulgarian and Rumanian immigrants, and the Soviet-style cultural elements of the party old guard, as well as the Arabic cultural elements of its large Palestinian membership and, to a lesser extent, the more educated and elite Palestinian leaders. The arrival of the native-Israeli Sneh men prompted a cultural effort to create "a new Communist Israeli Left."[3] This attempt was received with wariness by the party old guard and was a source of constant tension within MAKI, eventually tearing it asunder in 1965.

The diffusion into the Communist subculture of Jewish motifs was also accompanied by the reinvention of symbols, myths, and rituals. Like other participants in the Socialist-Zionist cultural discourse, the Jewish Communists based their myths, symbols, and rituals on Jewish tradition, but gave them their own explanation. Using Marxism and what they perceived as popular and progressive Jewish traditions, they formed their own rituals, symbols, and myths.

The Holidays

Hanukkah

Hanukkah was undoubtedly the most important Jewish holiday to be celebrated by Jewish Communists. In the Zionist context, the story of

Hanukkah and the Maccabees became a narrative of national liberation rather than divine deliverance. Socialist-Zionist culture further interpreted the holiday from a Socialist class point of view, portraying the rebellion as having been carried out by the lower classes. The emergence of a national cult around Hanukkah was the background to the first Communist reaction to the holiday.

It came in the form of a booklet issued by the Young Communist League in December 1929, written by party leader Yosef Berger-Barzilai and a group of young Communist activists. Cumbersomely entitled *The Mufti Matityahu and the Great Peasants Uprising Two Thousand Years Ago*, the booklet uses the historical events of antiquity to launch a political attack against the British Mandate and the Zionist and Palestinian leaderships, which it criticized for their reactionary nature. Its main argument is that Matityahu and the Maccabees usurped the mass uprising of the poor peasants against the Greeks and their servants in Judea, fearing that "if the people would rebel against the Greeks and drive the foreign leeches from the country, and feel that they could do it without the 'clerks,' then nothing would remain of them and their donations and taxes."[4] Thus, the Maccabees exploited religious fanaticism to wrest control of the uprising, which made them kings of the land and enabled them eventually to sell out to the Greeks and Romans. This turn of events is contrasted to the present when the Communist Party will lead the peasants and workers in driving out the present-day Greeks and their collaborators.

Beyond its thinly veiled political metaphor, the 1929 booklet is a cultural statement. It condemns the heroic role assigned by Zionism to the Maccabees, and in that it reflects the anti-Zionism of the Communists. At the same time, the booklet rejects the religious narrative of the holiday, portraying it as a ploy to "stupefy the minds of the youth with foolish legends."[5] As anti-Zionist as the booklet is, though, it is nonetheless part of the Socialist-Zionist cultural discourse of Hanukkah. That is most evident in its class analysis of the Hanukkah narrative. Despite the sharp criticism of the Maccabees as an antique version of bourgeois Zionists, the uprising of the poor peasants is presented as a popular guerrilla struggle. The whole text is steeped in terms of class as a social category and anti-imperialism; it depicts the Syrian Greeks' rule over Judea as a "Greek 'Mandate,'" contrasts the peace-loving peasant masses to their exploitative religious leadership, and ultimately rejects the idea of Jewish heroism originating from antiquity.

The booklet marks the start of the Jewish Communists' use of Marxist terms in describing the narrative of Hanukkah. The archaic nature of this explanation is justified by the basic Marxist explanation of history as the struggle between classes. Albeit relatively awkwardly, in the hands of the Jewish Communists the Marxist historical portrayal was used, as will be seen later, as a basic myth justifying Hanukkah, and indeed many other Jewish holidays, in their eyes. The use of Marxist categories, as cumbersome as it may seem to present-day readers, shows us how Jewish nationalist motifs diffused into the Communist subculture. To a political collective that in essence rejected Jewish nationalism and Zionism, only Marxist language could make a myth like Hanukkah palatable. Paradoxically, this connected the Jewish Communists to Socialist-Zionist culture.

The 1941 German invasion of the USSR dramatically changed the position of the Communist Party in Palestine. After having been hunted by the British from the start of the war due to the party's objection to the war, blindly following Moscow's line, the party was legalized, only to split up into its national components in 1943. The war changed the way Jewish Communists in Palestine viewed Jewish heroism. Soviet Jewish soldiers in the Red Army were covered regularly in the Communist Party press. The acclamation of Soviet-Jewish heroism was not missing either from the pages of the Young Communist League organ *Kol Hano'ar*. In its January 1943 issue, a long item was dedicated to the story of Haim Diskin, a young Soviet Jewish gunner "who without fearing death . . . with all his bodily strength, as a hero, in boundless dedication,"[6] destroyed five enemy tanks and was wounded fourteen times. Despite the hyperbolic language of wartime Soviet propaganda in the style of "Ivan killed 100 Germans with a spoon," this stress on Jewish national heroism opened the Jewish Communists to a more positive appreciation of the Hanukkah myth.

Next to the item describing Haim Diskin's heroics, an article simply entitled "Hanukkah" presented the new Communist myth of the holiday. Signed by one Samuel from Jerusalem, it is a historical-political metaphor, as was the 1929 booklet. It begins with the question: "Hanukkah, the day of the victory of the Maccabees . . . what does this glorious chapter in our people's history symbolize?"[7] The answer consists of a long historical narrative in which class and national heroism are interwoven. One line of connection between the 1929 and 1943[8] texts, and between them and Socialist-Zionist culture, is the class analysis of the events in antiquity. In accordance with Marxist ideology, along with the penetration of commerce into Judea came "the language of commerce, Greek, and the defenders of commerce, the Greek gods."[9] The new economic order both destroyed the Jewish peasantry and caused an internal class war within the ruling class between the old landowning elite and the new commercial class. This situation became more entangled when the Seleucid Empire intervened on behalf of the new, culturally Hellenistic commercial elite. In an attempt to impose Hellenistic culture and religion, it tried to ban the practice of Judaism, resulting in a war of popular liberation led by Judah the Maccabee.

This Marxist narrative of the Hanukkah myth differs from the 1929 booklet in its positive approach to the Maccabees. The Hasmoneans and Matityahu, negatively portrayed in the late 1920s, have become "a family of country clerks from a small town . . . who rejected the foreign ways." Judah the Maccabee is "the man who was able to be the leader of an entire population. He was the man that symbolized the national pride of the people of Judea."[10] Like the 1929 text, the historical narrative ends with the morals of history for the present. Nevertheless, whereas in the 1929 booklet the idea of Jewish heroism was rejected, in 1943 it was embraced. Hanukkah became an example of past Jewish heroics inspiring Jews, now in the midst of mortal struggle, to fight on. Leading this new fight was not the Zionist Yishuv, however, but "liberated Soviet Jewry . . . fighting alongside the rest of the USSR people against the Nazis."[11] Here the Jewish Communists gave expression to their own genuine feelings of sympathy with the plight of the Jews in Europe. At the same time, they were being used as a tool of Soviet policy that sought to mobilize Jewish public opinion in the West on behalf of the Soviet war effort. The rosy, idyllic portrayals of Jewish heroism disregarded the fact that anti-Semitism still existed in the USSR.

This diffusion of Jewish nationalist elements into the Communist myth of Hanukkah gathered pace during the 1940s. Under the influence of the Holocaust and the Yishuv's struggle against the British, Jewish Communists began framing Hanukkah more and more in Jewish nationalist terms. This is evident in the December 1947 article "To the Sons of the Maccabees." At that point, soon after the Gromyko speech, delivered by Soviet ambassador to the UN Andrei Gromyko in support of the 1947 UN Partition of Palestine, the Jewish Communists identified almost completely with the Yishuv, which was in the midst of an escalating war with the Palestinians. Like its predecessor in 1943, the 1947 text starts with a question: "What is the meaning of Hanukkah for us?"[12] What follows is a historical narrative of the events in Judea, almost identical to the class-based account delivered in 1943. The Mityavnim (Hebrew: Hellenistic Jews) are described as having been driven by their class interest to cooperate with the Greeks. The uprising is described as a popular peasant revolution motivated by class and nationalist interests.

The 1947 article "Lebney Hamakabim" (To the Sons of the Maccabees) differs from its predecessor in two main respects: the image of the Maccabees and the present-day political moral to be drawn from history. In 1943 the approach to the Maccabees was still somewhat reserved. They are described as a landowning elite, driven by internal class warfare to lead the uprising. In 1947 they become completely identified with the uprising, being portrayed as "the vanguard of the people's war against its oppressors."[13] They also became part of a Jewish heroic lineage ending with the ghetto fighters in Europe. In 1943 the Jewish Communists accepted Jewish heroism, but only in the context of World War II, presenting Soviet Jewry as the heirs to Maccabean bravery. By 1947, having become committed to the political "independence" of the Yishuv, they were describing the present-day political lesson of the holiday in nationalist terms: "The bravery of the Maccabees and their fight is a symbol to us now—a symbol and a command—with the coming of independence."[14]

The Communist myth of Hanukkah came into its own in the 1950s to the mid-1960s. In a section of *Kol Hano'ar* from November 1956, in the midst of the Sinai War and the Hungarian Revolution, the contrast between past and present dominates. The Jewish Communists were isolated by their objection to the 1956 War, and their propaganda fell on deaf ears. In reaction to their isolation, they internalized the holiday myth. A collage of literary pieces, poetry, and short articles, the section is informed by the dichotomy between past and present as phrased in the traditional way, "in those days, at this time." The anti-imperialist rebellion of antiquity, a fight in which the people of Judea "struggled alongside the peoples of the Middle East," is contrasted to the present day "when the peoples of the Middle East have broken the yoke of the robber empires in the freedom and independence struggle,"[15] while Israel was aligning itself with the decaying empires of France and England. The contrast between past and present is also cultural. Whereas in the past the people fiercely defended their national culture, fighting Hellenization, at present American culture was a corrupting influence allowed to rage unabated. Finally, a contrast is struck between the popular revolt of the working masses headed by the Maccabees and the war frenzy of 1956.

From the contrast between past and present the article draws its final conclusion that the legacy of the holiday belongs to "those on whose flag peace and independence are inscribed,"[16] meaning the Communists. The *Kol Hano'ar* article reiterates the elements evident in the previous articles: the popular class nature of the rebellion, recourse to the past as a repository of political morals for the present, and recognition of the Communists as the true heirs to the myth of Hanukkah.

The myth of Hanukkah was disseminated among the young Communists not only by Banki's public organ, but by its instructors' brochures as well. The latter offer a window into the cultural world of the young Communists. In the case of Hanukkah and other Jewish holidays, they show how elements of, respectively, Jewish tradition and Soviet and left-wing European culture were expressed and changed by Banki members, and how Socialist-Zionist discourse, in this case the narrative of Hanukkah, was adapted into Communist cultural practice. Indeed, the basic medium of Socialist-Zionist and statist culture, the *Masechet,* became the commonplace way for Jewish Communists to express their cultural inclinations.

The instructors' brochure of November 1955, like others used by Banki, was built on the *Masechet* model as a collage of literary, theoretical, and theatrical pieces revolving around one or two subjects. The section that deals with Hanukkah opens with a quote from Meir Vilner, who strings together the Hasmonean and Bar Kokhva rebellions as part of a "progressive revolution of the Jewish people."[17] As in other Banki texts, he contrasts those Jews who wished to become Hellenistic to those who stood firm against foreign rule and culture. He also asserts that the example of the ancient rebels should be used to educate the young Communists, as it holds a moral for the present, and Vilner encourages Communists to defend Israel's independence and Jewish honor against present-day Mityavnim.

The text moves on to a historical description of the Maccabean uprising. The historical narrative exhibits many of the typical characteristics of the Communist myth of the holiday. The revolt is described as a popular uprising that pitted the people against the Greek mercenaries and their Jewish lackeys. The identification of the Maccabees with the people, as its leaders, is also evident. The political moral is not forgotten at the end, either. After comparing the Seleucid Empire to Western imperialism and equating the Hellenization of antiquity with bad American culture, the text concludes that "our period is very much like the Maccabean. Then and now, those who want peace and independence, the patriots, must unite and fight for Israel's independence against pre-emptive war, for world peace and peace between Israel and the Arab states."[18]

The next instructors' brochure to deal with Hanukkah is dated November 1956. At this very politically sensitive moment for the Communists (the only political force in Israel objecting to the 1956 Sinai War), the authors of the brochure stressed "that according to Banki's secretariat resolution there is the utmost importance to organizing public celebrations that are devoted to Hanukkah."[19] In the *Masechet* style, the booklet is constructed around the motifs of just and unjust war and the traditional Hanukkah blessing, "in those days, at this time." It contains everything from an essay by Mao to a poem by Natan Alterman. Of the literary pieces focusing on Hanukkah, two came from sources of cultural importance to the Communists.

First are two poems by Ḥaya Kadmon, the party's undisputed poet laureate and one of the most romantic and tragic figures in Communist circles. Kadmon held an influential cultural position within MAKI. Her knowledge of Hebrew and world literature made her a principal contributor to *Kol Ha'am*'s cultural supplement. Both poems in the 1956 instructor's brochure express motifs already established in the Communist myth of Hanukkah. The first, "Yet Again as in the Time of Modi'in," continues to pursue the theme, in poetic form, of striking a parallel between antiquity and the present, as the following lines well demonstrate: "Yet again as in the days of Modi'in / the enemy besieges the land/ and the pig of Mammon enters the Temple / Once more a handful of seated parasites / burn incense for foreigners and bow to their words." Another motif expressed in the poem is the popular nature of the Maccabean revolt: "Common people, poor priests / will awaken the spirit of revolt." This motif, taken from Socialist-Zionist culture, is also related to the present: "Once more the Hasmonean fires burn / From Judea to the Galilee; / 'The days of slavery shall end.' "[20]

A second important source is the book *My Glorious Brothers* by Howard Fast, an American Communist writer who occupied an enormous place in the cultural consciousness of Banki members in the 1950s. Shoshana Shmuely refers to it as the "Bible" of Hanukkah. She recalls that her copy of the book was repeatedly marked with the sections to be used on Hanukkah.[21] It provided material that would be read to the younger age groups by their Banki instructors or acted out in the form of plays, serving in effect as a manual for their activities with the younger members.

The holiday featured diverse practices, including plays and scout games, which extended to the movement's clubs. In a circular from the early 1950s, it is suggested that the local club be decorated "in Hanukkah lamps and dreidels." Instructors are advised to conduct a menorah-making contest, and that one entry at least should be "against the background of the (Soviet) Pioneers symbol."[22]

From the late 1920s, Hanukkah acquired growing symbolic importance among Jewish Communists. Its message of national liberation, of revolt against oppressive foreign rule and traitors at home, suited the Communists' cultural and political needs. The high point of the integration of the Hanukkah myth into Banki came in the early 1960s, as an attempt to produce a unified guide for the holiday in 1963 makes evident. Like many of Banki's instructors' brochures, the 1963 booklet begins with a historical narrative of the holiday. Once more the same elements can be found. The uprising was carried out by the poor and downtrodden pitted in a class war against a parasitic elite of clerks, merchants, and tax farmers. Judah the Maccabee is positively described as hailing from a peasant family. The uprising is linked to a progressive Jewish tradition of freedom fighting as another link in the chain stretching from the revolts against Rome in antiquity to Israel's war of independence.

As in the earlier texts, the contrast between the Mityavnim and the Maccabees is a motif with meaning that extends to the present day, as the young Communist should learn "that there was not and cannot be any unity between Mityavnim and Maccabean, between the lovers of Rome and the Zealots, between Judenräte and the ghetto fighters, between the servants of imperialism and those who oppose it."[23] And there is a final moral that history presents. In contrast to the past, "today when a third of the world is inhabited by liberated peoples, and in the rest of the world the people are marching safely toward their complete liberation—under the constant guidance of the working class—in the twentieth century, the century of Socialism and Communism—one oppressor will not be replaced by another."[24]

The 1963 booklet is divided into three main sections, featuring poems appropriate for the holiday, stories, and plays, respectively. The first section opens with a poem by Alexander Penn, the most important cultural figure in the Communist subculture of the 1950s and 1960s. Penn joined the party in 1947 and very quickly became "the party's great poet, its high priest."[25] His performances reading his poems at party events left a lasting impression on those who witnessed them.[26] His poems in *Kol Ha'am*, dealing with the politics of the day, were a regular fixture throughout the 1950s and 1960s. In his contribution to the 1963 booklet, *Brothers' Light*, the main motif is light, one well connected to Hanukkah, the Jewish festival of lights. The light in the poem is ignited "from the Volga to the Vistula," connecting Soviet heroism with the "light of our brothers and glorious heroes," alluding to the Maccabees. Thus, a motif that first emerged in World War II reappears in poetic form in the early 1960s.

The booklet's contents illustrate the cultural shaping of Hanukkah in the Jewish Communist subculture. The holiday was interpreted through a cultural reinvention of antiquity to suit the Marxist version of history. The aim of such varied cultural elements was to implant the holiday in the young Communists' minds in terms that were ideologically permissible in a Communist movement, thus creating a Jewish Communist progressive narrative of Hanukkah.

As celebrated among Jewish Communists from the 1920s, Hanukkah featured an alternative ritual that, despite being rooted in Jewish tradition, had a distinctive Communist aspect. The main ritual traditionally associated with the holiday is the lighting of candles. Zionism and Zionist Socialism took this ritual, usually performed in the privacy of the family, and turned it into a national public event. The Communist subculture followed the same path, and the lighting of the candles became a ritual performed in Banki's clubs. The uniquely Communist aspect of the ceremony was the recitation of blessings with the lighting of each candle. The young Communists replaced the traditional blessings with ones featuring Communist content, such as blessings for the USSR, Communist parties worldwide headed by the Soviet Party, and so forth.[27]

There is no evidence indicating that the ceremony was performed in the early days of Communism in Palestine. This kind of open activity was only possible in conditions of legality. Tamar Gozansky dates the start of the ceremony to the merger of the Left with MAKI in the mid-1950s. Yoram Gozansky, on the other hand, believes it to have existed long before the 1950s.[28] The earliest visible evidence is a photograph of the ceremony in a 1956 issue of *Kol Hano'ar*. It shows three members of the Tel Aviv branch, a young girl and two boys; the girl is lighting the Hanukkah candles. Above the three youngsters hangs a banner with the slogan: "We will follow the Maccabean way on the path of struggle for the homeland's independence!" The caption below the photo reads: "Members of the Tel Aviv Banki branch light candles in memory of the liberation from the yoke of the invaders." Although both slogan and caption adduce nationalist motifs, giving the old Jewish ritual new national content, the symbols surrounding the ceremony are Communist. To the left is the Banki emblem—made up of the national flag signifying the local Israeli element—the Red Star, and the Sheaf of Wheat signifying the progressive, internationalist, and Soviet Socialist element. To the right is the emblem of the World Federation of Democratic Youth (WFDY), betokening interracial solidarity and universality. These symbols give the ceremony its uniqueness. It is a traditional Jewish ritual with nationalist content as performed by Zionist Socialism, but in a Communist setting.

Though there was no uniform protocol for the Communist ritual of Hanukkah, the blessings accompanying the lighting of the candles featured a common content and orientation. In Yad Hana, the only kibbutz affiliated with the party, the ceremony was performed in front of the congregated kibbutz members; the blessings over the candles included "a candle for freedom, which the heroic Maccabees enjoined us to fight for no matter what the cost, a candle for peace between nations, a candle for toil, a candle for fraternity between humans and between nations, a candle for the love of the homeland, a candle for the party that lights our way, a candle for all children and a candle for our Yad Hana."[29] According to the testimony of a former Yad Hana member, the ceremony also included the acting out of parts of Howard Fast's *My Glorious Brothers* by the kibbutz children. The ceremony was conducted under a banner that read, "A great revolt happened here," no doubt a repudiation of the traditional slogan, "A great miracle happened here." In Tel Aviv the same basic pattern was followed. Candles were lit for the true independence of Israel, for Arab-Jewish fraternity, and in condemnation of the military government. The ceremonies were conducted in the local Banki club on a stage decorated with a large candelabrum. The members took turns lighting the candles and reciting the blessings over them. The ceremony was followed by a party. Elements of Communist and Socialist solidarity also had a place in the Hanukkah ceremony. Some of the testimony describes candles being lit for the Soviet Union and MAKI, and a candle lit in solidarity for national liberation struggles like the Vietnam War. Local Communist struggles were not forgotten either, as candles were lit for the Arab brethren and in condemnation of the military government imposed upon them.[30]

By the mid-1960s Hanukkah had become a central Communist holiday. A short ceremony with detailed blessings was featured in the 1963 booklet, apparently in an attempt to apply uniform practice in all Banki branches. The ceremony was to begin with the playing of a tune or song. Then the candles were to be lit; the first one, the *shamash*, was to be lit "for the great deeds that were done and are being done by the fighters for freedom, peace and independence in those days at this time." The blessings over the candles that follow exemplify the different aspects of Communist subculture and identity in Israel as they developed from the late 1920s. The first blessing connects the holiday to the Jewish heroic lineage from "the Maccabean bonfires, from the fire of the Zealots' revolt and Bar Kokhva, from the flames of the ghetto's rebels and the fire of Israel's independence struggle." The text equates the present-day with past oppressors and calls for an intense struggle against "the oppressors external and internal, the heirs of Antiochus and the Mityavnim."

Solidarity with other peoples is expressed in the blessings over the second candle, which was to be lit for all the people struggling for freedom, and over the fifth candle, to be lit "for all the people of the Middle East, who are casting off their chains." Loyalty to the Soviet Union and the Communist movement is expressed in the blessing over the third candle, to be lit for "the People of the Soviets" and the nations of the Peoples' Democracies. The fourth was to be lit for "the Communist parties worldwide, and for the lighthouse—the Communist Party of the Soviet Union." The sixth, seventh, and eighth candles were to be lit on behalf of local party constituents. The sixth candle was for "our dear friends from Nazareth, the Triangle and the villages of the Galilee," and the blessing vowed to keep alive the struggle to end the military government. The seventh candle was for "the humiliated and exploited toilers of Israel." Here the blessing vows to bring to them the words of the Communist movement, "the word of truth that rouses to struggle." The ceremony was to end with the singing of the Zionist secular Hanukkah song, "We Are Carrying Torches."[31]

Victor Turner defined liminality and communitas as part of the ritual process meant to neutralize crisis points within the social structure such as the differences of status and gender. The ritual carries its participants outside of the normal social structure into a liminal state where they are in effect between and betwixt the social structure, thus creating an anti-structure, an alternative to the day-to-day structures of society. In this condition, those taking part in the process are outside their social roles. Through the ritual and symbol enacted in this liminal condition, a generalized social bond of communitas is revealed, in juxtaposition to the social political order.[32]

The Hanukkah rituals performed by the Jewish Communists bear all the characteristics of the rituals of communitas and liminality. The Jewish Communists were persecuted, relegated to the margins of Israel's political, social, and cultural structures. But even when they were marginalized, MAKI and Banki members shared Jewish cultural concepts with the broader society. The Jewish Banki members were mostly young, Hebrew-speaking, native-born Israelis. This closeness on the one hand and remoteness on the other placed the Jewish Communists between and betwixt the social structure. This position with the tension it brought was enhanced by the performance of rituals that expressed affinity with Jewish traditions. At the same time, the Jewish Communists sought to reinvent those traditions to fit their ideological sensitivities. They did so by giving them new, progressive, secular content. Thus their holiday rituals were meant to bond them together in rituals that combined Jewish traditional motifs with Marxist ideology. The rituals were meant to elevate their status, making them the heirs of the progressive revolutionary aspect they found in Hanukkah.

The Hanukkah ritual had no equivalent in ritual practices in the USSR and Eastern Europe. Its ritual language[33] was made up predominately of local elements from the Socialist-Zionist culture and Jewish tradition. Nonetheless, into the content of their various Hanukkah rituals the Jewish Communists amalgamated both nationalist and Communist elements. Thus it came about that over the lighting of the holiday candles there were blessings for the USSR and the party as well as for the fallen of the IDF. These rituals reflected the attempt by the Jewish Communists to create a Jewish-Israeli Communist subculture structured, as the Hanukkah blessings show, on a delicate equilibrium between local Israeli, mostly Socialist-Zionist elements, and Communist ones. This cultural hybrid could only exist when its various elements were balanced. By the early and mid-1960s, when under the influence of the Left Men the Jewish Communist subculture came to resemble Socialist-Zionist culture, its existence became untenable.

The integration of the Hanukkah myth into Banki's Communist subculture culminated in the early to mid-1960s. Banki, which by then was controlled by the veterans of the Left party, made an attempt to change the movement's ritual calendar and posit Hanukkah as a central occasion for its members. Yair Tzaban's proposal to enroll new members to the movement during Hanukkah sent a shock wave through the party,[34] highlighting the cultural differences between the Left Men and its old guard. This symbolic act brought into the open the conflict between the two approaches to Socialist-Zionist cultural practices in Banki and MAKI: the more Zionist approach brought by the Left Men and the one stressing Communist and class motifs. With the balance between those elements disrupted, Jewish Communist subculture lost its uniqueness and its reason to exist.

The recasting by Zionism of the holiday—which already as a religious celebration had a strong ethnic character—into a powerful national cult dictated the Communist reaction to it. As such, the old-new language of Zionist holidays was interpreted differently by the Jewish Communists. They moved from a repudiation of its Zionization to an acceptance of it under their own terms. These terms were Marxist and local Israeli—not Zionist—trying to imagine Hanukkah in different non-Zionist Israeli national motifs. Doing that shows how potent was the new nationalist culture Zionism created. Strength that led even a group of Jews who fundamentally rejected Zionism to reconstruct a national imaginary of their own.

Passover

Passover is one of the main holidays of the traditional Jewish cycle. It combines elements of a spring celebration passed down from antiquity and the biblical narrative of the Exodus of the ancient Hebrews from Egypt. The main ritual connected with the holiday is the reading of the Haggadah during the family Passover Seder. In the kibbutzim, in the 1930s, a radical experiment was undertaken, an attempt to rewrite the Haggadah and restructure the Seder itself. The holiday myth of the Hebrew slaves' struggle for freedom suited the Jewish Communists' class and national sensibilities. Freedom and liberty became the catchwords of their version of the holiday. The Communists also used the nature elements of the holiday such as its associations with spring and the sowing of the land.

The myth of the holiday was accepted by the Jewish Communists as early as World War II. In an article entitled "From Slavery to Freedom," author Het Vilner attributes the biblical story to the hostility of Jewish

Figure 2.1. Hanukkah party in a Banki club in Tel Aviv in the 1950s.

nomads to settled habitation. The holiday is described as a holiday of Jewish nomadic tribes—the author uses the word "Bedouin"—that preserved the idea of liberty. Despite the rejection of the biblical story as unhistorical, the writer acknowledges the importance of the holiday to Jewish culture and its progressive nature. From this love of liberty sprang the Jewish progressive traditions, from the Maccabees through Masada and ending with the Jewish revolutionaries in Tsarist Russia. The text goes on to make the connection between the holiday and the present, using the biblical Pharaoh as a metaphor for capitalists and the Amalek as a parallel to Nazism. The article ends with the prediction that the end of the war would bring with it the end "of the rule of parasitic capital over creative, working human beings," at which time humanity would celebrate "the 'great Passover—The Passover of the future.'"[35]

The April 13, 1949, issue of *Kol Ha'am* devoted an article in its cultural section to Passover. Written by Yehudit Veniar, it dealt with the history of the Passover customs and rituals. It traces the origins of the holiday to a spring celebration of the Hebrews in which an archaic manner of sacrifice was employed to symbolize tribal unity and the ancient spiritual independence. The article goes on to portray the development of the holiday through Jewish history, having always preserved the popular abhorrence of slavery and its national identity. It ends with a call for a change in the holiday "in accordance with the demands of the times."[36] This phrase shows the flexibility in regard to Jewish tradition that the Jewish Communists absorbed from Zionist Socialism. They too wanted to add new meaning to Passover, meaning that was progressive and universal as well as nationalistic. The 1949 debate was heavily influenced by the patriotic stand taken by the Jewish Communists during 1948, thus stressing elements of national identity and freedom.

All through the 1950s and early 1960s, two elements dominated the Jewish Communists' perception of Passover: first liberty, and second, the natural cycle connected with the day. The young Communists shared this stress on freedom and nature, and both these elements of the holiday appear in a 1956 article, where they are connected to universal motifs like the Spring of Nations and the spring of all mankind heralded by the Russian Revolution. Liberty was also associated with Jewish heroics like the Maccabean Revolt and the wars against the Romans.[37] The emphasis on the nature elements of the holiday was derived from Socialist-Zionist culture, mainly as instantiated in the kibbutzim. The connection between youth and nature originated in Europe, in the romantic Free German youth movement, the Wandervogel, which had a profound influence on the Socialist-Zionist youth movement.[38] Thus practices imported from Europe were adopted into Banki's celebration of the holidays.

Passover did not inspire much ritualistic activity by Banki. The Jewish Communists seem to have made no concerted attempt to create an alternative to the traditional interpretation of the main rituals of Passover, the Seder meal, and the reading of the Haggadah. Nevertheless, two pieces of evidence suggest that Banki and MAKI members did write a proletarian Haggadah. In a 1957 cultural section of *Kol Ha'am*, one page was devoted to a Hagadat Pesaḥ Begirsa Hamatima Leshe'ifot Hapo'alim Vekol Tomḥey Hashalom (Passover Haggadah in a Version Suited to the Aspirations of Workers and all Supporters of Peace), in the form of a *Masechet* drawn from various sources, ranging from the biblical to the Communist poets Penn and Kadmon. On the basis of the traditional Haggadah blessings, the Jewish Communists use the motifs of liberty and spring to create a Jewish Communist text. One piece states that "as the Passover is the spring of the year, so Communism is the spring of humanity." The message of freedom and justice is connected to a lineage of Jewish heroes ending with "Communists everywhere struggling to destroy the evil kingdom and free all the slaves in spirit and in body."[39]

In an interview, Nissim Calderon recalled the use of such texts. Since he was a member of a unified Banki during 1962–1965, it may be speculated that under Yair Tzaban the cultural resemblance between Banki and Socialist-Zionist culture reached its height, and this Socialist-Zionist practice previously unknown to Banki was borrowed.[40] Although uncorroborated and unattested to in the archives, such a custom would conform to the process of diffusion of Socialist-Zionist cultural practices into Banki. The symbolic language of the holiday clustered around two main symbols.[41] The first, liberty, was invoked through both nationalist, popular themes and universal ones. The second, spring, was used as it was in Socialist-Zionist culture to stress nature motifs, but also as a symbol of political rejuvenation as exemplified by Communism. Once more like the Socialist Zionists, the Jewish Communists took Jewish tradition and reinterpreted it in their own way. Thus they made Pharaoh a symbol of capitalism and posited the fight for liberty as part of a worldwide struggle, not just one for national freedom. The Jewish Communists used their own language, symbolism, and myth to absorb Jewish traditions into their subculture. Other Communist movements confronted their own national traditions in similar ways.

It was not just the Jewish Communists who faced ingrained religious or cultural traditions. European Communists in the Soviet Union and East Germany developed strategies to cope with traditions that were well established among a majority of their subjects. One of the ways devised by Communists to counter traditional symbols and rituals was to invent their own. This was common in the Soviet Union in the 1920s and in the post-Stalinist era. In response to the survival of religious beliefs within the Soviet citizenry, in the 1920s and again in the late 1950s Soviet cultural organizers and politicians tried to shape life-cycle rituals, and to reinvent and recast alternatives to the established church holidays like Christmas. The Israeli Communists never followed, or likely were unable to follow, such a course of action. Denied any real power, marginalized, and often persecuted, they could not mount the resources to form an alternative Jewish ritual.

But the Soviet attempt at revising the calendar was not the only way to approach tradition, and in this matter the Jewish Communists' course bore a greater resemblance to the way the German Communists dealt with *Kultur*. At first intensely antibourgeois, the German Communists rejected this middle-class concept. Nonetheless, from 1935 onward the KPD adopted *Kultur*, making it part of the KPD ethos, later to become part of the East German state cult. The adaptation of *Kultur* was accompanied by a process attributing progressive value to German cultural figures like Johann Sebastian Bach and Johann Wolfgang von Goethe. The Jewish Communists followed a similar path. They rejected Jewish and Zionist interpretations outright, only to later reinterpret and co-opt them into the Communist subculture. The cultural heritage of Judaism and Jewish history was given progressive value. Jewish heroes like the Maccabees and Bar Kokhva, and Jewish myths like Passover and the ancient revolts against the Seleucid Empire and Rome, were incorporated into a revolutionary lineage that led up to and ended with the Communist Party. Thus the Jewish Communists asserted themselves as part of an alternative history of the Jewish people. Their version of events viewed Jewish history as culminating not in Zionism, but in MAKI. Much like the Zionists, they saw it as a continuing struggle for national freedom, but one carried on by the underclass against its oppressors, be they Jews or not. Thus the Jewish lineage they imagined was progressive, moving in Marxist fashion to a higher level of understanding and struggle and leading up to themselves.

This co-opting of tradition is clearly seen in Communist holiday practices. The gradual absorption of Hanukkah and its myth by the Communists from the 1920s was accompanied by a process of reevaluating the holiday's main elements. The Maccabees became a symbol of popular revolt. Their revolt itself was transformed from a fight for religious freedom into a people's war of the underclass for national liberation. Passover became a holiday centered on liberty. Its main text was reinvented in proletarian form.

The Jewish Communist identity oscillated between two poles: rejection of Jewish religious and national culture and attraction to progressive motifs in Jewish history. This complex identity crisis resulted from a social crisis resembling the one described by Clifford Geertz in his 1957 article "Ritual and Social Change: A Javanese Example." There the change from village life and the rise of modern ideologies rendered the inhabitants of one Javanese village unable to perform their traditional funeral rites.[42] A similar crisis swept over Jewish communities in nineteenth-century Europe and made them unable to perform Jewish rituals.

Jewish Communists were the heirs to two secular ideologies, which appeared among the Jews as part and parcel of the secularization crisis: Marxism and the Jewish Enlightenment (Haskala). The Marxist critique of religion and claims of scientific certainty gave the Jewish Socialist a quasi-religious ideology, a substitute for the old certainties. The Jewish Enlightenment's criticism of the Jewish community released the first Jewish Socialists from the constraints of Jewish tradition. Nonetheless, these secularizing ideologies did nothing to alleviate their identity crisis. Some chose to assimilate into the world of revolutionary Socialism, disregarding their Jewish origins. Others chose to reinvent their Jewish identity and became nationalist Jews, particularly Zionist. The Jewish Communists in Palestine were at the crossroads of this complex identity crisis: socialist and internationalist in spirit, but living in the heart of the Zionist nation-building project.

The Jewish Communists rejected Zionism as a nationalist, anti-internationalist ideology and at the same time discarded some Jewish traditions as unfounded fraud. Nevertheless, they did not utterly reject their Jewish origins. Using the cultural mechanisms of Zionist Socialism, they reinvented their Jewish identity and poured new content into the old vessels of Judaism. But they did not adopt the Socialist-Zionist secular identity, instead assimilating into their Communist identity Jewish motifs that they deemed progressive, popular, and rebellious. A Jewish Communist was thus able to identify with Jewish heroes of antiquity and myths of Jewish heroism and feel as though they were his own. The rituals, symbols, and myths extant among Communists from the 1920s to the mid-1960s were the manifestations of this Jewish progressive identity.

Hanukkah, the main Jewish holiday celebrated by the Jewish Communists, exemplifies the process of formation of this identity. At first, the myth of Hanukkah elicited from the Communists their ingrained rejection of Jewish culture, be it religious or Zionist. However, even then their interpretation of the holiday bore some resemblance to Socialist-Zionist discourse. From that point on, Socialist-Zionist and traditional Jewish elements, transformed and reinterpreted in accordance with political circumstances, gradually diffused into the Communist identity, bringing to the fore an attraction to particular elements of Jewish history. During World War II, the Jewish Communists accepted Jewish heroism as part of the Hanukkah myth, but saw it as being exemplified only by Soviet Jews in modern times. By the late 1940s, however, they found themselves supporting the Israeli war effort and adopted the myth as an integral part of their identity. In the mid-1950s, isolated by their objection to the 1956 War, they finally became the true heirs to the holiday's national-patriotic legacy.

The high point of the assimilation of the Hanukkah myth into the Jewish Communist identity was in the 1950s to the mid-1960s. The growing influence of the Left Men, mainly in Banki, prompted the evolution of the Hanukkah myth into a Communist ritual, integrating traditional Jewish symbols and customs with Marxist-style myth. The full integration of Hanukkah into the Communist identity symbolized the end of the quest for a Jewish progressive identity. Hanukkah came to be celebrated by the Communists very similarly to the Socialist Zionists, indicating that by the time of the split-up in 1965 the Communist Jewish progressive identity had become very much Socialist Zionist.

The same process can be seen with respect to Passover, reflecting the changing nature of Communist identity. It exemplifies the degree to which Socialist-Zionist elements penetrated the Jewish Communist identity. During World War II, through the 1950s and into the early 1960s, the holiday's main theme was liberty. By the early 1960s, however, the young Communists of Banki, like the Socialist Zionists of the 1930s kibbutzim, may have created their own Haggadah. As in the case of Hanukkah, the Jewish Communist had become akin to the Socialist-Zionist identity.

The Jewish Communist identity eventually became simply too similar to Socialist-Zionist identity and lost its distinctive nature. MAKI and Banki were multicultural organizations, and behind the ideological unity diverse identities found expression. Those diverse identities were held together by Arab-Jewish internationalism and their rejection of Zionism. The quest for cultural hegemony by the Left Men, who tried to forge those identities into one Israeli identity, ended up violating this basic tenet. When that happened, it became one of the contributing factors in the schism of Israeli Communism.

Chapter 3

Holocaust, Independence, and Remembrance in Israeli Communist Commemoration

The Holocaust in Communist Consciousness and Narrative

The Communist subculture emerging in Palestine since the 1920s was in constant contact with Zionism's national culture and inescapably confronted by the turbulent Jewish history of the twentieth century. The Holocaust memory of the Jewish Communists was shaped by a few primary motifs. The first, mirroring attitudes in Israel of the 1950s, was the emphasis on the armed resistance of Jews in Europe, mainly the Warsaw Ghetto uprising. The Jewish Communists stressed Communist participation in the resistance, though they did not fail to extol the participation of Socialist Zionists as well. The second motif was the role of the USSR in fighting Nazism and saving Jews, and the third related to the political conflicts concerning the Holocaust prevalent in Israel in the 1950s. The 1960s saw a change in the Communist discourse about the Holocaust. As Israeli society moved toward greater identification with the "passive" Jewish victims of the Holocaust, so too the tone of Communist discourse started to change, expressing a greater empathy with the victims.

The Holocaust hit the Jewish Communists hard. Most of them were of Eastern European origin. The Nazi extermination of European Jewry wiped out the close family members of many Jewish Communists. The severity of the blow is all too evident in a short literary piece named *Grodno* by

Eliyahu (Alyosha) Gozansky, where the writer recalls his Polish hometown's tragic fate in a series of episodes portraying the life and death of the Jews of Grodno. In one of the last episodes, Gozansky describes how his father, Yitzhak Gozansky, a progressive-minded lawyer, was marched to his death along with another three thousand Jews, leading the death march dressed in a clown's hat while two Jewish minstrels played wedding tunes beside him. The morbid march was filled "with a chorus of thousands of voices, made up of hysterical outbursts, desperate cries, the wailing of mothers and their children, interrupted by the rasp of lashes and gunshots."[1] The book is written in a tone of nostalgic longing for the dead father and helpless horror at the barbaric treatment of the Jews of Grodno by their Nazi murderers, which well conveys Gozansky's pain at the loss of family and friends.

Grodno exhibits many of the elements that would dominate the later perception of the Holocaust by the Jewish Communists. First of these is the element of revenge, which Gozansky talks about in almost mystical terms: the spilled blood cries for revenge, which would be meted upon the Nazi murderers by anti-Nazi fighters from all of Europe. Another element is the joint fate of Jews and non-Jews. The Communists, as internationalists, rejected the conclusion that the Holocaust proved it was impossible for Jews and non-Jews to live together. In all their writing about the Holocaust, the Jewish Communists stressed the common cause of Jews and non-Jews. Gozansky expressed this element by saying, "In the mass grave of Klabsin Jews and 'Gentiles' lie together. Jews and 'Gentiles' were murdered together, and together they fought the German."[2]

As upon other occasions, the Jewish Communists preferred to disregard the complexities of history in favor of an ideologically based narrative. The historical reality of World War II in Eastern Europe was that many collaborated with or did nothing to hinder the Nazi genocide. By the Jewish Communists, however, this phenomenon was confined to elements that were politically disfavored in the new People's Democracies. They did not allow the fact that a grassroots anti-Semitism existed in many of the places occupied by the Nazis, as well as in postwar Poland, where it manifested in the Kielce pogrom, and in the USSR of the late Stalinist era, to muddle their picture of an internationalist fight against Fascism. The stress on the joint fighting leads to another key element, the emphasis on active resistance. On this point the Jewish Communists shared a common idea with Socialist-Zionist culture, which commemorated its members' role in European resistance movements, mainly the Warsaw Ghetto uprising. Gozansky gives early expression to this element as he glorifies five Jewish partisan women.

Gozansky glorifies the Red Army, an element that would become commonplace in Communist documents concerning the Holocaust. The Jewish Communists praised the Red Army for saving the remaining Jews in Europe and defeating Fascism. Gozansky expresses this element together with the element of revenge, saying, "On the mass grave in Klabsin the victorious Soviet armies marched. Revenge and victory mean—death to the murderers."[3] These same elements, which were expressed in literary form in *Grodno*, found expression in many publications of MAKI and Banki from the mid-1940s to the 1960s. The admiration for the Red Army was not confined to the ranks of the Communists, as will be dealt with in detail in the next chapter, and Gozansky's remarks were probably not out of line in Palestine during the 1940s. However, it is highly doubtful that the Red Army was perceived as the main tool of revenge by Socialist Zionists.

As early as 1937, articles in *Kol Ha'am* called for free immigration to the democratic countries of the West for Jewish refugees from Germany. As the magnitude of the massacre in Europe became known to the Yishuv, the Communists' call for revenge became more pronounced. In a leaflet from 1942, as the Nazis were exterminating the majority of Jews in Warsaw, the Young Communist League urged the Jewish youth of Palestine to join the war effort. The young men of Palestine were called upon to join "the companies of the destroyers of the ghettos" in order to pay back the Nazis: "Blood for Blood! Death for Death!"[4]

From the late 1940s and into the 1950s the main focal point of the Communist commemoration of the Holocaust became the Warsaw Ghetto uprising. An internal letter of 1946 issued on the third anniversary of the uprising shows how elements that had appeared in earlier years were changed and added upon due to the events in Warsaw. The text was political in nature, informing party members and its candidates of the party's line in regard to the Warsaw uprising.

The letter develops the element of heroic armed resistance to the Nazi war machine. The importance of the uprising lay in "the defense of the national and human honor of the Jews, showing that the Jews would not be led like sheep to the slaughter"—a phrase lifted straight from Abba Kovner's famous manifesto, further connecting the Communist perception of the Holocaust to that prevalent among Socialist Zionists. The text stresses that the USSR saved the largest number of European Jews during the war and that the uprising came after the Battle of Stalingrad, which encouraged and inspired the rebels. It hails the cooperation between the Jewish underground in the ghetto and the democratic (i.e., left-wing) Polish underground and praises the support lent to the Jewish Combat Organization (under its Polish acronym ŻOB) by the underground organizations of the Polish left, mainly the Armia Ludowa (People's Army). This support translated into political support of "the new Poland established on the ruins of Hitlerism and Polish reaction."[5] The Jewish Communists disregarded the survival in Poland of anti-Semitism, which would resurface as a state policy under Gomułka in 1968.

The 1946 political letter expressed for the first time the anti-Fascist unity of all the Jewish political parties in the ghetto. It asserts that in the ghetto the "Workers Committee," consisting of Communists, Bundists, and the Socialist Zionists, worked with a "National Committee" that included the liberal Zionist and Orthodox parties. All of these diverse political forces had struggled together in the uprising. Another new element to appear was the contrast between armed resistance and passivity, later developed into an even sharper contrast between the heroic underground and the treacherous Judenräte.

In Israel of the 1950s Holocaust commemorations were sidelined. Israelis had a complex relation to events in Europe. Their image of European Jews as passive victims who went to their deaths without resistance was complicated by guilt over the little help lent by the Yishuv to suffering European Jewry and the Zionist negation of the Diaspora, making Israeli society myopic to a more sensitive approach to the Holocaust. This indifference, however, does not mean that the Holocaust was not debated politically during Israel's formative years. Israeli society during the 1950s was overtly political, leading to the politicization of aspects of life beyond what is customary in liberal democracies. One such aspect was the Holocaust and its victims. Far from being a source of unity, the topic elicited "unending political strife."[6] Three main issues stood at the center of this political debate: the reparations from West Germany, the shaping of the commemoration of the Holocaust, and the Kastner trial.

The latter involved Israel Kastner, a MAPAI official and one of the leaders of Hungarian Jewry during the war, who was accused by one Malchiel Gruenwald of dealing with SS officers to save around a thousand Jews at the expense of the mass of Hungarian Jews. Kastner lost his libel suit against Malchiel Gruenwald in 1953 when the judge determined "that he sold his soul to the devil."[7] He was assassinated by radical right-wing extremists in 1957. In 1958 the Israeli Supreme Court overturned the lower court decision and acquitted Kastner of the allegations against him. The Kastner case and the reparations from West Germany were used by MAKI and Banki to mount a radical opposition to the MAPAI-dominated governments. The commemoration of the Holocaust was used as part of a political and cultural struggle to preserve the memory of Communist Jewish resistance in Europe within the Socialist-Zionist culture.

From the early 1950s, the Israeli government negotiated with the West German government over compensation for Jewish life and property destroyed during the war. The negotiations culminated in an agreement signed in September 1952 between the German chancellor Konrad Adenauer and Israeli minister of foreign affairs Moshe Sharett. The agreement was opposed by both the extreme right and the extreme left. For MAKI, opposition to the agreement accorded with the Cold War rivalry between East and West and furthermore was a development of the revenge motif into boycotting West Germany, in their eyes the successor to Nazi Germany. All through 1952 the party ran an anti-German campaign in its organ and in the streets, constantly reporting on demonstrations and rallies against the negotiations with Bonn.[8] When the reparations issue subsided, the Communist press continued to attack West Germany and the Israeli establishment's growing ties with it. The main bone of contention for the Communists was the rearming of Germany as part of the North Atlantic Treaty Organization (NATO). The Kastner trial also left an impression on the politics of MAKI. The Communists took a radical stand when Kastner lost the libel trial and demanded that the state prosecute him. The party press published the verdict in the trial and MAKI, together with the right-wing Herut party, delivered a vote of no confidence in the MAPAI-led government.

The political debate was not confined to the realm of the day-to-day politics of the Jewish Communists. It also influenced the Communist subculture and its commemoration of the Holocaust. The Jewish Communists commemorated the Holocaust as a way of criticizing Israel's predilection for the West and opposing MAPAI's political hegemony. Their memory of the resistance would serve to carve their own niche in the memorial culture of the Holocaust, which was dominated by the Socialist Zionists, and toward that end they used their press.

The focal point of the Communist commemorative subculture was the Warsaw uprising of 1943. The yearly reminders of the day of the uprising in *Kol Ha'am* and in *Kol Hano'ar* at first hailed its importance as an uplifting experience. *Kol Hano'ar* explained its importance as a heroic battle for Jewish national dignity. In a document issued to mark the tenth anniversary of the uprising, stress is placed on the fact that the Jews stood armed to defend their human dignity. The text clearly expresses the elements present in Communist consciousness of the Holocaust since the 1940s. The uprising is said to have been inspired by the Soviet Army. The ghetto rebels were heartened by the victory at Stalingrad and gave an example of political unity in battle. The uprising was also an example of internationalist heroism of Jewish and Polish anti-Fascist fighters. Whereas the Polish left aided the rebels, the Judenräte betrayed its own people and collaborated with the Germans. And the uprising also carried a contemporary political message, with young Banki members being told that American imperialism was reviving Fascism, while the Israeli government by agreeing to reparations was legitimizing the neo-Nazi West Germany. It was incumbent on them to fulfill the "legacy and example of the ghetto rebels"[9] by increased agitation among the youth and denouncing the present-day Judenräte.

The Communist narrative of the ghetto uprising starts with the establishment of the first underground groups at the initiative of Jewish Communists as early as 1941. The first underground organization, the Anti-Fascist Bloc, was formed in February 1942 by two Jewish Communist activists, Pinkus Kartin (known by his underground name, Andrzej Szmidt), a veteran of the International Brigades who was parachuted into Warsaw by the Soviets in 1941, and Josef Lewartowski, a veteran Communist activist.[10] The bloc was an example of political unity among different political parties. Andrzej Szmidt's lieutenant was Mordecai Anielewicz from Hashomer Hatza'ir, who would lead the uprising in 1943. The Communists took great pains to demonstrate their part in the uprising and complained bitterly when it was ignored. On the sixteenth anniversary of the uprising, Adolf Berman, one of the surviving leaders of the uprising and a MAKI Knesset member, stated:

> We must regrettably note . . . that the press of MAPAM and Ahdut Ha'Avoda-Po'aley Zion and their institutions are distorting the history of the struggle in the ghettos. In the rallies in Kibbutz Lochamey Hagetaot and Yad Mordecai, they do not tell the historical fact that the first organization of armed resistance in the Warsaw Ghetto was the Anti-Fascist Bloc that was initiated by Communists and the PPR [Polish Workers' Party].[11]

The stress placed on the Warsaw Ghetto uprising and the central place it occupied in the Communist commemorative effort show that the Jewish Communists wanted to integrate within the Socialist-Zionist commemorative culture rather than oppose it, as both political groups emphasized armed resistance in contrast to passivity. While on issues like the Kastner trial and the German reparations MAKI and Banki did not pull any political punches, in regard to Holocaust commemoration they stressed what united them with Socialist Zionists. One glaring example is the cult MAKI developed around the figure of Mordecai Anielewicz, the ultimate Socialist-Zionist hero, who was placed alongside the Communist founders of the resistance in the ghetto. The same inclusive approach is noted by Yair Tzaban, who remarks that although the party stressed the role of Communist resistance heroes, it still "treated Anielewicz with a great deal of reverence."[12]

In contrast to the heroism of the Jewish rebels stood the Judenräte; for the Jewish Communists, those assigned to head them and the Jewish police were nothing short of traitors. The Judenräte were perceived by the Jewish Communists as a tool for the extermination of Jews. Their effort to appease the Nazis is described as being part of a long Jewish tradition of passivity leading to national betrayal. There were class-related motivations behind this approach to the Judenräte. The Warsaw Ghetto is described in Marxist terms as having preserved the class differences of prewar Polish Jewish society. Those who suffered in the ghetto were the masses, while a small minority lived a good life despite the conditions in the ghetto. The basic class difference that manifested during this period shows the "animalistic nature of the Jewish bourgeoisie" and its institutionalized expression, namely, "the community [the Judenräte] the entirety of whose activity is one injustice that cries to heaven, an injustice to the poor."[13] The collaborative behavior of the Judenräte is opposed to the heroic underground: one exemplifies weakness and degradation, the other human and national dignity. A more sensitive stand toward the Judenräte was precluded by the one-dimensional narrative that the Jewish Communists created. Even when a more balanced and redemptive approach to them emerged after the poet Natan Alterman called for their rehabilitation, igniting a public debate, the Jewish Communist stand remained simplistic and unchanged.

The narrative of the Warsaw uprising was targeted at both MAKI and Banki members in order to instill a lesson of a political nature, concerning three main themes: the reparations, the Kastner trial, and Israel's blossoming relations with West Germany. In a speech made at the founding of the Anti-Nazi Fighters Organization (ANFO),[14] Avraham Berman denounced Israel's ruling classes for cooperating with Hitler's successors for "thirty pieces of silver during the reparations."[15] The Kastner trial was also addressed in

Berman's speech, which asserts that "all those who suffered in the camps and ghettos felt the crimes of the 'Kapos,' the 'Judenräte,' and the ghetto police. The victims of Nazism in Israel must speak up and condemn Kastner and the policy of Kastnerism."[16] He accuses government circles of attempting to produce witnesses from Europe in order to clear Kastner's name.

Banki also internalized the narrative of the Holocaust. In a speech to a youth rally on April 17, 1954, the uprising is portrayed as having been inspired by the victories of the Red Army. The handful of rebels saved the honor of the Jews, in contrast to the Judenräte who sold them out. The rebels shared a common cause with the "Polish anti-Fascist underground." The Judenräte were aligned with Kastner. The victims and rebels left after them the command "not to forgive and not to forget what was done to the Jewish people by German Fascism."[17] This legacy would be fulfilled through political struggle by the youth against the rearming of West Germany and Israel's relations with that country.

This one-dimensional and extremely judgmental stance with its overtly political aim prevented the Jewish Communists from developing an alternative consciousness of the Holocaust. Echoing the East German anti-Fascist myth in which brave Communists battled the Nazis to the exclusion of all others, the Jewish Communists, instead of sympathizing with the Jewish victims, preferred to glorify the few cases of armed resistance. Instead of trying to understand more deeply the complexities of survival in conditions of a breakdown of civilized society, they adopted a one-sided dichotomy of resistance versus Judenräte. What motivated the Jewish Communists to construct such a narrative? One reason may be an inability to explain the unexplainable. An event of such magnitude cried out for explanation, yet the Jewish Communists found themselves at an ideological shortfall. The dichotomy of resistance versus Judenräte is therefore understandable, as for them it represented some kind of Marxist explanation. The stress on the Red Army and the internationalist cooperation of Jews and non-Jews can be explained by the acute sense of weakness and victimization that the Jewish Communists as well as other Jews experienced in the wake of the Holocaust. But lacking the recourse of the Zionists to the creation of Jewish sovereignty in the form of the Israeli state, the Jewish Communists turned to their own source of empowerment—the Soviet Union's heroic struggle against Nazism. The political legacy and involvement of MAKI and Banki in the politics of the Holocaust reconnected them to Israeli society of the 1950s. Even more so, it can be said that in the case of the Holocaust, unlike cultural and political issues such as Palestinian-Jewish relations or the Soviet Union, the Jewish Communists mirrored the prevailing attitudes of a society that was ambiguous and conflicted with regard to the events in Europe. However, these societal attitudes were about to change, and the Jewish Communists would change with them.

The problematic attitude the Jewish Communists adopted, motivated as it was by an inability of ideology to explain the Holocaust, was not restricted to them only. Zionists and Orthodox Jews grappled with the same issue. For Zionists the judgmental approach to the victims of the Nazi mass murder was rooted in myths about the passivity of the exilic Jews. This image "was one of the extreme manifestation of the 'Negation of the Exile' idea."[18] Like the Communists, Zionists stressed the armed resistance of members of the Socialist-Zionist youth movements, contrasting their activism to the perceived passivity of the Jewish masses.[19] Indeed there were other voices—mainly among the Zionist religious Mizrahi movement—that were more empathetic to the masses of Jewish victims. However, overall, the Socialist-Zionist elites shaping Israel of the 1950s voiced stands similar to the Jewish Communists. Roni Stauber explains this attitude in "the current attitudes and problems of Israeli society in her first formative years."[20] While not disregarding this explanation, I explain it, also, as a breakdown of Zionist values and ideology.

This crisis of values and ideas was even more apparent in Orthodox Jewry's response to the slaughter of European Jews. Its most straightforward justification of the horrors consisted of "explaining the tragedy as a punishment for the Jews' sins."[21] Rooted in the biblical texts, those who held this view found the root cause of the Nazi genocide in Jews' preference for Reform Judaism, Zionism, or just their disavowal of the covenant between God and his people. Other explanations, trying to avoid the judgmental reproach of millions of innocent victims, were found in such biblical sources as the Binding of Isaac, the book of Job, or the idea that God turned his face away from his people.[22] As was the case with Zionists, this reasoning revealed a deep crisis of accepted value systems when confronting a man-made disaster that defied understanding. The Communists' condemnatory attitude was but one expression of the theological and ideological crises that visited the post-Shoah Jewish World.

The 1960s were marked by a change in the attitude of Israeli society toward the Holocaust. In a process that started in the late 1950s and culminated in the Eichmann trial, the Israelis opened up to the stories of survival and passive resistance that burst into the public sphere during the trial. The Jewish Communists' perception of the Holocaust started to change and a new tone started to emerge as the survivors' stories were told during the trial.

The Eichmann trial was covered extensively by *Kol Ha'am*. From the first announcement of Eichmann's apprehension, through his arrival in Israel and trial, to his execution, MAKI demanded that the judicial process include the "many Eichmanns that exist in the world,"[23] namely, ex-Nazis who, according to the Communists, held top positions in the West German establishment. Another criticism aimed at the trial was the fact that the proceedings did not sharply distinguish between Kastner's conduct and the armed resistance of the Jewish underground.

Just before Eichmann's apprehension in 1960, in the Communists' yearly commemoration of the Warsaw uprising upon its seventeenth anniversary, the same motifs from the war years are still evident. The ANFO issued a public statement that "the shameful meeting between Ben-Gurion and Adenauer that constitutes the desecration of the memory of the ghetto fighters and the victims of Nazism . . . is an expression of the Judenräte policy that the ghetto rebels fought against."[24] In an editorial on the same page, the uprising is described as having been inspired by the Soviet victory in Stalingrad.

However, beside the motifs of armed resistance, national honor, pro-Soviet glorification, the Cold War and Israeli politics, new voices could be heard. As Israeli society started to take a more subtle view of the Holocaust, so did the Jewish Communists. In that year's customary Holocaust Day issue of *Kol Ha'am*, beside the narrative of armed resistance in the Warsaw Ghetto, two new items appeared. The first was a portion of a diary describing life in Bergen-Belsen, devoid of any heroic content. The second was a poem entitled "The Butterfly" by a boy inmate in Theresienstadt.[25] Both gave expression, however small, to groups other than the partisans and ghetto fighters, namely, the camp inmates and children.

A real change in Communist consciousness came with the opening of proceedings in the Eichmann trial followed by the testimonies of the prosecution witnesses. The trial was accompanied by a wide range of public activities by MAKI and the ANFO. Two days before it opened, at the conclusion of the fifth conference of the ANFO, the participants marched through the Tel Aviv streets wearing armbands with yellow stars, some of them dressed in the striped uniforms of the concentration camp inmates. This public display on the eve of the trial placed at its center not the heroics of the Holocaust, but its supposedly passive victims. When the evidentiary stage of the trial arrived, the Israeli public was exposed for the first time to the stories of the witnesses. One of them was the leading Jewish Communist spokesman, Avraham Berman. As one of the surviving leaders of the Warsaw uprising, Berman testified on the uprising and the events leading up to it. Nevertheless, a large part of his testimony dealt with the fate of the children of the ghetto, most of them murdered in Treblinka. As head of CENTOS, an aid organization for the Jewish children in the Warsaw Ghetto, he was able to shed light on the civic aid activities in the ghetto besides the active resistance of the underground. At the emotional highpoint of his testimony, to the sounds "of sighs and quiet weeping,"[26] Berman held up a pair of children's shoes found in Treblinka.

The change in the way the Jewish Communists perceived the Holocaust raises two questions. First, why did the Communist attitude change? Second, what were the implications of this change for the Jewish Communists' subculture and their perceived place in Israeli society? The Jewish Communists' change of tone can be explained by the change that Israeli society as a whole underwent from the late 1950s in regard to the Holocaust. Like all other Jewish Israelis, the Jewish Communists heard and participated in the Eichmann trial and the change this event effected was reflected in their subculture; the change to a more sensitive appreciation of the Holocaust beyond physical valor reflected the deep link between the Jewish Communists and their cultural social surroundings. Thus, the events of World War II that had helped connect the Communist Party to the Yishuv from the early 1940s accomplished the same in the early 1960s.

The new tone in the Jewish Communists' commemoration of the Holocaust did not, however, oust the dominant discourse of armed resistance in the ghettos. The final instructor's brochure from 1963 crystallizes all the elements of the Communist narrative of the Holocaust. It provides a jumble of readings and scout activity—mainly a version of the Hare and Hounds game, the object of which is to find Mordechai Anielewicz's bunker and read his final letter—fun-filled activity, no doubt. The brochure sought to instill in the young Bney Amal the true meaning of the Warsaw Ghetto uprising as part of the anti-Fascist struggle, or in the words of the text: "To inspire in them a hate of Fascism, and instill in their hearts respect and appreciation of the ghetto fighters and partisans and hate and contempt of the Judenräte . . . to fight against the renewed danger of Fascism and war and struggle against the relations between the Israeli government and the neo-Nazi government in Bonn."[27] The brochure concludes by listing the points that need to be emphasized to the members. Under "the ghetto class struggle,"[28] the ghetto is described as having been torn by class warfare between the Jewish bourgeoisie and the Judenräte and the Jewish left-wing organizations. The text stresses the role of the Communists in forming the "Anti-Fascist Bloc" and the cooperation between the Polish left and the ghetto fighters. The USSR is also glorified, especially for the emancipatory and liberating role of the Red Army. The text ends with the customary political edict to denounce Israeli polices of allying with West Germany, the embodiment of neo-Nazism.

Independence and Remembrance in MAKI and Banki

Israeli independence and the 1948 War posed a dilemma for the Jewish Communists. The support they lent to the creation of a Jewish state contradicted their anti-Zionism and the Palestinian-Jewish character of the party. In order to resolve the contradiction, the Jewish Communists accommodated Israeli independence by composing it into an anti-imperialist ideological and cultural narrative. That narrative in turn sustained Communist critical loyalty to the state of Israel and spawned an entire range of cultural practices, from hero cults to mass rites that created and reflected an anti-Zionist Israeli patriotic identity.

From its formative period in the 1920s, the Communist Party was anti-imperialist. Ideologically influenced by Leninism, the Jewish Communists developed a militant anti-imperialism, its discourse at first aimed against the British Empire. The Jewish Communists stressed the connection between Zionism and imperialism. They suggested a joint Palestinian-Jewish struggle to throw off the yoke of British imperialism and achieve independence. Thus the concept of independence was immanently connected in Communist discourse to anti-imperialism. In the 1930s and 1940s, as the Jewish Communists increasingly were co-opted into the Yishuv, they started to emphasize the role of the USSR in achieving independence. British imperialism was replaced by the growing American presence as the nemesis of Israel's newfound independence. In the 1950s and 1960s, the anti-imperialist discourse was further elaborated as the Communists attacked Israel's growing tendency to lean on Western powers, thus reshaping their attack on Zionism's connection to imperialism. The Communists constructed, through their anti-imperialist stands, a narrative of Israel's independence as an unfinished revolution and vied for position as true patriots. The joint Palestinian-Jewish anti-imperialist struggle was reshaped into a call for

Israeli-Arab peace and the implementation of the UN resolutions for the creation of a Palestinian state.

The anti-imperialist stand is evident in the early written manifestations of Communism in Palestine. A 1923 pamphlet points to the organic connection between the British and the Zionist bourgeoisie, asserting that in order to "sway the Jewish worker from revolution,"[29] the latter was using British imperialism to establish a Jewish state. In 1924, in an internal memo sent to the Eastern department of the Comintern, British rule in Palestine is defined as a "military colony, meaning strategic colony, which ensures the land route to India."[30] Pointing to the growing economic interests of British companies in Palestine, the party saw it as "its historic role to organize the Jewish and Arab toilers for a joint struggle against British imperialism."[31]

In the 1930s, which saw the increased Arabization of the party, there was no lessening of the anti-imperialist discourse. In the 1930 party conference resolutions, the Jewish members of the party were ordered "to expose the true aim of the Jewish bourgeoisie, and the fact that together with the Jewish minority in Palestine under its influence, it is the main instrument of oppression by the British occupiers against the native Arab population."[32] Nevertheless, the increasingly Palestinian nationalist stand of the PKP, looking upon the Palestinians as the revolutionary force in Palestine, was not received well by the Jewish members of the party. While the Arab Revolt of 1936 was defined as anti-imperialist, by the end of the 1930s the Jewish Communists were arguing that immigration to Palestine and the growing displacement of Palestinians made the Yishuv a national minority. From that ideological stand, the Jewish Communists demanded an end to the British Mandate in Palestine and the creation of a unified binational democratic country. Increasingly participating in the Jewish Yishuv's politics and culture, they became involved in the escalating confrontation between the British and the Jews of Palestine.

A wall poster issued by the Young Communist League in 1946 expresses the growing affinity between the Yishuv's demands and those of the Jewish Communists and their anti-imperialist discourse. It also points to the internalization of the anti-imperialist discourse in the formative stage of Banki in the 1940s. The poster, issued for the November 7th anniversary, describes British behavior in Palestine as being driven by imperialist interests "to strengthen their power to turn our country into a British military base to oppress the Yishuv and the peoples of the Middle East and the Soviet Union."[33] In order to achieve these aims, British imperialism and its agents incite Arabs and Jews. The leadership of the Yishuv was accused of capitulating to British terror, preferring cooperation with imperialism and offering it military bases. The way to win the struggle against British rule is by a creating a democratic binational state with full national rights for Palestinians and Jews.

In the midst of escalating violence between Palestinians and Jews, the Jewish section of the party and its youth movement identified completely with the Yishuv's war. The new motifs are evident in a handbill from 1948 calling on the youth to enlist in the war. The UN resolution of November 29th is described as a victory achieved with the aid of the USSR and the People's Democracies. The war raging all over the country is said to be the result of a conspiracy by the British government, Arab gangs, the remains of Anders' Army and Nazi agents, banded together by imperialism to prevent Jewish as well as Palestinian independence and restore British rule. The handbill warns against a return to foreign rule or the substitution of an American dependency for real independence. The Palestinians, until then partners in the fight against imperialism, are now presented as the victims "of the foreign ruler and its accessories—the men of Arab reaction with their gangs of killers."[34]

The change of attitude toward support for the creation of a Jewish state was not just the result of the Soviet policy change. It reflected a long-term process in which the Jewish Communists, internalizing the idea through anti-imperialist terms, recognized the existence of a Jewish nation in Palestine as well as a Palestinian one. This recognition came just as Palestinian society was being destroyed in the 1948 War. The paradigmatic change in politics was therefore correlated to a new view of the Palestinians as victims of imperialism, mirroring the complexities of MAKI's stand during the 1948 War. The party explained the plight of the Palestinians as being due to the evil deeds of imperialism, and in part the historical reality since 1917 justified this stand. At the same time, the destruction of Palestinian society in 1948 was as much the fault of Zionism. But MAKI, as part of the new state with Zionism at its center, could not offer that explanation.

As the fighting intensified into open warfare with the regular armies of the Arab states neighboring Israel, the anti-imperialist discourse became more pronounced.[35] In their publications the Jewish Communists stressed Soviet aid to the new state and the menacing role of American imperialism—substituting for British imperialism.

By the end of the 1948 War and into the 1950s and '60s, the Jewish Communists developed their anti-imperialist discourse into a narrative of an unfinished revolution. According to them, the events of 1948 were by nature anti-imperialist. The Jews of Palestine had thrown off the yoke of British rule and achieved independence. Yet Anglo-American imperialism was not ready to grant Arabs and Jews their freedom. Using the local Palestinian reaction at first and then the armies of the Arab reactionary regimes, British imperialism had tried through war and invasion to destroy the new state. American imperialism on its part had attempted to prevent independence or diminish it by political means. But with the political help of the USSR and military aid from the People's Democracies, the state of Israel had prevailed and achieved its independence. This independence, however, was not full. The tendency of the Zionist leadership to lean on imperialism, first British and then American, had estranged Israel's one true friend, the USSR, and as a result the country's freedom had been sold out to foreigners.

The same motifs are evident on the tenth Independence Day. Analyzing the deterioration in Israel's international standing as a result of its growing affiliation with colonial rulers on the world stage, an article in *Kol Ha'am* ascribes the initial support for the state to democratic, Socialist, and Communist forces. The creation of the state is seen as part of the global postcolonial wave that swept the world after World War II. However, despite the anti-imperialist nature of the Israeli independence struggle, "the world confronts the paradoxical phenomenon that the government of the state of Israel that was established as part of the breakdown of the colonial system is standing by the doomed colonial forces."[36] The text goes on to demand that Israel amend its relations with the USSR by ascribing to a policy of nonalliance.

The anti-imperialist discourse was not limited to the older MAKI members, but well ingrained in the consciousness of Banki members as well. In a document intended to provide background to discussions of independence for the young and mid-age levels of the movement, the anti-imperialist discourse is intertwined into the text. Independence from Britain is viewed as a result of the Soviet victory over Germany and the weakening of British imperialism. The 1917 Balfour Declaration, in which Britain promised a National Home for the Zionists, is perceived as a way for Britain to control Eretz-Israel. The Zionist leadership recognized Britain's aims and implemented a policy that separated Arabs and Jews, arousing hostility between the peoples. From the 1930s, the Jews of Palestine became a nation developing on a capitalist foundation. The British Empire was interested in exploiting the Eretz-Israeli industry on one hand, and on the other hand stopping it from competing with British economic interests.

On that economic basis, the antagonism between Britain and the Yishuv developed, resulting in the UN resolution that ended, with the help of the USSR, British rule in Palestine.

But imperialism did not abandon its attempt to deny the Jews their independence. The British wanted to prevent the possibility of a Jewish state being founded by provoking bloody conflict. While the British provided weapons to the Arab states, the Americans placed an embargo on arms sales to the Middle East. In the war, the Jewish people fulfilled its right to its own independent state, established through a struggle against British imperialism and its Arab allies. Yet political independence would not be complete while the Israeli-Arab conflict remained unresolved. As long as the conflict continues, "imperialism will exploit it and meddle with it." Peace is dependent on "saving Israel from the dependency on imperialism."[37]

The young Jewish Communists of Banki internalized cultural motifs of the 1948 War that were identified with the Palmach (Strike Force), the Yishuv's pre-1948 elite unit, as well as the anti-imperialist dictates of party ideology. This reflected the growing cultural and political influence of the Left Men, many of whom were veterans of the Palmach, which, despite being identified with the kibbutzim and Zionist Socialism, consequently gained increasing popularity among Banki members. Banki's instructors' brochures clearly show the cultural mix of Israeli Communism and Palmach culture. The 1964 brochure, entitled *Artsenu Hayafa—Zar Lo Ishlot Ba* (Our Beautiful Land—A Foreigner Won't Rule It), opens its selection of materials with an exchange of telegrams between Moshe Sharett, the Israeli foreign minister, and Vyacheslav Molotov—a text meant to remind the young Communists who supported Israel in 1948. The brochure ends with excerpts from the words of the fallen in the war and a poem by Haim Gouri, a poet closely identified with the Palmach and its culture. The song booklets also express this fusion, featuring Soviet songs and May Day songs alongside songs about Dudu from the Palmach and a love poem to Eretz-Israel by the poet Rachel.

The fusion between the Palmach culture and the Communist subculture is most evident in Banki members' veneration of the figure of Yitzhak Sadeh and use of his writings. Sadeh, the founder of the Palmach and one of the most able commanders of the 1948 War, was ideologically identified with MAPAM, making him acceptable to the Communists, albeit not very easily for veteran party members. In his personality, Sadeh merged not just military skills but those of an educator and a writer. Shoshana Shmuely recalled that his writings were used as part of the cultural mix designed for

Independence Day as well as other holidays.[38] Despite his Socialist-Zionist views, his figure was memorialized on the pages of *Kol Ha'am* where his defense of the Soviet Union and his humility were stressed.[39]

The anti-imperialist myth created by the Jewish Communists served a number of political and cultural purposes. It enabled them to give an ideologically acceptable reason for the foundation of the State of Israel. Rejection of Jewish nationalism ran deep in the history of Soviet Communism. It began in the early days of Bolshevism, when Lenin debated against the Bund demand for separate Jewish representation within the Russian Social Democratic Labor Party (RSDLP), and later against its claim to represent the Jewish workers in the Russian Empire and secure their cultural national rights. From the time of that debate, Soviet Communism rejected Zionism.[40] The Jewish Communists in Palestine inherited these ideological concepts and the harsh negation of Zionism and its drive for a Jewish state in Palestine. But then the imperial interests of the USSR changed, as did the Jewish Communists' approach to Jewish nationalism, and it supported the founding of Israel.

Heroes of the Anti-Imperialist Struggle

The years of underground activity against British colonial rule in Palestine and the 1948 War left MAKI and Banki with a legacy of party heroes. Held up as paragons of proper Communist behavior, Yael Garson, Siyoma Mernonynski and Eliyahu (Alyosha) Gozansky were to become focal points of Communist rite and myth.

The earliest hero to emerge from the underground years was Yael Garson. Born in Palestine, Garson from an early age showed an inclination toward social activism. At the age of twelve in 1927 she led children in a demonstration against the closure of her elementary school's eighth grade. Harassed by the British police, Garson went to France in 1936 and was active in aiding the Spanish Republic. In 1940 she came back to Palestine and was arrested by the British authorities. She was incarcerated in a Bethlehem prison, where she contracted pneumonia that was badly treated by the prison authorities. Complications of the disease resulted in her death on February 9, 1941, at the age of twenty-six.[41]

The figure of Garson and the myth and rite that developed around her would be the prototype for local Communist Israeli heroes to come. From the very first eulogies of Yael Garson in the 1940s, she was depicted as a tireless Communist activist working diligently for the movement and the working class. Her death had not been in vain, the text promises, as she died for a free Socialist Palestine, and the party would respond to her death with increased struggle against "imperialism and Zionism."[42] While her memory along the same lines—presenting her as a devoted, humble Communist and anti-imperialist—was kept alive on the pages of *Kol Ha'am* into the 1940s and 1950s, by the early 1960s interest in her waned. Since her cult was not supported by living family members, it was somewhat forgotten, which did not reflect the place she held in Banki. Evenings in memory of Yael Garson were still being held in 1964 and one of the movement's clubs was named after her.

The ritual that developed around Yael Garson became the basic model for other party heroes. As early as 1942, members of Banki visited her grave and in a simple ritual laid a flower wreath on it emblazoned with the slogan "Yael Garson, the brave anti-Fascist fighter—the victim of police terror," and made "modest speeches filled with pain and deep love."[43]

The next hero of the Jewish Communists' anti-imperialist struggle was Siyoma Mernonynski. Mernonynski was born on March 12, 1908, in the city of Tiraspol in Moldavia, then part of Romania. He was radicalized already in Romania and banished from the university in Bucharest after his first year. In Palestine he became a worker and joined the underground PKP. At first he was active in Antifa, the organization established by the Left in Palestine to aid Republican Spain; later he joined the underground cadre of the party and became the secretary of the Tel Aviv branch. In this capacity he was arrested in the summer of 1941 by the British CID (Criminal Investigation Department) and taken to its headquarters in Jaffa. There he was beaten to death and his body thrown into the sea near Bat Yam.[44] Since there was no grave to serve as a focal point for the commemoration of Siyoma Mernonynski, the pages of *Kol Ha'am* served in its stead.

The image of Siyoma Mernonynski as portrayed by the party was that of an all-around Communist "who was a guide to workers in the class struggle."[45] The motif of the tireless Communist was reasserted, and like Yael Garson, he was elevated to the status of a martyr on the altar of independence and the anti-imperialist struggle. In the 1951 eulogy for Mernonynski, he is memorialized as a hero of independence,[46] and his death charged with meaning as having been part of the popular struggle against the collaborators with imperialism. The commemoration of Mernonynski continued to be marked by anti-imperialist discourse well into the late 1950s and early 1960s. In 1961, his death was linked to anti-imperialist struggles worldwide, for "imperialists will not be able to sustain their rule by spilling the blood of the freedom fighters—not in Algeria, not in Angola, nor in any other colonial country."[47] While Yael Garson was held up as a model for Banki, Siyoma Mernonynski was considered a hero of the party. One of the party's clubs in Tel Aviv was named after him. In Banki his name too was memorialized. However, in both MAKI and Banki no ritual tradition developed around him. The absence of a known grave and the fact that the party could not find the resources to erect a monument in his name contributed to the relatively smaller place that Siyoma Mernonynski occupied in the Communist memorial culture.

The third Communist hero of independence was Eliyahu (Alyosha) Gozansky, one of the most gifted workers' leaders that the PKP produced in the 1930s and 1940s. He was born in Petrograd (Leningrad) on August 1, 1914, to Freda and Yitzhak Gozansky, the latter a progressive lawyer. The family moved to Grodno (Poland) in 1917. As a young secondary school student, Gozansky exhibited both a tendency to stand up for the weak and an emerging political awareness, arguing with his history teacher about anti-Semitism. At that stage, like many future Communist leaders, he joined Hashomer Hatza'ir. In 1930 Gozansky immigrated to Palestine. After a short stay in Kibbutz Glil-Yam, he started to study at the Mikve Israel agricultural school. There he was radicalized and joined the underground Communist Youth. In 1936 he came back to Grodno to learn to be a surveyor, and there he joined the Polish Communist Youth. As an activist in the Polish Communist Youth, he was caught by the Polish authorities and sentenced to eight years in prison. Acting on his father's advice, he exercised his Palestinian citizenship and was deported back to Palestine.

In Palestine Alyosha became an activist of the underground PKP. Under the cover of his work as a surveyor, he disseminated Communist propaganda in the army camps and among workers. In 1941 he was arrested by the British police. After his release, he started to work as a diamond polisher. Having worked in this industry for less than a year, he organized a strike and from then on became a union organizer involved in all the union conflicts in Palestine in the 1940s. The union work brought out Alyosha's organizational skills and ability to mobilize workers from different backgrounds and of divergent political stripes to fight for their rights. Apart from his union work, Gozansky was also active within the party, taking the initiative to turn *Kol Ha'am* into a daily from 1946. As the conflict between the Yishuv, including the PKP, and the British escalated, Gozansky's attention, as well as the party's, turned to forging connections abroad. He traveled in the newly established People's Democracies in Yugoslavia, Bulgaria, and his homeland Poland, cultivating contacts with the new regimes. With the outbreak of the 1948 War, Gozansky was active in support of the Israeli war effort, giving interviews to Eastern European media and public speeches in Jewish communities. His last public appearance was at the unification conference of the Polish Socialists and Communists in December 1948. On December 21, 1948, he died in a plane crash over Greece at the age of thirty-four.

Gozansky's death marked the start of a ritual tradition that would last through the 1950s until the schism of 1965, presenting Alyosha as the symbol of the party's patriotic stand in the 1948 War. The veneration of Gozansky and his association with the struggle for independence started with his funeral. News of his death was announced in an obituary on the front page of *Kol Ha'am*, stating that Gozansky had died serving the people and the party. The obituary briefly described Alyosha's life, stressing that he "worked hard to mobilize sympathy and aid for the Yishuv's war for independence."[48] The first ritual connected to Gozansky's hero cult was a wake in his memory immediately after the news of his death. It was a simple rite, attended by Alexander Penn, at which the party's Ron choir sang and MAKI secretary Shmuel Mikunis delivered a eulogy.

From the very first speeches, obituaries, and rites, the image of Gozansky, as projected by MAKI, was already taking shape. Again the tireless Communist appears, Gozansky being praised for having had "above all a boundless and diverse capability for work."[49] Neither is the connection to the struggle for independence neglected. Gozansky had been chosen by the Central Committee to head the party delegation to Eastern Europe "to mobilize material and political help,"[50] and had worked tirelessly to get it to Israel. Gozansky's funeral was the starting point for the rites that would enshrine his name as the Communist hero of the 1948 War. It was also a way for MAKI to project its own image at that historical moment.

After the body was flown in from Greece, the coffin lay in state in the party club in Tel Aviv, draped with MAKI's flag. The walls of the club were covered in red flags and the white and blue Israeli flag. A big picture of Gozansky giving his last speech in Eastern Europe was hung on the wall. The funeral procession set out from the party's club, led by a company of IDF soldiers and officers. The coffin was borne by MAKI Central Committee members. The procession was made up of Palestinians and Jews, representatives of the Histadrut and various unions, representatives of the workers' parties, and workers and representatives of the newly established Czech and Polish People's Democracies. Marching in the rear were party and Communist youth members. The funeral march stopped at two symbolic spots: the Workers' Council of Tel Aviv in Brenner House and the Histadrut Executive Building. At each point, eulogies were delivered by prominent party members. The connection between Gozansky and the struggle for independence was reasserted, Meir Vilner stating "that many who are present here are here thanks to the recruitment of comrade Gozansky in the People's Democracies for Israel's War of Independence."[51] The ceremony ended in the graveyard with a eulogy by MAKI's general secretary and the laying of wreaths.

The funeral march embodied the Jewish Communists' conception of themselves and their party. MAKI was a single entity made up of Arabs and Jews, symbolizing the internationalist solidarity of party ideology and practice; it consisted of two main bodies, the party and its youth movement. It was rooted in the Israeli working class and part of its center of power, the Histadrut. The party was also a participant in the patriotic struggle for independence and in the main tool for its attainment, the army. In essence, this symbolic procession expressed the ideal self-conception of the Jewish Communists for the years ahead. It also reflected the symbolic centers of power MAKI drew upon: the Israeli working class (Palestinian and Jewish), World Communism, and the Israeli state.

From the start, the cult surrounding Gozansky was characterized by a stress on the association between his deeds and the struggle for independence. The inscription on his gravestone noted that he'd died "on a mission to recruit help for Israel's war of independence at the age of thirty-four."[52] The sign of the Hammer and Sickle hung from the stone.

The first anniversary of Gozansky's death was marked by a memorial that consisted of speeches by MAKI leaders, the reading of poems devoted to Alyosha, and choral singing. The speeches about Gozansky's life stressed, among other things, his recruitment work in Eastern Europe on behalf of the Israeli independence struggle. The memorial rally would become the main fixture in Gozansky's cult for years to come. In a long speech, Meir Vilner sketched Gozansky's image as the Communist hero of independence and a paragon of the Jewish Communist, portraying Gozansky as the "driving force of the party,"[53] a political activist who had been behind every major party enterprise, and the "theoretician and the leader of our party in its union-class struggle."[54] He went on to praise the fallen party secretary for having been "a true Marxist and revolutionary . . . devoted to the cooperation between the Jewish and Arab workers."[55] Vilner glorified Alyosha's hatred of Fascism and imperialism, stressing that he'd been loyal "to the land of Socialism, an admirer of the Bolshevik Party and comrade Stalin."[56] He described Gozansky's trips to Eastern Europe to aid the Israeli war effort and his support of Israeli independence in accordance with MAKI's anti-imperialist discourse, stating that Gozansky "headed our party activity to recruit comprehensive aid for Israel's war of independence in the People's Democracies."[57] Gozansky's patriotism grew from his internationalism. He had embodied the patriotism of the Communist and internationalist, on the understanding that the pro-imperialism of the Zionist leadership did not overshadow what was objectively an anti-imperialist war. This characterization of the 1948 War was meant to alleviate, through the image of Gozansky, the contradiction between the Jewish Communists' anti-imperialism and the need to rationalize their participation in the state-building enterprise. In the following years, the cult surrounding Gozansky's figure was standardized in a way similar to the commemoration of Yael Garson. In the 1950s an attempt was made to celebrate Gozansky's memorial closer to Israel's Independence Day, but by the 1960s it was set on December 21, the date of his death. The motifs established in the formative stages of the cult did not change as the years passed. From the late 1940s on Gozansky was presented as a tireless, devoted Communist activist, internationalist and patriot, and the embodiment of MAKI's ideals.

Banki members participated in the rituals that were organized by MAKI and commemorated Gozansky's name as well in evenings that were devoted to all three heroes of the anti-imperialist struggle. Still, despite the calls by party leaders for the study of Gozansky's legacy, the evidence does not point to any widespread cult around his figure. The image of Alyosha that Banki members internalized was in essence the one that MAKI propagated, as one of the movement's ex-members testifies.[58] The fact that Banki did not develop an independent cult around the fallen party secretary points to the movement's organizational independence. At the same time, it relates to the cultural similarities between Banki and its mother party, as the figure of Gozansky projected by MAKI was shared by its youth movement.

The cult that developed around the martyrs of the anti-imperialist struggle validated the anti-imperialist myth that lay at the heart of Jewish Communist patriotism. Garson and Mernonynski, who had been victims of anti-Communist repression, were at first portrayed as above all Communists and anti-imperialists, the independence of the country as only a by-product of their sacrifice. They were portrayed as tireless, well-organized revolutionaries to be emulated by party members young and old. This portrayal was then extended to Gozansky and expanded to include all his life's work. However, despite the continuity in both content and ritual, Alyosha's cult exhibited a new element: Gozansky was not just a model Communist and anti-imperialist, but a patriotic hero of the War of Independence.

This new element was integrated into the ideological codes of the Jewish Communists. Alyosha's patriotic national image was framed in the language of two ideological principles: anti-imperialism and internationalism. Connecting his figure to the anti-imperialist myth meant that the Jewish Communists attributed to Gozansky a proper understanding of the 1948 War as anti-imperialist by nature. Gozansky could be both an Israeli patriot and an internationalist. He could be nationalist and Communist. He could assist the Israeli war effort and work for Arab-Jewish unity.

On the face of it, the contradictions in the figure of Gozansky and the clash between internationalism and nationalism that he represents are hard to reconcile. However, a look at the practices of other Communist parties in Europe and the ideological tenets of the Jewish Communists may place the actions of the latter in context. The German Communists, mainly in the years after 1945, adopted German nationalism and sought to present themselves as the force leading modern German nationalism.[59] In that sense, the Jewish Communists' actions in the late 1940s and afterward were justified in the context of World Communism. To the Jewish Communists themselves, there was no contradiction between their internationalism and nationalism; or, as Nissim Calderon phrased it: "Nationalism was welcomed not as a negative phenomenon: we accepted it. There was a Communist tradition of the move of the Soviet Union to accept nationalism and, moreover, pride that the Bolsheviks gave freedom to the peoples that had been under the Tsarist yoke."[60]

Developing a non-Zionist Jewish nationalism and manifesting it through anti-Zionist patriotism enabled the Jewish Communists to resolve the clash between nationalism and internationalism. They could thus present Gozansky as both an Israeli patriot and an internationalist at the same time.

It is hard to determine the extent to which the participants in Gozansky's commemoration truly believed in the myth that arose around him. However, the centrality he occupied in MAKI's commemoration culture suggests that he truly represented a figure that could resolve the party's ideological and political contradictions regarding the 1948 War. It is telling that Gozansky was memorialized in an NLL obituary in *Kol Ha'am* "on the death of the dear comrade Eliyahu Gozansky."[61]

Around twenty-five MAKI and Banki members were killed in the 1948 War. The party and Banki never developed a cult around them; perhaps due to the strength of the state memorial that developed around the fallen, they were only memorialized in a yearly obituary in *Kol Ha'am*. Gozansky, who had been a civilian and not directly involved in the fighting, became the independence hero of the party. In part, that may be explained by the fact that he was a leading figure in the party.

Apart from the rites connected to the fallen Communist heroes, the Jewish Communists, like most Israelis, took part in the mass celebrations of independence in the streets of Israel. These celebrations were described by Maoz Azaryahu as having given rise to a feeling of closeness and solidarity. As for the connections made in the ensuing spontaneous atmosphere of the public sphere, "some of them look unlikely and even impossible in the rigid structure of day-to-day life."[62] This communitas, with its accompanying liminal state, allowed even the marginalized Jewish Communists, Banki members in particular, to take part in the celebrations. This did not mean, however, that the young Communists blended in with the crowd. For even as they participated in the gatherings and group dancing, they stood out in their white shirts and red ties.

A photograph taken by Teddy Brauner on Independence Day in 1950 shows MAKI and Banki members standing on a truck, some of them dressed in the Banki uniform, holding up the national and class flags in their clenched fists. The dancing of Banki members in Mograbi Square, then the center of Tel Aviv, is documented in Ron Barkai's semi-autobiographical book *Like an Egyptian Movie*. As the protagonist of the book approaches the square, he sees the members of the Socialist-Zionist youth movements in their blue uniforms dancing and singing in circles. Then some confusion breaks out at the edge of the square and draws him over to a new circle of dancers. In the face of the audience's hostile reaction, "boys and girls in white shirts with red ties around their necks"[63] dance, singing a revolutionary song.

While Barkai's book describes a hostile and violent reaction of the audience, and it is likely that in the 1950s the reactions to Banki's appearances were hostile, by the 1960s the communitas formed during the mass celebrations included the young Communists too. One ex-member of the movement recalled that while Banki members were seen as a bit odd, they still were "absorbed by the size"[64] of the massed crowds. The dances were performed with great enthusiasm by the young Banki members, eager to show off their nationalist zeal and to surpass the rival youth movements.

Figure 3.1. Banki members celebrating the 1950 Israeli Independence Day.

Ritual, Narrative, Discourse, and Identity

From the 1920s and '30s, the Jewish Communists developed their own rites, as well as a discourse around the two defining events in modern Jewish history: the Holocaust and the establishment of Israel. In the process of developing this side of the Communist subculture, they shaped a Jewish Israeli identity uniquely their own. Their comprehension of the Holocaust and independence was dominated by the two meta-narratives of heroic resistance and anti-imperialism. The Holocaust became part of a narrative of heroism and resistance, posing as an example of total self-sacrifice that the Jewish Communists were supposed to follow. The Jewish Communists ignored the overwhelming majority of Jewish victims and concentrated only on the minority of cases of armed resistance. At the same time, they did not shy away from imparting to party and Banki members their own unique motifs. The uprising in the Warsaw Ghetto was connected to the victory of the USSR in Stalingrad. Soviet aid to European Jewry was emphasized. The help the Jewish underground received from the Polish left was praised as an example of internationalism, and the cooperation between Communists and Zionists was stressed.

The Communist narrative of the Holocaust was meant to create an identity that integrated Jewish pride and internationalism. It did not differentiate between Jews and non-Jews—unless the latter belonged to the wrong political party. There is no evidence that internationalism, so fundamental to Communist thinking, became blurred when a more victim-oriented narrative started to emerge. First, the heroic narrative was still the dominant one in the early 1960s and internationalism was an important element of it. Second, the new narrative was in the process of taking form and its elements were still in flux.

The Jewish Communist narrative of the Holocaust was constructed around a basic dichotomy of good versus evil. The ultimate evil was Nazism; the Jewish Communists "Other" was the Judenräte. Reflecting attitudes common in Israeli society, the Jewish Communists viewed the Judenräte as collaborators with the Germans. As Marxists, they described them as a class manifestation of the Jewish bourgeoisie, in contrast to the Jewish resistance that was identified with the Jewish working class. The emphasis on the class nature of the ghetto and the hatred of the Judenräte were meant to reinforce in the Jewish Communist identity the premise of a basic Marxist category such as class warfare. When it came to explaining the Holocaust, the Jewish Communists turned to their ideological tenets, rejecting religious and nationalist Zionist explanations.

For the Jewish Communists, independence from the British was closely connected with anti-imperialism. From the late 1930s onward, they were increasingly integrated into the political culture of the Yishuv, this process reaching a high point at the end of the 1940s. As the relations between the

Yishuv and Britain broke down, Jewish Communists identified the struggle as being objectively anti-imperialist. Influenced by the Marxist-Leninist stress on imperialism and the Soviet support for Jewish nationhood in Palestine, they supported the Yishuv's anti-British struggle and joined the Israeli war effort in the 1948 War.

According to the narrative constructed by the Jewish Communists, the 1948 War was the result of conspiring British and American imperialism. British imperialists had sent the armies of the reactionary Arab regimes to invade the newly established State of Israel. American imperialists had tried to prevent complete independence by embargoing weapons shipments to Israel and engaging in political maneuvering in the United Nations. Israel's only true friends were the anti-imperialist USSR and the People's Democracies that had provided the new state with arms and political aid. While the struggle for independence was anti-imperialist, Israel's leadership was not. The Zionist leaders very quickly sold out hard-won independence to American imperialism, subjugating the new state politically and economically. The Jewish Communists saw the 1948 War as an unfinished revolution, which would be completed only when Israel threw off the American yoke and aligned itself with the Eastern Bloc. The "independence" narrative was used to instill in MAKI and Banki members a Communist version of Israeli patriotism. The stress on anti-imperialism enabled the Jewish Communists to remain loyal to the state, while at the same time negating its leadership, ideology, and policy. Independence, maintained the Communists, had been achieved by the masses, and with that act of creation the Communists could identify.

The anti-imperialist discourse produced its own local Israeli heroes and a tradition of rituals connected to them. Their lives and deaths were to inspire in Banki and MAKI members a devotion to the party and instill in them a militant anti-imperialism. The most extensive and prolonged hero cult was the one that developed around Eliyahu Gozansky. His image as the perfect Jewish Communist and the hero of independence was meant to resolve the contradictions that MAKI's stand in the war had created. Gozansky could be an Israeli patriot and an Arab-Jewish internationalist at the same time.

The identity that emerged from the Jewish Communists' preoccupation with the Holocaust was underlain by a dialectics of opposing elements: identification with the Jewish victims of the Holocaust versus idealization of armed Jewish resistance; Jewish pride with its attendant drive for vengeance and refusal to compromise with the Germans versus an internationalism that encompassed Jews and non-Jews. The narrative and rites surrounding the 1948 War and its heroes were meant to instill in the Jewish Communists a militant anti-imperialism, and consequently a Communist version of Israeli patriotism. These two layers of identity spoke to two of the core values of Communism in Israel: loyalty to the Soviet Union and to Marxist-Leninist ideology. At the same time, the Jewish Communists, like parts of the Haredi community, formed a limited loyalty to the State of Israel. In contrast to the Haredim, however, whose limited loyalty to the Zionist state earned them a political stake in shaping it, the Jewish Communists did not influence the state, staying at the margins of its politics and culture.

At the heart of the Jewish Communists' approach to Jewish nationalism lay not a conflict between Zionism and Communism, between Jewish identity and Red assimilation, but the harmonization of Jewish and Israeli identities and internationalist and class approaches. Remarks by the late Dani Peter-Petrziel, a veteran of the 1948 War, an ex–Left Man and an active Communist to his last days, express this point well:

> In the party we received . . . with the internationalist and class approaches—also Israeli patriotism. At the 11th party conference held in 1949, Meir Vilner delivered—and it is important to stress that it was him—the main ideological lecture, in which he stressed the Israeli patriotic aspect. It was not in contrast to the other two approaches, but part of them.[65]

He also adds that the party was anti-Zionist at its core, regardless of its actual politics. He justifies those statements using Stalin's definition of a nation:

> In my opinion the party was ideologically anti-Zionist because it was Stalinist to both its Arab and Jewish audiences; it was Stalin who defined what a nation is and what an ethnic entity is . . . ethnicity according to him has four hallmarks: common language, common territory, common history and common economy. According to these hallmarks, it is obvious that the Jews are not a nation.[66]

He did not exclude the Palestinians from the anti-Zionist tenets of the party. When asked, "Could it be that it (the party) was anti-Zionist when approaching the Arabs, and not Zionist or a little more Zionist when approaching Jews?" he answers unequivocally: "No. It was anti-Zionist when it approached Jews."[67]

Chapter 4

Workers' Utopia and Reality in Israeli Communism

Communism among the Jews in Palestine never matured into a mass workers' movement. The Communists were alienated from the well-organized Jewish working class due to their anti-Zionism, their organizational weakness, their preference for dealing with the USSR and resolving Palestinian and Jewish relations rather than class war, and their exclusion from the Histadrut by the Socialist Zionists who controlled it. These factors made the Jewish Communists a small minority that in most cases operated at the margins of workers' politics in Palestine and later Israel.

In contrast to that reality, the Jewish Communist subculture made the militancy of the working class an imperative. May Day was celebrated as one of its central holidays. When MAKI and Banki members marched in the main Histadrut parade, they were engaging in a long-standing ritual from the early 1920s that expressed their cultural affinity with the working class. What had started as a revolutionary counter-ritual was transformed into a militaristic parade as the Jewish Communists, elaborately displaying Soviet and European left-wing symbols, enacted a marching Socialist vision of their society.

The Zionist Working Class and the Jewish Communists

The Jewish Communists never controlled the main Jewish union in Palestine, the Histadrut. In the early stages of the formation of Communism in Palestine, the MPSA enjoyed relative success in union and class politics. The first groups of Jewish Communists participated in the founding of the Histadrut. In the elections to the founding conference, they won 303 votes out of 4,433 or about 6.8 percent of the electorate.[1] Although it represented only a small minority outside the mainstream of Zionist workers' parties, the MPSA achieved an influence in a few trade unions, mainly the tailors' union and the sand-workers' union. The nascent Communist movement also tried to penetrate the most advanced group of workers in Palestine, the railroad workers, presenting radical demands, such as the inclusion of Palestinian workers in the union, and objecting to connections with the international Zionist movement, which was controlled by the Jewish bourgeoisie.

Worried about the influence the Jewish Communists were gaining, the Zionist leadership of the Histadrut broke it by force. The MPSA club in Haifa and its cultural circle in Tel Aviv were attacked. By infiltrating loyal workers, the Histadrut took over Communist-controlled unions. By 1921, the MPSA's hopes of a large-scale class struggle spearheaded by the Histadrut were dashed, and they left it. By the mid-1920s, as they became increasingly anti-Zionist, so the influence of the Jewish Communists within the Jewish working class diminished. However, they continued to maintain their presence within the Histadrut. At the second Histadrut convention in 1923, the PKP ran a non-party list named "the Workers' Faction." The faction was controlled by Communists and was essentially a front of the PKP. It won 250 votes and sent three delegates to the conference.[2] The marked decline in voting for the Communists can be attributed to their internal divisions. The expulsion of the faction from the Histadrut signaled the pariah status of the Jewish Communists, and at the margins of Socialist-Zionist culture and organization they remained.

The World War II years opened up new prospects for Communist union work, even among sections of the Jewish working class. The dislocation of the diamond-polishing industry from its traditional centers in the Netherlands and Belgium and the inaccessibility of European polishing centers to the De Beers raw diamond cartel, combined with British influence and interest in this industry, which was vital to financing the war and spurring local initiative in Palestine, led to the foundation of an extensive polishing industry. Its founding by Jewish capitalists ensured that the venture would employ Jewish workers, in accordance with the Hebrew work policies of the Zionist establishment in Palestine. The Jewish character of the industry did not mean, however, that the Histadrut penetrated it. The industry was in the hands of private owners who shortened the time of internship of the largely youthful workforce, and the Histadrut influence—traditionally exerted on workers and interns through its work bureaus—was limited. That meant that all the different political unions, from the Revisionist right to the Orthodox, organized the workers. It also meant that workers from "marginalized" groups who had trouble finding work through the Histadrut work bureaus were able to find work. As a result, a relatively large number of right-wingers and Communists were employed in the diamond-polishing industry. Divided into different unions and paid by the piecework method, unusually young and restless, the diamond workers were more predisposed to strike than other workers in Palestine.[3]

A leading Communist activist was Alyosha Gozansky, probably the most capable organizer the party ever had among Jewish workers. A diamond worker himself, Gozansky led the workers in the industry in their struggles during 1942–1946. Some describe him as endowed with boundless energy and an uncanny ability to work with workers of different stripes. He became a voice for Jewish workers. During the 1940s Gozansky was also involved in the struggles of the British camp workers who worked for the British Army and the civil servants' struggles. In his union work he stressed the need for the Communists to integrate into the Histadrut.

In 1944 the Jewish Communists got their first chance to do just that. For the first time since its expulsion from the Histadrut, the PKP was allowed to work openly as one of the union's parties. Readmittance to the Histadrut marked the start of a flurry of activity by the Jewish Communists. In a Haganah secret agent report on a conference of committees of the PKP in June 1945, Alyosha is quoted as saying that "when the party wished to participate in the election to the Histadrut convention (1944) it was able to collect, in two days, the three hundred required signatures of Histadrut members."[4] He also called on party members to join the union and organize, and he announced that a special party department was being established for Histadrut activity that would be the mainstay of Communist work. The hectic activity among Jewish workers culminated in the report delivered by Alyosha in the name of the Central Committee to the September 1945 PKP conference.

The report was the most methodical attempt, thus far, by any Jewish Communist to understand Palestine's working class and its economic surroundings. Its analysis is based on statistical data charts, the industrialization of the country during the war, and the policies and behavior of private capital and the British colonial government. It also describes the conditions of life and work of Jewish and Palestinian workers, arriving at the conclusion that "the foreign monopolies, in partnership with the local and big bourgeoisie helped by the colonial government,"[5] were lowering workers' living standards and impairing Palestinian industry's ability to compete in both the local and foreign markets. The report is imbued with Marxist ideology, but at the same time Gozansky's practical experience in the diamond industry is evident.

The upsurge in the Jewish Communists' involvement in and leadership of union struggles was short-lived. As the conflict between Palestinians and Jews deteriorated into open warfare from the mid- to late 1940s, the Jewish Communists' attention was diverted to it. Even Gozansky's relentless efforts were redirected to the party's connections with the new Communist regimes, and later to helping the Yishuv's war effort. When he died at the end of 1948, the Jewish Communists felt they had lost one of their most gifted leaders. Even the gains won by Jewish Communist union activity in the 1940s remained limited. Communist involvement in the diamond industry stemmed from the special position the workers in this sector occupied in Palestine's economy during the war. When those circumstances ceased to exist after 1945, Communist influence evaporated. During the 1950s and early 1960s, the Jewish Communists maintained their representation in the Histadrut and became a permanent opposition to the longtime hegemony of MAPAI. The main struggle they engaged in was opening the union ranks to Palestinians with Israeli citizenship. This campaign can be seen as not just purely class based but part of the struggle for equality of Palestinians within Israel.

The only purely class-based struggle that MAKI was involved in was that of the merchant marine sailors. In 1950, when Israeli sailors rebelled against the Histadrut and its powerful Haifa machinery, electing their own separate representation, they were broken by the union and the MAPAI establishment. Many of the strikers, ex-members of the Palmach naval unit, found their way to Sneh's men and MAKI. Aside from that, the Communist Party embarked upon intense activity among the new immigrants that were coming into the country. To the distress of these newcomers, separated from the mainstream of Israeli society of the 1950s by cultural and language barriers and the pains of immigration, MAKI and Banki gave voice.

Again, however, neither the party's gains among the new immigrants nor its participation in the sailors' struggle were long lasting. The sailors' strike never materialized into a large-scale revolt against the hegemony of the Histadrut. In regard to the new immigrants, every "step up the economic ladder, leaving the overcrowded immigrants' towns, getting out of the swarming slums,"[6] meant also that they were abandoning the Communist Party. The party was ideologically and culturally committed to working-class militancy and struggle, but in practice, its agenda was aimed at "the Soviet Union, the Arab population, and only after them—the class struggle."[7]

Despite the Jewish Communists' modest achievements among workers, their symbols, rituals, and myths did not reflect that reality. Like other Communist parties worldwide, MAKI perceived itself as the vanguard of the working class. In Banki one of the main points of the movement's education was to instill in the young Communists an understanding of and sympathy toward the workingman. This identification with workers was reflected in the holiday connected with workers' militancy, May Day.

The main ritual connected with workers was the May Day march that MAKI and Banki participated in as part of the Histadrut's central march. The march was accompanied by a plethora of rallies and get-togethers that spread MAKI's messages nationwide. It was steeped in symbolic and mythological motifs taken from Soviet traditions but also showing local influences.

May Day

May Day was celebrated in Palestine for the first time in 1906 by members of the Po'aley Zion party. Its symbols came from International Socialism, mainly the Red Flag, the workers' march, and the singing of the "Internationale." Alongside the borrowed Socialist symbolism, the Socialist Zionists tried to integrate Zionist symbolism into May Day as well: "The White-Blue flag was raised alongside the Red Flag, national slogans were added to the class ones, and two anthems, the national and that of the Labour Movement, were sung together with the 'Internationale.'"[8] The holiday was institutionalized from the 1920s onward by the Histadrut, which turned it into a display of its growing power within the Yishuv.

From the early 1920s the Jewish Communists marched on May Day. But since they were nevertheless operating at the underground margins of workers' politics, it was for them a day of protest, an incursion into a hostile public sphere, an occasion when, like the revolutionary movement in Tsarist Russia, they burst out into the open. There they violently encountered their political rivals and the forces of the British colonial state. In 1921 the MPS (Socialist Workers Party) parade became embroiled in a skirmish with the participants of the Ahdut HaAvoda march. By a dismal coincidence, the brawl in Tel Aviv occurred just as Jaffa Palestinians began to attack Jews in what became known as the "1921 Riots." The Communists were wrongly accused of provoking the riots, giving the Mandate police justification to persecute them.

The testimony regarding later May Day demonstrations during the 1920s stresses their underground nature. Nachman List described the PKP May Day demonstration in Tel Aviv as an exercise that involved sending a group of members to lure the police away from the intended site. The decoy was so successful that when the demonstration started, only one policeman, the one responsible for fighting Communism, chased after the demonstrators on his bicycle, whistling and shouting, "Disperse." The rituals accompanying these raids into the public sphere were simple: the demonstrators waved "the Red Flag and marched singing the 'Internationale,' "[9] and the singing was accompanied by a speech. The demonstration ended with arrests.

A less humorous tone is found in the testimony of Bullas Farah regarding the same May Day in 1925, but in Haifa. The Communist-led parade clashed with the police, as the "security men tried to disperse the demonstration and grab the Red Flag from a young man carrying it at the head of the marchers."[10] When the flag-bearer punched the officer in charge, it only provoked the police into violently attacking the marchers. In Haifa we see again the same elements featured already in the Tel Aviv May Day demonstration: the Red Flag as the main symbol and the clash with the forces of the state.

In the streets the PKP activists clashed with Socialist Zionists and the forces of order. The handbills clandestinely distributed by the party were imbued with the same militant spirit. From the start, the Jewish Communists defined May Day in transnational terms. Psychologically compensating for their weakness and small numbers, they used May Day to demonstrate their belonging to the world proletariat headed by the "magnificent edifice of the Soviet Socialist Federation."[11] In a 1921 pamphlet, the Jewish Communists call upon the Hebrew workers to celebrate their day of struggle as working-class rule is being born around the world. The Socialist-Zionist parties are accused of betraying the Jewish workers of Palestine by collaborating with the Jewish bourgeoisie and the British. The pamphlet cites struggles ranging from "the countries of the East—gigantic China, great India, Egypt, Syria, and Lebanon" to "countries with a large working class"[12] like England and France.

As the PKP became increasingly anti-Zionist, as it moved more and more to the margins of workers' politics in Palestine, so the language of its pamphlets became more radical. Well into the early 1940s the Jewish

Communists continued to embellish the militantly working-class, universalistic, and pro-Soviet terms that they had been using already in the 1920s.

In the formative stage of Communism in Palestine, three distinct elements of a Communist May Day emerged. The first was its nature as a counter-ritual where the Communists emerged into the public sphere, violently clashing with their political rivals and the forces of the British colonial state. The second was the core meaning of the holiday as the day of international working-class militancy. The workers of Palestine were called upon to join a global class struggle in which Palestine was merely one small front. The third was the pride of place held by the USSR in Jewish Communist awareness. In the context of May Day, the Soviet Union was perceived as a workers' paradise, a place where workers held political power and solved national and economic problems. The emphasis on the international working class and the USSR was undoubtedly compensation for the realities of Palestine: the PKP was a small and oppressed minority, with few gains among the only substantial working class in the country, the Jewish one, which stayed staunchly loyal to Zionism.

The turning point in the form and content of May Day came with the legalization of the PKP on June 22, 1941. For the first time, the Jewish Communists' counter-ritual was allowed into the public sphere. Visual evidence of the 1944 May Day parade shows that it had been transformed

Figure 4.1. Communist marchers, May Day 1944, Tel Aviv. Photograph courtesy of Yoram Gozansky.

from a counter-ritual into an orderly, militaristic parade. Emulating Soviet parade practices, which had frozen into a rigid militaristic format since the early 1930s, the Jewish Communists in late-1940s Palestine marched in orderly military fashion. The first photograph shows the Communist marchers in three columns, headed by a flag-bearer dressed in Banki uniform. They are carrying the Red Flag, the symbol of working-class militancy. A second photograph shows the same march passing along Tel Aviv's seashore promenade. As in the earlier photo, there are three rows of marchers, made up of Banki members dressed in their white shirts and red ties and older party members dressed in civilian clothing. At their head, under the Red Flag, march party leaders Alyosha Gozansky and Uzi Borshtain.[13]

The new, open way in which May Day was celebrated in the mid-1940s may point not only to the change in the party's status, but also to the persistence of a hampering reality. Now legalized, having participated in labor struggles during the war, and prompted by the need to work with Socialist Zionists to aid the USSR and their identification with the plight of European Jewry, the Jewish Communists discovered a growing affinity between them and the Yishuv. At the same time, this new openness did not change the basic fundamentals of the reality in which they operated. They were still a small minority within the Jewish working class. They were still held suspect by most parties in the Histadrut, and the gains they had made among workers during the war were not long lasting; although legalized, in many ways they remained marginalized.

The changes in the form of the May Day march can also be explained by the change in the activity and legal status of the party. The counter-ritual had been the product of the underground circumstances of a small sect of believers rushing into the open public sphere in a revolutionary charge. Legalization meant that the PKP became one of the parties of the Histadrut and a participant in the political system created by the Yishuv, both in the Histadrut and in the instantiations of Jewish autonomy in Palestine. It meant that the Jewish Communists had to persuade people of the validity of their ideology and political stands and not just violently agitate for a workers' revolution. In this new reality, a dynamic but orderly and disciplined ritual was needed.

Communist May Day's new and orderly form, from the mid-1940s, did not mean that the holiday entirely lost its counter-ritual character. While Communists did not directly engage with the forces of the state, which did not prevent them from marching and intervened only to maintain order, they still confronted their political rivals. May Day was a contentious issue between left-wing and right-wing Zionists. For Zionist Revisionists especially the holiday was an abomination and, as early as 1928, they skirmished with Communist May Day marchers.[14] The street skirmishes with the right are the background to the persistence of May Day's countercultural nature even after legalization.

In an article commemorating Alyosha Gozansky, the writer describes how the activists of the PKP in Tel Aviv were ordered on May Day 1943 to "hang large cloth placards in central spots in the city."[15] One such spot was a school located in the old heart of the city near Allenby Street. The task fell to some young Communists who hoisted a red banner bearing portraits of Lenin and Stalin and the Hammer and Sickle. That ignited a protracted street battle between Beytar (acronym of the Yosef Trumpeldor Alliance, the Revisionist youth movement) members and the Communists. This incident bears all the hallmarks of the Communist counter-ritual of the 1920s. The Communist youths and older party members burst into the public sphere with the symbols of the Soviet Union painted in the red of the working class. Their incursion led to a clash with their political rivals and the forces of order, and the police tore up the placards that caused the ruckus.

The most important development in the evolution of the Communist May Day in the era after legalization was the inclusion of the party in the Histadrut procession. As early as 1944, the Histadrut lifted the ban on accepting Communist members to its ranks, in fact recognizing the PKP as one of the union's parties. In late March 1946 the party sent to the Histadrut executive a telegram demanding "the participation of our representatives in the performances and rallies of the Histadrut"[16] on May Day. The demand was granted, but not fully. In Tel Aviv the main procession went smoothly, but in Haifa *Kol Ha'am* reported that the members of the Communist youth movement were not permitted to march with the rest of the union.

The main parade in Tel Aviv, where both the party and its youth movement marched, featured the elements that had come to characterize the Jewish Communists' May Day since legalization. The PKP and the Communist youth marched in separate blocs. The march was headed by a truck "decorated with Red Flags and a big star made out of vegetation and flowers."[17] The first bloc consisted of youth movement members "dressed in white shirts and red ties, marching in uniform lines."[18] The second bloc consisted of the party's Central Committee and veteran members, with the flag of the Tel Aviv PKP branch waving at the forefront. The rest of the marchers were war veterans and the veterans of the International Brigades.

The party marched separately from the Communist youth, as was customary in Histadrut May Day marches—where the workers' parties paraded ahead of their youth movements.

One element that carried over from the 1920s was the use of working-class and Soviet symbolism, preeminently the Red Flag. The Red Star made of vegetation expressed the spring motif of the holiday and echoed the first parades of the Russian Revolution where flora had been used to decorate the horses of the Red Army. Another Soviet element straight out of the Stalinist vocabulary was the carrying of portraits of Lenin and Stalin. The quasi-Stalinist symbolism and rigidity of the youth march especially were accompanied by carnival-like elements, as for example when the bloc of soldiers and veterans carried cartoons mocking the veterans' sad state. This element was more akin to the first revolutionary festivals in Russia and the USSR of the 1920s.

The content of the holiday remained internationalist, militantly working class, and pro-Soviet, as in the 1920s. In the party's holiday slogans one finds, side by side, "Long live the Soviet Union!" and "Long live the freedom and independence struggle of the peoples of Indonesia and India and all colonial peoples!" Another slogan calls for "progressive work and social laws."[19] Overall, May Day was used to showcase everything the Jewish Communists stood for. In slogans and in symbols, they showed their loyalty to the Soviet Union and Arab-Jewish fraternity, and the party's sympathy for anticolonial and working-class struggles, local and international.

After 1948, May Day was characterized by an increased effort on the part of MAPAI to "direct its ceremonies from above and to shape the holiday patterns so they will contribute to the advancement of its values and the strengthening of its position."[20] That called for the regimentation of the preparations for and execution of the holiday. At the same time, MAPAI tried to nationalize the holiday and create a symbolic identification between it and the state. These tendencies were partly absorbed by the Jewish Communists. While the Communist holiday was already self-regimented ideologically and organizationally, the Jewish Communists refused to bow to MAPAI's demands. In that sense, May Day maintained some of its counter-ritual spirit, as the Communists clashed with their political rivals inside and outside the Histadrut.

During the 1950s the elements of Communist May Day, which had first appeared in the 1920s, became entrenched. The holiday march displayed a mix of Soviet elements and features of local Israeli origin. The main event of May Day was without a doubt the mass march and the assembly. Like the other holiday events, they too were tightly organized by the Histadrut. The Communists participated in the march in two blocs, the one reserved for the workers' parties and the closing bloc of the parade made up of the youth movements. The main demonstrations were held in Jerusalem, Tel Aviv, Nazareth, and Haifa. While MAKI members marched in relatively loose fashion,[21] Banki's march was an exercise in orderly discipline. All through the 1950s until the mid-1960s, the youthful marchers served as the showcase of the party and the entire movement, it being noted that "their fighting character and fair form . . . are respected by the crowds."[22] Already in 1944 the Communist march had shown signs of militaristic order, but from the 1950s this element became increasingly evident. Further to the process of co-optation of the Jewish Communists into the political system of the Histadrut, it marked the Communist subculture's internalization of motifs from statist and Socialist-Zionist culture.

There was a grassroots mobilization of Banki members to add aesthetic flair to the march. In many ways, the marked change in the appearance of the May Day march was the result of the collective work of Banki members, mainly the late Yoska Valershtiean, a survivor of Theresienstadt and Auschwitz who was sent to Palestine as part of a unit recruited by the Czechs and MAKI to aid Israel in the 1948 War. A devout Communist and a graphic artist, he used his talents in the service of the Communist movement. On May Days he was responsible for the design of the slogans and displays carried by the marchers: handheld placards showing the detonation of an atomic bomb, peace doves with their wings flapping, and a globe four meters in diameter highlighting the Eastern Bloc and the USSR.[23] Valershtiean's ideas were executed by the members of the Tel Aviv branch of Banki, who would turn the movement's club into a workshop where they made the displays for the march and even trained drummers and trumpeters. It was a grassroots effort similar to that which accompanied the revolutionary marches in NEP-era Russia.

While the mobilization of Banki members may have echoed early Soviet models, the Banki marches came straight from the visual world of Stalinism and the post-Stalinist USSR. Yoska Valershtiean admitted as much, saying, "I put all my experience from the Czech Republic and my impressions from the May Day demonstrations in the Socialist countries and the USSR"[24] into the design of the marches in Tel Aviv. Another ex-member makes the connection even clearer: "Look at the marches in the USSR of November 7th or May Day. Clearly it is not to the same extent, and without the arms it is only a small fraction of that."[25] The orderliness and discipline of the

Figure 4.2. Banki display, May Day 1957, Tel Aviv.

Figure 4.3. May Day 1958, Tel Aviv.

parade earned the respect of even the non-Communist press, as *Kol Hano'ar* was happy to report: "The impression that the Banki demonstration in Tel Aviv left can be estimated from the article in *Ma'ariv*, which had to report (much to his regret, in his words) 'the most impressive performance was that of the Communist Youth—Banki . . . it was a colorful march with its big displays and devices.' "[26]

Marching publicly in the streets, the Communists encountered a certain level of resistance and violence. Jacob Markovizky asserts that most Communist May Day demonstrations "ended with no bloodshed or violent confrontations,"[27] but a closer look reveals a more complex reality. First to erect barriers to the conduct of the marches was the Histadrut. Anxious to imbue May Day with Zionist content, the MAPAI-dominated union tried to invalidate the slogans proposed by MAKI. On one glaring occasion in 1960, the Histadrut's nationalization of May Day came into direct confrontation with MAKI's socialist principles. Claiming that the holiday overlapped with Remembrance Day, Histadrut secretary general Pinhas Lavon passed a resolution in the Histadrut institutions annulling it. For MAKI this was sacrilege. It accused Lavon and the union of attempting to detach the holiday from its intended anticapitalist and antiwar contexts.

Other harassments were of a more violent nature. The main focal point of hostility toward the Communist marchers was in Haifa. Ruled by MAPAI boss Abba Hushi, Red Haifa welcomed the Communist marchers with physical and verbal abuse. Bottles were thrown at the marchers, and Hushi's and the Histadrut's strongmen attacked them. In Tel Aviv the Banki demonstrators clashed with Beytar members when the procession of the former passed one of the strongholds of the latter near where the Banki club was located.[28] Clashes with political rivals were frequent in the formative stage of Communist May Day in the 1920s and continued after legalization. This aspect of the holiday seems to have persisted, at least until the 1950s.

The visual evidence remaining of the Banki processions also points to the Soviet influence on May Day. The photographs of successive events reveal elaborate visual effects that the displays were planned to create. The parade included everything from abstract displays to graphically sophisticated placards, illustrating such themes as nuclear war, workers' solidarity, the Eastern Bloc, and Arab-Jewish fraternity. Other important elements were the written slogans, marching bands, and the extensive use of national flags side by side with the Red Flag. Vehicles carrying displays also participated in the marches.

Figure 4.4. Banki section in the 1953 May Day march.

Figure 4.5. Banki members' parade on May Day 1957.

What was the purpose of the Jewish Communists' elaborate display? Clifford Geertz maintains that ritualistic processions are displays of symbols of power emanating from symbolic centers of power. In that sense, the use of Soviet symbols and practices is understandable. The militaristic uniformed procession, the profiles of Lenin and Stalin, the Hammer and Sickle, and the oversized displays all derived from the Soviet Union; they were the trappings of power that the Jewish Communists wished to present. The Jewish Communists also resorted to the symbolic system of the international working class, mainly the Red Flag. Hoisted at Communist May Day demonstrations since the 1920s, it was prominent as the symbol of the international working class and can be considered a dominant symbol,[29] connecting the Jewish Communists with another symbolic center of power, the international and local working class. These symbols of power clearly stood in contrast to the reality of the Jewish Communists as a small, sometimes persecuted minority with little representation in the mainly Jewish working class. They were meant to alleviate this contradiction by identifying them with a worldwide class and a superpower.

At the same time, the Banki parades also had a local symbolic aspect. Two local symbols were used foremost, the Israeli flag and the Arab-Jewish duo showing Palestinian and Jewish figures standing side by side symbolizing Arab-Jewish friendship. There is no evidence as to when the Jewish Communists started to use the national flag, with its obvious Zionist context, in their May Day procession. The scant visual evidence from the mid- to late 1940s gives no indication that the Blue and White was used before 1948, but since it does appear from as early as 1958,[30] it may be assumed that it was in use at least since 1948. In carrying the two flags together, the Jewish Communists were following the practice of the other Zionist workers' parties that waved the two flags. The existence of this practice manifestly shows the growing affinity between Socialist-Zionist culture and the Jewish Communist subculture subsequent to legalization. However, the use of the flag was not indicative of an outright Zionization of Banki. The Jewish Communist subculture was permeated with local forms of Israeli nationalism that critiqued Zionism as a manifestation of the Jewish bourgeoisie, and which did not recognize the Zionist nationalization of Jewish communities worldwide. In that context, the raising of the Blue and White may not have been a Zionist but rather an Israeli nationalist gesture, constituting recognition of the power of the state.

The other symbol used by Banki members, the Arab-Jewish duo, was borrowed directly from the symbolic vocabulary of Israeli Communism.

Widely used to symbolize Arab-Jewish fraternity, one of MAKI and Banki's core identity values, it played an important role in May Day. The Communist May Day demonstrations manifestly stressed their Arab-Jewish identity. The Palestinian members of Banki dressed in the traditional keffiyeh and marched side by side with their Jewish comrades.[31] Yoska Valershtiean recalled that Banki members insisted that the Palestinian members wear the keffiyeh, thus deliberately identifying them as Palestinians and stressing the Arab-Jewish character of the march.[32] These practices seem to have had obvious Orientalist undertones; however, they were not used as a way to stereotype the Palestinian. The Jewish Communists wanted to stress the presence of Palestinians in their midst to a wider audience, and the wearing of the keffiyeh served that purpose. The representation of Palestinians in the march marked them all as a dynamic modernized collective.[33] It is in this context that the Arab-Jewish duo emerges in the May Day Banki procession. In a photograph from the 1957 May Day march,[34] we see a vehicle mounted with a display of two youths, one Palestinian, the other Jewish. Both figures are in Red Banki ties and one of them is clad in a keffiyeh. Beneath them a caption reads, "Long live Jewish-Arab fraternity!" flanked by the Banki logo, which incorporated the national flag with the Red Star, the Hammer and Sickle, and a sheaf of wheat. At either side of the display, the Red Flag and the Blue and White flag are waving. The entire display, bedecked with the plethora of Jewish Communist symbols, points to the set of cultural traits that Banki wished to convey to the spectators and other marchers.

Geertz asserts that royal processions and political rituals were codified with cultural signifiers that portrayed an idealized view of the universe, the nature of the ruler's charisma, or the expectations of the ruled from the ruler. The symbolic language used by Banki members was codified in symbols of Soviet Communism, working-class militancy, Arab-Jewish fraternity, international peace, and liberation struggles. It depicts a Socialist utopia, one where Israel would be "independent, democratic, and peace-seeking,"[35] a land that gave "happiness to its builders—workers and Jews and Arabs, Ashkenazi and Sephardic [. . .] living together in equality and fraternity with no military government and no discrimination."[36] In fact, the young Banki members' march represented a veritable Socialist utopia.

Since the early 1920s, the Communist May Day had been framed in militantly internationalist working-class terms. This language is clearly evident in Banki's instructors' brochures dedicated to May Day. Like much of Banki's instructional material, they were constructed as a *Masechet* of literary and educational segments. One text from the late 1950s is made up of articles on the origins of May Day, plays and poems. A central theme in the brochures is the history of May Day. The young Communists were taught that its origins lay in the Haymarket Massacre, where clashes in Chicago between the police and workers demanding an eight-hour workday gave birth to May Day, and the Second International resolution of 1889 that established May Day as the day of struggle and celebration of the working class. The historical sections of the instructors' brochures contained a detailed history of the holiday. The historical narrative was meant to instill in the young Communists a militant identification with the international working class. The identification with the workingmen was, from the 1920s, couched in an internationalist language. Quoting Lenin, Banki members proclaimed that "Jew and Christian, Armenian and Tatar, Pole and Russian, Finn and Swedish, Latvian and German, all march together under the joint banner of Socialism."[37]

The poems, plays, and allegorical stories abounding in the brochures were used to get the young Communists to internalize the day's values. The literary segments included antiwar sections, stories about the sufferings of Israeli workers, anticapitalist allegories, and poems by Ḥaya Kadmon, Alexander Penn, and Nâzım Hikmet as well as other Communist poets. The literary pieces, together with the historical parts, instilled in Banki members the identification with workers and their plight and with national and class liberation struggles. The Soviet Union, ever present in the Jewish Communist mind, was not denied a place either. One booklet stressed the fact "that since October 1917 . . . the workers of Russia started celebrating in their own state."[38] An internal memorandum of Banki's Education and Culture Department, in the wake of the Twentieth Congress, asserts the "achievements of the USSR and the Eastern Bloc" in the face of all criticism. The memorandum represents the image of the USSR, held by the Jewish Communists since the 1920s, as a utopia fulfilled. By 1960, the text boasts, the USSR will have moved to a six-hour working day for young workers (which in fact happened only in 1967) and free education.[39]

A 1962 Bney Amal booklet claims that the "Red Flag will be waved in victory all over the globe." The Red Flag, part and parcel of Communist subculture since the 1920s, is emphasized in the instructors' booklets of the 1950s and early 1960s. In the 1962 Bney Amal booklet, in a section named "suggestions for diversifying activity," the Red Flag is given a central role and is connected to workers' militancy. The instructor is advised to connect the talk with the young Communists to stories about the Red Flag, to collect newspaper clippings on the background of the Red Flag, a map of the Socialist countries marked with Red Flags, and "essays and songs on the subject—*what does the Red Flag tell me?*"[40] Furthermore, the Red Flag was also internalized by means of poems and allegorical stories.

The Communist May Day posed a sharp contrast to reality. MAKI and Banki members had almost no influence on the masses of Jewish workers, who remained deeply committed to Zionism. The young Jewish Banki members were encouraged by their parents to become intellectuals rather than workers. Their few attempts to make contact with Israel's underclass failed dismally.[41] Nonetheless, despite the flaws in the Jewish Communists' day-to-day contact with workers, their May Day represented the possibility of a different Israeli society, one that respects its workingmen, where Palestinians and Jews could live and work free of nationalism and exploitation. It was a direction that Israeli society never took.

Working-class militancy, symbolized through Soviet and local motifs, ritualized in what was undoubtedly the main rite of MAKI and Banki, had a profound effect on the young Communists. Marching through the main streets of the cities left diverse and conflicting impressions on the participating youngsters. As in other public appearances of the Communists, mainly in the 1950s, the reaction to them was abusive and sometimes violent. Some, like Carmit Gai, recall the exposure to the hostility of the crowd as a negative experience:

> May Day marches, in white shirts with blue and red ties, are engraved in my memory as a terrible nightmare. Marching in step left-right, the national or the class flag in hand, or some slogan in favor of fraternity, freedom, and peace, shouting slogans in unified, confident chorus in the city street, to the sound of shouts of scorn and the cursing of passersby, added to the activity in the movement a dimension of exposure that I could not bear.[42]

In a gentler tone, Nessia Shafran recalls, in contrast to her friends, that "May Day demonstrations were for them a great release, a sort of yearly catharsis," and that she felt "held back in such collective shouting."[43] At the same time, Shafran admits to being excited, as a child, as she watched her father marching in the main street of her hometown. Nissim Calderon fondly remembers the youthful enthusiasm that accompanied the preparations for the march. Yoram Gozansky also recalls the hard work and the pride that the young Banki members felt when the other Socialist-Zionist youth movements passed by.[44]

Whatever the young Communists' feelings and doubts may have been about May Day, MAKI and Banki used the holiday to further the movement's indoctrination and instill in them a sense of identification with the workers' struggle. The stress on the symbols and myths of working-class struggle was intended precisely, despite the personal ambivalence some Communists may have felt, to develop that sympathy toward workingmen.

Sympathy did not translate, however, into a sense of belonging. The Jewish Communists never managed to recruit a large enough number of workers to develop a proletarian identity. Their contacts with the underclass of Israel in the 1950s, made up mainly of non-European Jews streaming into the country after 1948, were limited and short-lived. The "attempts to work among the youths in Kfar Yona Bet did not go well," recalls Carmit Gai. The young Banki members from Yad Hanna approached the unemployed youngsters of the slum with real enthusiasm, intent on introducing them to Socialism and solidarity. Nonetheless, when those youngsters hinted at a romantic interest in the girls, "we were startled and clammed up like a hedgehog."[45] Nessia Shafran describes her group's attempts to connect to the local juvenile garage workers as driven by good but impractical intentions. The lack of a proletarian identity was reflected in MAKI as well as in Banki. The history of the party shows a tendency to deal more with the national question and relations with the Soviet Union than with the class struggle. A glaring example of that is the fact that Yair Tzaban was reprimanded by the party for allocating too much space in an article in *Kol Hano'ar* to the exploitation of young boys picking cotton, and for not allocating more space in the issue to the October Revolution.[46]

Why did the Jewish Communists lack a proletarian identity? Above all, there were objective reasons. Since the 1920s the Communist Party had been forcibly marginalized within the Jewish working class. The PKP's inability to propagate its views openly certainly contributed to its inability to recruit workers in such numbers as to give it a proletarian character and identity. By the time the party was allowed to operate openly among the Jewish working class, the Zionist Histadrut was already entrenched, giving the Jewish working class a Socialist-Zionist identity. Thus, the PKP and later MAKI were unable to emplace an alternative working-class identity.

The structure of the Histadrut itself prevented the Jewish Communists from attaining a meaningful place within the ranks of Jewish workers. The Histadrut wielded a combination of economic and ideological powers that were vital to the Zionist project. The potent combination of Zionist nationalism and socialist ideology that was meant to serve it made the Histadrut a powerful body. It organized the workers to such a degree that there was no place for the Communists to create class alternatives. This factor clearly prevented the development of a true Jewish Communist workers' identity.

A last factor that prevented the Jewish Communists from forming a proletarian identity was the nature of political culture and conflict. Palestine's political culture evolved around the conflict between the Zionist settler society and Palestinian nationalism. The Jewish Communists were more preoccupied with the fight against Zionism and dealing with the sway that nationalism had over them than with diverting their energies to class warfare. Thus another barrier was erected to the creation of a proletarian identity among the Jewish Communists.

The lack of a working-class identity does not detract from the cultural importance of the Jewish Communists' identity structure, as is evident from the amount of educational and other materials dedicated to May Day. The Jewish Communists identified with the plight of working people. The mythical, symbolic, and ritualistic dimensions of that identification played an important role in shaping the Jewish Communist subculture. The Jewish Communists' presence within the Jewish working class may have been small—but it was there. The struggles of people like Alyosha Gozansky and countless unknown others wrote a hitherto unknown page in the history of the Israeli working class. Theirs certainly was not the hegemonic Zionist narrative that preferred to forgo class distinctions in favor of class harmony in building a Zionist state and nation.

Chapter 5

Revolution and the Soviet Union among Israeli Communists

The Jewish Communists, the Philo-Soviet Community, and the USSR

The link between the Soviet Union and the Jewish Communists assumed a vital political, organizational, and cultural role in MAKI and Banki. The myth that legitimized this link was based on two historical events: the October Revolution and the Soviet-German War of 1941–1945. In ritual, myth, and symbol, the Jewish Communists shaped their identity and subculture around a pseudo-religious perception of those events. Glossing over Stalin's horrendous crimes and the excesses of the Revolution, they created a myth of the USSR consecrated in ritual that was both Soviet and local at same time.

From its formative stages in the 1920s, Communism in Palestine and later Israel was based on loyalty to the Soviet Union. The first contacts between Bolshevik Russia and the fledgling Jewish Communists were formed between 1920 and 1922. The Po'aley Zion Left party tried to join the Comintern, presenting a political program with mixed Zionist and Communist elements. This first contact ended in failure, as the Comintern rejected the overtly Zionist Po'aley Zion Left. Contacts between the Jewish Communists in Palestine and the Soviet Union were resumed in February 1924 when the Comintern recognized the PKP as a section of the Third International. A letter from the Palestinian subcommittee says: "It was resolved: to acknowledge the PKP as a section of the Comintern."[1] From then on the Jewish Communists took their orders from Moscow; nonetheless, their obedience was not as blind as Zionist historians portray it.

From the moment the PKP became part of the Comintern in 1924, Moscow, trying to firmly implant the party in the majority population of Palestine, demanded it's Arabization. For ideological justification, the Comintern quoted Lenin's edict regarding Soviet Communist work in the East, namely, that the Russian Communists should be the helpers and not the leaders of their Central Asian comrades. That process culminated in the aftermath of the 1929 Riots when the Jewish leadership of the party was disbanded on Moscow's orders and a new Central Committee with Moscow-trained Palestinian activists was installed. Although the party had been making efforts to penetrate the Palestinian masses of Palestine, its Jewish leaders were reluctant to give up their control. The clash between Moscow and the leadership of the PKP came to a head after the 1929 Riots when the Comintern compelled the Jewish Communists to Arabize. By the 1930s, the now Arabized PKP was operating under Soviet tutelage in the shape of the Comintern. However, from 1937, the party had no further contact with the Soviet Union until the first Soviet delegation to Palestine in 1942. In a report to that delegation on PKP internal politics by one Sash Philosoph, the writer states that "for several years the party has had no contact with the Communist International," adding that "a detailed report, referring to the period up until September 1939, was sent to the Comintern committee in April 1940 by a messenger . . . but it never arrived."[2]

From the early 1940s, the reconstituted contacts between the Communists in Palestine and the Soviet Union were severed once again after the split of 1943, to be restarted when PKP members Ruth Lubitz and Alyosha Gozansky made contacts in Yugoslavia and other People's Democracies. Besides their sputtering relationship with the USSR, during World War II the Jewish Communists laid the foundations of a larger philo-Soviet community,[3] made up of Jewish Communists, Socialist Zionists, and unaffiliated intellectuals. While the Communist Party was linked to the Soviet Union, ideologically as well as culturally, the philo-Soviet community was not necessarily ideologically reliant on the USSR. It fostered a wider system of cultural ties that were captioned as Soviet-Israel Friendship.

During World War II the Jewish Communists and the growing philo-Soviet community in Palestine sought to institutionalize aid to the USSR. An internal document of the Young Communist League asserts that "there's a need to develop a wide movement of sympathy toward the Soviet Union."[4] Russian culture and the Russian Revolution had long been incorporated into the culture of the Yishuv's workers and youth movements, and World War II added to the existing cultural and political ties between the Socialist-Zionist left and the USSR, stimulating the growth of the philo-Soviet community within the Yishuv. On October 18, 1941, the V League was established by a group of Haifa-based intellectuals, led by the author Arnold Zweig. In parallel to it, a group led by the Communist poet and writer Mordechai Avi-Shaul was formed in Tel Aviv. On May 2, 1942, the Haifa and Tel Aviv groups were united to form the V League for Soviet Russia (hereinafter: the V League).

The V League had three stipulations in its platform, stressing its wide appeal: "1. The league is a nonpartisan organization. 2. Its role is to provide help to the Red Army. 3. It should foster a mutual understanding between the USSR and the Jewish and Arab communities in Eretz-Israel."[5] The league immediately undertook extensive activity on behalf of the Soviet war effort. In a series of fundraising events, it collected mainly medical aid, including field ambulances and money. The aid was delivered to the USSR by a delegation to the Soviet ambassador in Teheran. Posters of the V League reveal the nature of its activity. Alongside drives to purchase bandages and ambulances, it held a Russian art exhibition, celebrations of the foundation of the Red Army and the Revolution, and even a soccer match whose proceeds went "to aid the Red Army."[6]

Though the first impulse behind the V League was immediate help to the Soviet Union, by the end of the war it had become a cultural agency of the Soviet Union in Palestine and the foundation of a cultural political philo-Soviet community. The change in the character of the V League was accompanied by a change in its makeup. As late as November 1945, the national conference of the organization was attended by prominent Socialist-Zionist politicians. Men like David Remez from MAPAI and Yitzhak Tabenkin from Ahdut HaAvoda participated in the conference alongside PKP secretary general Shmuel Mikunis. But as the tensions of the Cold War mounted and Israel increasingly allied itself with the West, the Socialist Zionists left the organization, MAPAI's representatives in 1949, and those of MAPAM after its loyalty to the Soviet Union was shaken by the Communist regime's anti-Zionism and the 1953 Doctors Trials.

With the Socialist-Zionist parties gone, the renamed Friendship Movement Israel–Soviet Union (hereinafter: the Friendship Movement) became more closely connected to MAKI. Nonetheless, the Communists, now at the helm of the Friendship Movement, tried to leave it open to others who were not necessarily party members. The platform of the reconstituted organization reflected that the Friendship Movement was open to people with different worldviews. The Friendship Movement became the principal channel through which the Jewish Communists and the philo-Soviet community publicly maintained their contact with the USSR, primarily in the form of a constant stream of delegations to the USSR.

Wall posters from the 1950s and early 1960s demonstrate the Friendship Movement's activity. One poster offers a thirty-day tour in the USSR, including four days on a Soviet passenger vessel. Besides tourism, the Friendship Movement sent delegations to Soviet scientific and youth gatherings. Soviet and Russian culture also had its place in the activity of the Friendship Movement. A poster of the Haifa Friendship House from 1963 announces a lecture marking the hundredth anniversary of Constantin Stanislavski's birth. MAKI and Banki sustained their own contacts with the USSR. A 1950 poster proclaims a "V. I. Lenin Evening" to mark the twenty-sixth anniversary of his death. Meir Vilner's speech at that event was dedicated to the publication of *The Short Course*. Like the Friendship Movement, Banki sent delegations to the USSR. In a 1964 pamphlet, signed by Banki, the public is encouraged to "hear live impressions from an interesting mission to the Soviet Union."[7]

The bond between the Jewish Communists, the philo-Soviet circles around them, and the USSR was not without its darker sides. Any criticism of Soviet policies was branded anti-Soviet incitement. At times the Jewish Communists and other pro-Soviet circles were in the right, as in the case of the 1953 bombing of the Soviet embassy in Tel Aviv by right-wing extremists. In other cases they refused to admit the existence of institutionalized anti-Semitism in the Soviet Union, and they invariably portrayed life in the Soviet Union as progressive and free, disregarding the lack of freedom, continued persecution of dissenters, inability of the planned economy to provide a bounty equal to that of capitalist economy, and Soviet imperialism.

As the relations between the USSR and Israel deteriorated and as Israel turned to the West, MAKI acted behind the scenes, trying to establish a parallel friendship league in the USSR and to unite Soviet Jewish families with relatives in Israel. Though the party leaders did not agree with every single policy of the Soviets, especially as regards the freedom of movement of Soviet Jews to immigrate outside the USSR, they put on a show of complete loyalty and obedience for the sake of the party rank and file and the philo-Soviet public. That took a toll on MAKI's public image, most notably during the 1953 Doctors Trials and the Purge Trials in the People's Democracies, costing the party many Jewish supporters. It was not until 1967 that the Jewish MAKI broke with the USSR in the wake of its support for the 1967 War. The Palestinian-Jewish Rakah party remained loyal to the Soviet Union until 1991.

The importance of the USSR to the Jewish Communists and the philo-Soviet community rested upon two historical events: the Soviet-German War and the October Revolution. Both stimulated the emergence of unique symbols, myths, and rites to signify friendship with the Soviets.

The Colossus Triumphant

The celebration of the Soviet victory over Nazi Germany was above all a celebration of the USSR's military and political prowess and Soviet friendship. The glorification of Soviet power took root early in the history of Communism in Palestine. In a 1925 handbill, the PKP threatened the British with an international "army of the world revolution."[8] In a 1940 issue of *Kol Ha'am*, dedicated to the twenty-second anniversary of the founding of the Red Army, it was described as the defender of Communism and the accomplishments of the Revolution, an army that turned the country into a well-defended fortress. The article did not mention the debacle of the Winter War. Glossing over the unpleasant aspects of Soviet policy and of the Red Army's behavior during the war would come to characterize the myth of the war.

The myth of Soviet power was evident already in the first months of the war. In an article entitled "The Red Army in Battle," Soviet power is portrayed as defending the achievements of the Revolution: "The Red Army stands on guard. The peoples of the Soviet Union stand on guard . . . the Soviet soldier and Soviet men are fiercely resisting the distraction of the happiness accumulated over twenty-four years of persistent struggle and hard work."[9] The Jewish connection is not neglected, Jews being called on to join the fight against Fascist annihilation. Soviet failures in the war were glossed over, with *Kol Ha'am* asserting "that the Army of the Ukraine commanded by comrade Budyonny managed to prevent the encirclement in the Ukraine,"[10] whereas in fact Budyonny, one of Stalin's favorites, was responsible for one of the great Soviet disasters of the war. A March 1942 *Kol Hano'ar* article dedicated to the Red Army's anniversary has a different tone, placing stress on Jewish heroism in the framework of Soviet patriotism. The Jews were fighting among "Russians, Ukrainians, Georgians, Azerbaijanis, and Tartars."[11]

By the end of the war, the new patriotic tone of the discourse about Soviet power became more pronounced. In a booklet titled *The War of Liberation*, published as the end of the war drew near, the young Communists gave an account of the war from their point of view. The war had opened the way for the Jewish Communists in Palestine to adopt Jewish national motifs. Here Jewish heroism was intertwined with Soviet patriotism: Soviet Jewry "hand in hand with the other Soviet peoples" had fought against Fascism, reflecting "the great tradition of the Maccabean, Bar-Kokhba, and Rabbi Akiva."[12]

The symbols used by the Jewish Communists in their pro-Soviet propaganda and those used by the V League also glorified Soviet power. Taking their cue from Soviet wartime propaganda, Communist and V League publications were decorated with images of Soviet soldiers. A postcard distributed by the Communist youth shows Stalin with three representatives of the Soviet Army, Air Force, and Navy, seen against the background of the Soviet flag. The caption marries together Soviet power and Jewish plight: "The Salvation of the Jewish People Demands More Help to the Red Army!"[13]

The elements forged during the war sustained into the 1950s and mid-1960s. In the part of the Bney Amal booklet concerned with World War II, the young Communists are taught to emulate the individual sacrifices of Soviet heroes. The war itself is called, Soviet style, the Motherland War. The children are encouraged to prepare a diary of the war written by a Soviet soldier or soldiers. The cult of Soviet power found expression in the booklet in the form of a list of facts to be taught to the young Bney Amal members. In contrast to historical reality, the text downplays the importance of Western aid to the USSR. In accordance with historical reality, it claims that the bulk of German forces fought in the East, specifically Stalingrad. The connection between awareness of the Holocaust and the Soviet myth finds expression in the suggested activities, which the instructor is encouraged to construct around the aid lent by the Red Army to the ghetto fighters and the fact that the Soviet Union saved more Jews than any other country.[14]

The heroes that the young Communists were encouraged to learn from were self-sacrificing, simple-mannered, one-dimensional proletarian heroes. In a *Kol Hano'ar* article on the tenth anniversary of the victory, a Soviet soldier is depicted as carrying "his ever-present accordion and radiant optimism"[15] as he liberates thankful East Europeans. This mixture of kitsch and heroism—although Russian patriotism and heroism and the weight of Soviet losses could not be discounted—veiled the darker sides of the

Soviet war effort. The brutality toward soldiers and civilians, the rape and pillage committed by the Soviets outside the USSR, mainly in Germany, are completely absent from the Jewish Communist texts. By the mid-1960s the myth of the Soviet victory was well fixed in the Jewish Communist mind. No dissenting voices were heard either publicly or privately, as the Jewish Communists engaged in a mass rite that MAKI, Banki, and the philo-Soviet community had been developing since the early 1950s.

The Yishuv welcomed the news of the capitulation of Germany with a flurry of marches. On May 8, 1945, the Communist Party organized a victory march in which hundreds of party members and members of the Young Communist League participated. The parade in Tel Aviv, despite being the founding event of the Communist celebration of May 9, was later discontinued and replaced by a mass cult of a different kind in the Red Army forest, which, from the early 1950s, became a focal point for the cult of the USSR and the war.

At the end of the war, the V League initiated an enterprise to symbolically commemorate and pay tribute to the Red Army. The scheme reflected the League's new role as a cultural agency. The effort to raise money for planting a forest in honor of the Red Army was launched in an opening ceremony at the Mograbi Theater in Tel Aviv, where the nationwide sale of a victory badge was announced. By July, the Histadrut Executive Committee,

Figure 5.1. Victory parade, May 12, 1945, Tel Aviv.

in a letter signed by Golda Meyerson, had adopted the campaign and allotted it a period of two weeks. In the national convention of the V League, its chairman L. Tarnopler stated that its aim was to raise "3,000 pounds in Palestine, enough to plant a forest of 100 dunams around Jerusalem." He also announced a plan "for the building of a victory monument"[16] on the grounds.

After five years of fundraising and lobbying, on June 22, 1950, a planting ceremony and dedication of the monument was held. In Zionist ritual, the planting of trees was an accepted practice symbolizing the rerooting of the Jewish collective in its old-new land. In the case of the Red Army forest, however, the practice was pressed into service to show gratitude to an army and state beyond the national territory. The reason given for planting trees was the gratitude the people of Israel owed the Red Army. Yitzhak Gruenbaum, one of the principal Polish Zionist leaders before the war, expressed his feelings of gratitude toward the Red Army and his hope that the monument would symbolize Soviet friendship. Already in the planting ceremony, the speakers reminded the audience of their obligation not to forget the bloody struggle on Russian soil. The edict not to forget was connected to the memory of the Holocaust, as the Jewish anti-Fascist Committee's "great proclamation of faith in the internal mission, 'Thou Shalt Not Die, but Live,' "[17] was invoked.

The outstanding feature of the Red Army forest is the stone monument. From the late 1940s, Israeli national monuments increasingly became centers of the Israeli cult of the fallen. The Red Army monument was part of this cultural trend, in the sense that it became the center of a ritual of commemoration; however, the content of the memory was different. The monument symbolically manifests local nationalist motifs and Soviet European ones that characterized the Soviet victory myth. It is a typical *galed* monument made of one massive stone. In that respect, it poses a sharp contrast to the Soviet war monuments, which incorporate human figures, inscribed tombstones, and battlefield weapons, most notably seen in the massive Soviet war monuments in East Berlin. Nevertheless, the stone visibly references the symbolism of the Soviet state, as the Hammer and Sickle is mounted upon it. The symbols of the workers' state are presented against the background of the Red Star, another Soviet symbol. The inscription at the top of the stone further clarifies that "this forest was planted by the people of Israel in honor of the Soviet Army,"[18] reaffirming the gratitude motif.

Communists participated in the planting ceremony, as a picture in *Kol Ha'am* shows a prominent party member, Ester Vilenska, planting a tree. However, true to their tactics since the formation of the V League, the Communists emphasized the broad multiparty nature of the support for the USSR. Therefore, known Communists did not speak at the opening event and all the main speakers were Zionist, some of them state officials. From the early 1950s, the ceremony started to evolve into a mass rally with speeches followed by artistic performances. The 1951 ceremony, under the Israel-USSR Friendship League, now jointly led by MAPAM and MAKI, included speeches, poetry readings, choral singing, and folk dancing. The following year Ester Vilenska revisited the element of gratitude toward and prowess of the Red Army, lauding it as the "Army of Peace" that all "the peace-loving peoples of the world look to in gratitude."[19]

The ritual at the foot of the monument in the Red Army forest was elaborated with the waving of flags, speeches, and the presentation of floral wreaths, followed by artistic performances, eventually evolving into a three-part ceremony. The first, official part of the ceremony included symbolic acts like anthem singing, laying of wreaths at the foot of the stone, and the release of doves to flight. The second part consisted of artistic performances that, more often than not, included the party's choirs and poets.[20] The third part evolved into a popular celebration that included exhibitions, food stands, raffle booths, and a mass family picnic. The celebrations combined the solemn with the carnival-like, echoing the early Bolshevik rituals. The three-part structure of the ritual was meant to move the audience in a structured manner from the solemn to the carnivalesque. After the waving of flags, singing of the national anthem, and speeches, followed by artistic performances, the celebration ended with the complete release of tension as the crowds enjoyed a mass picnic.

The annual preparations for the victory celebration were complicated and demanded diligent planning and mobilization of the Friendship League and Banki. *Kol Ha'am* advertised the yearly event, reporting on extensive preparations for the ceremony. Most of the organizational work was done by the Friendship League, which registered the participants, distributed tickets through its branches, and arranged for transportation. The actual construction of facilities at the ceremony site was performed by Banki. As early as 1955, *Kol Ha'am* reported that the night before the mass rally "a youth rally was held commemorating the tenth anniversary of the victory over Hitler's Germany."[21] From then on, Banki members would gather at the monument the night before the main ceremony in order to prepare the site to receive the crowds. By the nineteenth anniversary of the victory in 1964, the gathering had evolved into a mass rite, including a bonfire, joint Palestinian and Jewish meetings, a film show, and singing and dancing.

Banki was following the common practice of the Zionist Left youth movements, which were influenced by the German Wandervogel with their hikes and gatherings in remote natural surroundings. In the culture of the Socialist-Zionist youth movements, such hikes and gatherings bore a distinctively national-Zionist content of "knowing the land through the legs." The most notable such hike was the pilgrimage to Masada in the pre-state era. Banki members engaged in similar activity, but they gave it their own exegesis. Instead of performing a Zionist pilgrimage to a site of mythological national heroism, they hiked to Palestinian villages or slums and promoted the myth of the USSR and the Red Army.

The May 9th celebration was a ritual of the communitas type. The pilgrimage[22] to the monument, which became a shrine for the cult of the Soviet Union, invoked a feeling of communitas, as reports by ex-party member Lillya Peter make evident. The feeling of unity erased the status distinctions between young and old: "Here are old friends whose friendship, solid and mighty, has withstood days and years confronted by waves of murky incitement; here are young friends who joined the great camp only yesterday." Echoing the words of Panfilov—"the motherland is you, your wife, and your children; the motherland is him and me—we"—Peter includes in her version of the motherland those of low status:

> The motherland is you, the simple worker who daily turns the wheels of toil of our country; the motherland is you the gray-haired mother who sighs at night, fearing for loved ones. The motherland is you the *fellah* whom they try to drive from your land . . . the motherland is the children who released white doves in the air! The motherland is everybody, everybody that yearns for peace.[23]

Lillya Peter describes how, as the pilgrims departed at the end of the ritual, "above them the Ruby and White-Blue flags kiss each other in the spring wind."[24] This short sentence encapsulates the dominant symbol used by the Communists and the philo-Soviet community to represent Soviet-Israeli friendship and the victory over Nazi Germany. The joined flags symbol made an early appearance in the war years. A postcard distributed by Banki during the years 1942–1943 shows a crowd depicted in silhouette holding up the Star of David alongside the Hammer and Sickle. The joined flags symbol reappeared in the late 1940s in a poster of the Friendship League welcoming the Soviet legation to the newly founded state, and again in the mid-1950s in a poster for the 1954 Soviet-Israeli Friendship Congress.[25] It was a prominent element also in the victory rite. In a 1960 diagram of the site, the entire clearing facing the audience is lined with what are termed double flags, meaning the Israeli and Soviet ones. The Red Army monument was also decorated with the same flags, as well as the Red Star and the Hammer and Sickle.[26]

This symbolic language alludes to symbolic power centers. For the Jewish Communists, lacking any real political power, both symbolic and real power lay in the USSR. Using the symbols of a state that, as a result of the war, was now a superpower empowered the small group of Communists in Israel. It also enabled them to be part of a wider cultural circle within the Yishuv and later Israel that sympathized with the Soviet war effort and state. Against that background, the use of the Israeli national flag and colors became possible. It represented the Jewish Communists' wish to unite their local national loyalty with their loyalty to the USSR and appeal to a wider audience. The use of the joined flag symbol in the central rite celebrating the World War II victory points to the two poles of influence on which the Jewish Communists and the philo-Soviet worldview leaned: Soviet power and the Israeli state. The symbolic presence of both served to highlight their existence on the same continuum, making the stress on the USSR's being vital to Jewish survival and Israeli independence understandable. The symbol of the joint flag also came to symbolize the harmonization of the international Soviet element with local Israeli patriotism. At the same time, it was a way of mediating the tension between what basically were, and eventually openly became, ideological and political rivals: a Zionist Western state on the one hand, and an anti-Zionist, increasingly pro-Arab Soviet state, on the other.

The Cosmology of Revolution

The shock waves sent out by the October Revolution sparked the founding of Communism in Palestine. For the Jewish Communists, as for Communists everywhere, the revolution was an event of cosmological proportions, the opening of a new chapter in human history; it was described as a popular uprising of the downtrodden, led by the Communist Party.

In a 1920 manifesto issued on November 7th, the Russian Revolution is perceived as the popular uprising of the underclass, the day itself a great revolutionary holiday. The revolution marks not just a political change, but the start of a new historical era. The manifesto is charged with messianic expectation, for "the hour has come; the world revolution awaits its fighters,"[27] and the Jewish workers are exhorted to shake off their passivity and fight the British and the bourgeoisie.

The messianic revolutionary tone was soon replaced by one stressing the centrality of the Soviet Union. In a 1927 pamphlet on the tenth anniversary of the revolution, the claim is made "that the balance of the last 10 years shows that the proletarian revolution and Socialist construction continue to march forward."[28] The same centrality of the USSR can be found in the late 1930s. The Soviet Union is described as the land where capitalism was destroyed by the building of Socialism.

The first years of World War II saw a resurgence of the revolutionary internationalist rhetoric of the Jewish Communists, reflecting the Soviet policies that culminated in the 1939 pact with Germany. The belligerent nations of the Allies and the Axis are belittled as two groups of imperialists fighting to redistribute the world's resources. Once again the Soviet Union is presented in the terms of Socialist construction: "The land of the Soviets has scored great achievements. Socialist industry and agriculture develop and expand from day to day. From one hour to the next, Socialist culture is taking root in every corner of the Soviet Union."[29]

The German invasion of the USSR changed the Jewish Communists' perception of the October Revolution. A pamphlet on the occasion of November 7, 1941, reverts to revolutionary language, invoking the revolutionary traditions and vision, as follows:

> For thousands of years men have been exploited by men. For hundreds of years the best in humanity has been looking for a system where there will not be master and slave, exploiter and exploited. For generations the workers' movement has been fighting for a Socialist regime where there will not be bourgeoisie and proletariat. Thousands have been killed and died in prisons, demonstrations, and uprisings. Every time the ruling class prevailed. Twenty-four years ago the Russian working class executed the undertaking that generations had fought for and dreamed of, the foundation was laid, the walls were built, and the Soviet people began to roof over the giant Socialist enterprise.[30]

The revolution was just one, albeit central, element of a more comprehensive European revolutionary tradition with which the young Jewish

Communists and party members were made familiar. Like the Bolsheviks, the Jewish Communists looked at history as a string of progressive revolutions leading up to the 1917 Russian Revolution. Through instructors' manuals and the party's paper, the traditions of the Paris Commune, the Vienna Uprising, and the 1905 Revolution were remembered. Each was seen as a stepping-stone toward the next revolutionary event. Each was analyzed for lessons in accordance with Marxist-Leninist ideology. The message delivered to the young Communists was that only the Soviet model of the revolutionary process could work, thus strengthening the image of the Soviet Union as the paragon of revolutionary success.

In Banki, the traditions of the Paris Commune and the Vienna Uprising were memorialized in two instructors' booklets. The instructor is told to pass on the narrative of the Commune by telling stories, drawing up a placard named the "Communards' Wall," and playing a symbolic game named the "Communards' Flag."[31] The subject of the Commune was directly connected to the October Revolution. In a section named "Why the Commune Was Defeated," the young Communists are taught, straight out of the Leninist handbook, that the Commune failed because the ideological diversity of the Communards was not based in Scientific Socialism. Only a revolutionary party based on a Marxist-Leninist worldview could lead the masses to power.

The Vienna Uprising of 1934 was also used to impart to the young Communists a sense of historical revolutionary continuity. In a June 1964 booklet, the aim of the subject is defined in familiar revolutionary cosmological terms: "We will give them the understanding and knowledge that the road to the fulfillment of Socialism was long, hard, and filled with sacrifice; that many heroic battles were fought and sacrifices made by workers in different countries, lost battles and glorious ones alike that marched humanity forward to the exciting achievements of Socialism."[32] The lesson was clear: the uprising failed because it was not organized in a Bolshevist manner due to the damaging influence of Social Democracy.

The Spanish Civil War loomed large in Jewish Communist consciousness. It had attracted around six hundred volunteers from Palestine, and the main hero to emerge from the war for the Jewish Communists was Mark Milman, a young Jewish student and Communist youth member who died in Spain in 1938. Communist writer Mordechai Avi-Shaul wrote a book in Milman's honor, *Jewish Captain in Fighting Spain*. One of Banki's clubs in Haifa was also named after him. In the literary legacy commemorating him, Milman is described as coming from a working-class background and, at the same time, being a sensitive poet. This echoes the way the International

Brigades volunteers were memorialized in Europe, as young middle-class intellectuals that fought for the ideals of international solidarity. But in contrast to the one-dimensional figures devoid of any human traits such as Hans Beimler, the object of a cult in East Germany, Milman's character was portrayed as surprisingly human and sensitive, with a tender love of his mother.[33] Milman's cult, propagated in the party's press and in Banki, corresponded with local and Jewish elements. Milman had dispatched the duty of Jews to fight Fascism. As a true Jewish Communist from Palestine, he had reacted to the 1936 Arab Rebellion by calling for an international struggle against the common enemy, Fascism. He had even sung in Hebrew accompanied by his mandolin to his fellow soldiers in Spain.

While Milman's cult did not conform to forms of commemoration coming from East Germany, it did bear some resemblance to Socialist-Zionist practices. The young Palmach generation that emerged from the 1948 War was epitomized by the figure of Aron (Jimmy) Shemi. Much like Milman, he was immortalized in a book titled *Friends Tell about Jimmy*.[34] Like the young volunteer depicted by Avi-Shaul, Jimmy is depicted as a young, violin-playing, sensitive man—albeit in the tough exterior guise of a sabra. Both are portrayed as having had deep, loving relations with their mothers. Both are described as espousing left-wing politics, Milman the Communist who becomes a commissar of his unit, and Jimmy the Socialist Zionist who explores the classical writings of Marxism—both even play musical instruments. Both men's military prowess and charisma as military commanders are emphasized. However the similarities are not complete. While Milman's socialism is described as arising from the circumstances of his life as a worker and experiences as a student in France, Jimmy's socialism is confined to theory and books; in practice he is much the dedicated Zionist. Whereas Milman—in accordance with Communist ideology—calls for Arab-Jewish fraternity in the face of the Arab Revolt, for Jimmy Arabs are a subject of surveillance—as part of the intelligence-gathering effort of the Yishuv on Palestinian communities—and subject to death as abstract enemies in the course of the war.

What was the reason for the striking similarities in the way these different men were commemorated? The answer lies in the fact that the Jewish Communists had taken part in the development of the native Hebrew commemoration culture since the late 1940s. As in other cases, the Communists took Socialist-Zionist cultural elements and changed them to suit their ideological sensitivities.

The anti-Fascist myth of Spain was commemorated yearly by *Kol Ha'am*, which publicized the memoirs of veterans, interviews with La Pasionaria, and vows to continue the fight. The Spanish war was part and parcel of the European traditions of working-class revolt that were instilled in the Jewish Communist mind. The foundation of the republic was described as a working-class revolt that ended in the overthrow of the monarchy. Anti-Fascism was presented in terms of class war. The reaction, Avi-Shaul asserts in the name of an unidentified Spanish politician, would "have to climb on the human wall of the masses of the proletariat that will rise against it. It will be a life and death struggle."[35] Thus the Spanish struggle of the International Brigades became the war of middle-class intellectuals, workers and farmers, a struggle carried on by those who "knew how to fight and die for freedom, as did their forefathers in former generations and years: 1789, 1871, 1917."[36]

The negative side of Communist and Soviet intervention in Spain was not discussed at all. The persecution of Trotskyites and Anarchists was ignored. The cold calculations that stood behind Soviet involvement in Spain and the Spanish Communists' de facto takeover of the republic were not openly debated. To the general public outside Communist circles, the commemoration of the Spanish war meant little. The Spanish republic had been supported by all the Socialist-Zionist parties, while the middle class remained largely uncommitted. Only a small minority at the extremes of the Revisionist right had supported the nationalists. However, sympathy for the Spanish republic on the part of the Socialist-Zionists did not mean sending men to fight Fascism in Spain; the Zionist project was far more important to them. In the 1950s and 1960s the memory of the Spanish war did not play an important part in their culture. The fact that most of the volunteers to Spain had been Jewish Communists contributed to the marginalization of their deeds. Thus the commemoration of the war was left mostly to the Jewish Communists, and any debate there may have been on the nature of the war in the Republican Zone did not change the status of the party.

The Jewish Communists' historical narrative of revolution culminated in the October Revolution. From the 1940s, the indoctrination among the Communist Youth followed the same lines as those of the mother party. In the 1950s to the mid-1960s, the October Revolution became a pillar of Banki's education. In a series of instructors' brochures and song booklets, the revolutionary tradition was transmitted to the young Jewish Communists.

In a booklet from the late 1940s, it is stressed that "the children should know well the contents of the holiday and feel it as one of the great and beautiful holidays."[37] It was to be celebrated with parties that included children beyond the immediate members of the movement. The meaning of November 7th was to be conveyed to the children by the use of songs, plays, recitations, and stories. Talks were to stress the principal elements of the Soviet myth, such as the Bolshevik Party and its organizational structure, Socialist construction after the revolution, and World War II. The revolution was viewed, as it had been since the 1920s, as a popular uprising of peasants and workers led by the party.

On the fortieth anniversary of the October Revolution, Banki issued an extensive amount of material about the USSR and its revolution. A 1957 booklet entitled *The Soviet Union* defined its aim as being "to broaden and deepen the knowledge about the Soviet Union, to intensify the faith and confidence in our Communist rightness, to invoke in the hearts of the comrades pride in being part of the right and victorious camp headed by the Socialist motherland—the USSR."[38] The instructor is advised to teach the subject for four months in an exciting and engaging way, while doing extensive reading himself. He is to engage the young Communists in a variety of activities such as viewing a Soviet film and playing a Soviet album.

The way the subject is structured in the booklet reemphasizes the cosmological perception of the October Revolution and the history of the Soviet Union. As in a story of redemption, it begins with a section entitled "In the Darkness of the Tsar Days," which is followed by "The October Revolution—The Dawn of Mankind": light is contrasted to darkness, freedom to slavery. The remaining sections impart geographical and statistical knowledge of the USSR alongside the achievements of the USSR and the victory in the war.

In the early 1960s an effort was made to standardize the educational process concerning the October Revolution. In the first booklet sent to the Bney Amal and Yasour (Petrel) groups of Banki, the instructors are encouraged to start off the subject with a story, followed by a talk stressing Soviet peace policy, its fight against anti-Semitism, and Soviet achievements. In groups unfamiliar with the subject, they are advised to talk in a lively and exhilarating way about the revolution. For the more mature Yasour group, the discussion was to start with the question: "Due to what did the Soviet Union change . . . from a backward country into a great power?"[39] A September 1963 brochure uses the same dispassionate tone. It advises the instructor to keep the teaching of the subject within a timeframe of two months; it recommends accompanying the activity with playing records, and so on. As opposed to the more passionate aims of the 1957 booklet, in 1963 the aim is "to provide an in-depth understanding of our relation to the Soviet Union." The brochure is organized almost like a teachers' manual with rehearsed questions, and it is even entitled "Educational Booklet No 1."[40]

The standardization of the Russian Revolution in Banki's educational routine can be explained by three factors. First, by the early 1960s the October Revolution had become a distant event, far removed from the experience of the young Communists and their instructors, its glory somewhat dulled by World War II. Second was the fact that Banki, by the early 1960s, was governed by the Left Men, who at that point started to doubt the validity of their faith in the USSR.[41] The third reason was the standardization process already evident in the Jewish Communists' treatment of other holidays in the Jewish calendar, most notably Hanukkah. This standardization can be seen as part of MAKI's growing assertion of organizational control over Banki.

Like the events connected to May 9th, the commemoration of the October Revolution was draped in the symbols of Soviet power. The main difference between the two holidays was the latter's lack of a local symbols such as the joined flags. This difference can be explained by the day's more universal nature, lacking the dimension of Soviet-Israeli friendship prevalent on May 9th. From the 1920s and 1930s no visual evidence or written testimony remains concerning the symbolism used to celebrate the revolution. Soviet insignia were first used in the context of the revolution's commemoration in the early 1940s. In two handbills from 1941, the symbol of the Hammer and Sickle appears at the top or bottom of the page.[42] From the 1950s onward, the use of Soviet symbols became much more prevalent in Communist publications for November 7th.

Communist posters from the 1950s reveal the way the Jewish Communists perceived November 7th through Soviet symbolism. One poster,[43] captioned in Arabic, shows the Kremlin's Senatskaya Tower. To the left of the tower, which is bedecked with the Red Star and the Hammer and Sickle, a Peace Dove is flying above the faces of three youngsters, representing the three races of the world. Soviet power, born out of the revolution, is thus symbolized as bringing peace to the people of the world. The poster reasserts the Jewish Communists' perception of the revolution as not just Russian, but a model with internationalist appeal. A second poster[44] from 1951 is in Yiddish. Beneath the profiles of Lenin and Stalin depicted on the background of the Soviet flag, it shows urban surroundings, a complex of modern skyscrapers and neoclassical buildings being built above a giant dam. The urban construction is flanked by a small sheaf of wheat. The poster revisits motifs such as Socialist reconstruction and the alliance of urban and rural, essential to the portrayal of the revolution. The use of the profiles of Lenin and Stalin and the Soviet flag connects the Jewish Communists to the symbols of global Communism fashioned during the revolution.

The eschatological cosmology of the revolution is again referenced in a 1957 poster[45] issued on the fortieth anniversary of the revolution. In the center it shows a globe held up by the Hammer and Sickle. The visible part of the globe showcases Eurasia, alluding both to the centrality of the

Figure 5.2. Poster commemorating the thirty-third anniversary of the October Revolution.

Figure 5.3. Poster for the thirty-fourth anniversary of the Russian Revolution.

USSR and the universality of the revolutionary idea. The caption at the top reads: "40 Years since the Great Socialist October Revolution." It is punctuated by another Soviet symbol, the Red Star, which has its own cosmological connotations. The caption at the bottom of the poster has the most obviously pseudo-religious utopian meaning, repeating a line from the "Internationale": "We have been naught, we shall be all."

The use of the symbolic system derived from the USSR in the November 7th imagery points to the Jewish Communists' perception of the world. At its center stood the Soviet Union, representing the revolution, revolutionary virtue, and its outcome of further revolution.

Figure 5.4. Poster for the fortieth anniversary of the October Revolution.

The Soviet Union was one of the central pillars of Jewish Communist identity. The continued indoctrination about the USSR in both respects—World War II and the October Revolution—propped up their belief. The pseudo-religious pilgrimages, the myth of 1917 as a cosmological event, and the rejection of any criticism as almost blasphemy are all reminiscent of religious thinking and practice. Nissim Calderon gives this aspect of identity clear expression: "It was in fact a cult. I would say that the Soviet Union was a replacement for the synagogue. It was not God, Communism was God, but it was the substitute for synagogue. It was where the thing is fulfilled and that was very important to us. We did not have only ideology; we had a living example that a third of the world's surface was red . . . We thought of the USSR as the Holy Temple, really in terms of sanctity."[46] He goes on to liken the ideological repetition of the narrative of the revolution to a prayer. Yoram Gozansky also terms the Soviet Union as "the fulfillment of our dream."[47]

Still, the dream was in many respects a nightmare. The Jewish Communists could not bring themselves to see the terrible repression overshadowing the Soviet Union's immense accomplishments. Abandoning their faith in the USSR would have meant a rupture of their identity as Communists. In that respect, the Left Men found it easier to doubt their belief in the Soviet edifice. Yair Tzaban claims to have started doubting the Soviet reality in the early 1960s, and Shoshana Shmuely claims that what primarily motivated her to join MAKI and Banki was not the USSR, but a vision of social justice. Yair Tzaban has eloquently expressed the depth of the attachment to the USSR, saying that it was "an intellectual addiction to a certain kind of Marxism."[48] Nessia Shafran pointedly asserts: "The faith in the Soviet Union was no different in essence from any other faith in which men have believed throughout history, and like many faiths people held to it with a strong and desperate strength, until at one point faith became stronger than any reality that contradicted it."[49] Tzaban's and Shafran's remarks point to the limitations of Israeli Communism, indeed of every Communist movement outside Soviet Russia since the 1920s: once Communism had become immanently connected with the USSR, without loyalty to that model nobody could be a Communist. Even Trotsky, the main rival of Soviet Stalinist Communism from the late 1920s, claimed to be loyal to Lenin's teachings and the early Soviet state. But he was persecuted, exiled, and eventually assassinated. Not until the schism in World Communism between China and the USSR and the emergence of Euro-Communism and the New Left in the West did other Marxist models appear. However, with MAKI and later Rakah remaining staunchly loyal to the USSR, no other model ever really took root in Israel until the collapse of the Soviet Union.

Chapter 6

Arab-Jewish Fraternity

Language, Perception, Symbol, and Ritual

Arab-Jewish Language and Symbol

The Language of Arab-Jewish Fraternity

Arab-Jewish fraternity lay at the core of Jewish Communist ideology, differentiating the Jewish Communists from the rest of Israeli society. From the early 1920s, the Jewish Communists developed cultural practices enabling them to engage with the Palestinian Other in a way unlike any other Jewish Israelis. As the relationship between the two peoples deteriorated into ever-escalating conflict, the Jewish Communists developed a language that described the Palestinians in terms of Marxist-Leninist thinking, civic rights, and Jewish historical traumas. This language was accompanied by symbols and rites that were uniquely Jewish Communist and primarily meant to create a bond between Jewish and Palestinian youths. As affirmative as it was, the Jewish Communist understanding of Palestinians was in terms that made Palestinians the object of a civil and human rights struggle. Their understanding of Palestinian national agency was, however, lacking. The Jewish Communists failed to fully appreciate or consider the Palestinian experiences of Zionism and the wide-ranging effect of the establishment of the State of Israel.

Interaction between Palestinians and Jews was one of the vital aspects of Communism in Palestine from its formative stages. Arab-Jewish fraternity was the one major difference between Socialist-Zionist practice and culture and the Communist subculture. Socialist Zionists increasingly practiced the exclusion of Palestinians from the labor market and their removal from lands marked out for Jewish settlement, culminating in the ethnic cleansing[1] of the 1948 War and the military government that followed it. The Jewish Communists, on the other hand, had been advocating for Arab-Jewish joint action and mutual interests since the 1920s. After 1948 they defended Palestinians' human, civil, and national rights, fighting for fair treatment and justice toward the Palestinian citizens of Israel, those left in the country after the 1948 War.

The relations between Palestinians and Jews in the Communist Party were not nearly as perfect as Communist propaganda described them. Palestinians were welcomed into the PKP from the 1920s. For most of its history until the 1965 split, however, the party remained mostly Jewish. As the existing evidence shows, in 1948 MAKI numbered 750 Jews and 300 Palestinians. In 1961 the Central Committee reported that the party had 1,600 members, 74.3 percent of them Jews and 25.7 percent Palestinians. These figures put the number of Jewish members at about 1,200 and the Palestinians at around 400.[2] Despite their small numbers, the Palestinian members of the party had a special place in it. As natives of the land, victims of Zionist colonization in the pre-state era, and a persecuted minority after 1948, they used the party to express their national identity and interests. This vocalization of Palestinian nationalism led to the Jewish members' discomfort with what they perceived as the prominence of Palestinian nationalism. This tension erupted twice in Communist history, in the 1943 and 1965 splits, which were partly motivated by ideological differences between the Palestinian and Jewish members.

Many ex-members of MAKI and Banki claim that the party always favored Palestinian nationalism. According to Yair Tzaban, one of the Left Men, "what became clear over the years to both Arabs and Jews was that the struggle against Jewish nationalism was to be mounted forcefully and without compromise, but the approach to Arab nationalism was lenient."[3] Nessia Shafran, the daughter of a Jewish party member, states that Palestinian victimization by Zionism resulted in a preference for Palestinian members.

However, the political reality of the Communist Party was more complicated than as described by the Left Men and other ex-members of MAKI and Banki. The party took action against Palestinian nationalism as well. It chastised one of its Palestinian leaders and ideologists, Emile Touma, for Palestinian nationalism. Touma, who opposed the official party line on partition, which recognized Israel's existence alongside a Palestinian state, was suspended from his party positions in 1949, only to be reinstated after self-criticism. The party was also suspicious of independent nationalist organizations outside its influence.

Relations between Palestinians and Jews were not confined to the political. The party and its youth movement were one of the few places where Jews and Palestinians met as equals. The social interactions brought with them close friendships and love affairs and even long-term marriages. One of the more famous cases involved Arna Mer-Khamis, an ex-Palmach member and the daughter of a well-known Israeli malaria researcher, who married Saliba Khamis, a prominent MAKI member in Nazareth, bridging the divide between Palestinians and Jews. Some of the Palestinian party leaders were married to Jewish women. Yoram Gozansky describes an intricate social network that included New Year visits to Nazareth, at times in open defiance of military government rules.[4] While the social interaction between Palestinians and Jews was not without its tensions, Jewish members who were interviewed for this book emphasized only close relationships.

From a historical perspective, the political and social interaction of Palestinians and Jews reflected the conflict between the two nations. It was a theater of human feelings and reactions, resulting from the meeting of two socially and ethnically dissimilar groups, whose differences were exacerbated by the conflict between them. Considering these circumstances, the Jewish Communists were able to create a more open and welcoming environment for Palestinians and Jews to interact in than any other part of Israeli society of the 1950s and early 1960s could offer.

The Jewish Communists believed that beyond their national identities, both Palestinians and Jews had a mutual interest as workers against their respective ruling classes. This joint interest decreed that Palestinians and Jews could achieve a political understanding living in the same state, as the PKP advocated until 1947, or in two separate states, afterward. The national conflict was perceived as not inherent to the two nations, but a result of the vile meddling of British imperialism, the Zionist bourgeoisie, and Palestinian reaction.

The first contact between the then Zionist Communists of the MPS and Palestinians was in the early 1920s. The Jewish members of the MPS, driven by what they considered the Jewish proletariat's mission to bring the revolution to the toilers of the East, at first sought a leadership role. This perception is evident in a 1920 report by MPS to the Comintern Executive Committee. Seeking recognition from the Comintern, it states, "Among the Arabs we have begun distributing propaganda for solidarity and unity of the working class and the consolidation of unions."[5] The budding Communist movement in Palestine, with its stress on the proletarians, addressed a relatively small number of Palestinian workers on the railroads, to which it did not appeal, and the European Jewish party members stated that they could not find able Arab workers to carry out party work. Three years later, however, in a pamphlet from September 1923, originally written in Arabic, the party Central Committee urges Palestinian workers to form an alliance of Palestinian and Jewish workers with the poor peasants. The pamphlet stresses the joint political action of Palestinians and Jews against Zionism and the British, stressing both groups' joint interest in fighting a common enemy.[6] The party's new tune came into play at the fifth party conference in 1925, where an unknown Palestinian worker appeared and talked about "the problems of the *fellah* and the prospects of activity among the Arabs."[7]

In a series of anonymous handbills from the 1930s, the Jewish section of the PKP called for an understanding between the peoples. The handbills were produced at one of the high points of the conflict between the Jewish Yishuv, the British, and the Palestinians: the 1936 Arab Revolt. They mostly contain slogans in reaction to the political issues of the moment, primarily the partition plan proposed by the British in 1937. One shows a map of Palestine across which two arms are clasped in a handshake. The caption above the picture reads, "Understanding between the Peoples," the caption below it, "The Solution: Understanding between the Peoples." At the side of the map there are slogans calling for "struggle for understanding between Jews and Arabs!" and "struggle against the alliance for Hebrew products!"[8] The document is signed by the Jewish section of the Palestinian Communist Party. A second handbill from 1939 condemns the St. James Conference convened in London in the aftermath of the Arab Revolt. It attacks British imperialism for having assembled "the representatives of Arab feudalism and the Jewish bourgeoisie" in a false charade of peacemaking. True peace would be achieved, according to the Jewish Communists, by "the workers and peasants of both peoples who have mutual interests."[9]

Both handbills feature three elements characteristic of the Jewish Communists' approach to Palestinians: a call for understanding between the peoples, the advocacy of Palestinian rights—in this case condemning the attempt by the Yishuv to push Palestinian produce outside the Jewish economy—and the assertion that political action of Arab and Jews together against imperialism would bring peace.

The 1930s were marked by an increase in the influx of Jews fleeing Europe to Palestine. The growing number of Jews and Palestinian fears of a radical change in the country's demography sparked the outbreak of the Arab Revolt. The Communist Party penetrated the Palestinian labor movement and started to attract larger numbers of young Palestinian workers. The entrance of new Palestinian cadres into the party came just as the Jewish members of the party started to recognize the national existence of Jews in Palestine. This is reflected in the handbills of the 1930s. The growing realization that the country was now binational and the only solution to the conflict was a political agreement prompted another change in the way the Jewish Communists viewed Palestinians, perceiving them now as a larger partner in an arrangement that would accommodate both nations. But the growing assertiveness of the Jewish Zionist Yishuv, which was trying to push Palestinians out of the job market, the economy, and their land, brought out a new element: advocacy on behalf of Palestinian rights. As the Palestinians lost their hold on the country, becoming a minority after the 1948 War, this element would become prominent in Jewish Communist discourse about Palestinians.

Although the documents of the 1930s reflect the reality of Palestine at the time, they do not reflect the growing differences between the Palestinian Communists and their Jewish counterparts. When the Arab Revolt broke out in 1936, the PKP supported it as an anti-imperialist fight. This position of the party's Central Committee alienated many of the Jewish party members, who felt the party did not take into account the existence of a new Jewish national group in Palestine. The Jewish members' ideological fissure with the Palestinian members split the party, but the split was temporarily mended in 1940 when the Jewish faction submitted to the discipline of the Central Committee. However, the reunification of the party did not last for long. The national tensions that led to the 1937 split resurfaced in 1943, splitting Palestinian Communism into Jewish and Palestinian parties that operated separately for the next five years.

An internal document from 1940 of the Jewish Emet (Truth) faction of the party discusses the approach toward the League for Jewish-Arab Understanding, an organization formed by moderate Zionist intellectuals and Po'aley Zion activists in the midst of the Arab Revolt. The first part of the document describes the stand of the Jewish Communists toward Zionism and the Palestinian question. Imperialist policy, it states, is aided by the division between the colonized peoples, and in Palestine it was using Zionism in order to maintain the divide between Palestinians and Jews, which blurred the real issues facing the two peoples, such as independence and class warfare. The control of the "Zionist ideology within the Jewish

Yishuv is blurring the real interests of the two peoples."[10] The interest, on the Jewish side, was to overcome the division between Palestinians and Jews in order to fight imperialism.

A document from 1942 resurrects the perception among Jewish Communists, originating in the 1920s, that the Palestinians, in this case the Palestinian youth, are potentially revolutionary. It discusses the ways of increasing the support and recruitment of Palestinians to the war effort, asserting that "in the last twenty years the Arab youth have been the vanguard of the national liberation movement in Palestine."[11] This inherent revolutionary tendency had been demonstrated, according to the text, in the struggles for their national rights in the 1930s. Zionism wanted to portray Palestinians as pro-Fascist, to deceive Jewish workers and conceal from them the principal revolutionary force in Palestine. The Jewish Communists alternately represented Palestinians as allies of the Jewish working class and as a revolutionary force.

The 1940s, mainly after the USSR entered the war, were the catalyst for the PKP's first major breakthrough into a substantial section of the Palestinian populace of Palestine. Drawn to the Soviet Union's anti-imperialist ideology and impressed by its stunning victories over Fascism after 1943, a group of young Christian Palestinians became intellectually and politically engaged as Communists. Men like Emile Habibi, Tawfik Toubi, and Emile Touma found in Communism a channel for political expression and the modernization of Palestinian politics. They differed from the young workers drawn to the party in the 1930s by its class ideology, and they became active among the expanding Palestinian working class. The new recruits to Communism in Palestine brought with them a greater stress on Palestinian nationalism and reignited the tensions of the 1930s, leading to the party split between Jews and Palestinians in 1943.[12]

Ever since the 1920s, the Jewish Communists had shaped their own view of Palestinians. Idealizing a complicated and sensitive reality in which Palestinians and Jews mixed socially and politically, they developed a positive stereotype of Palestinians: as partners in the Marxist struggle against imperialism, as political partners to a binational solution to the Palestine problem, and as inherently revolutionary. But this conception could not mask two facts. First, for the party, establishing itself among the Palestinian masses was a long and difficult process, which actually came to fruition only in the late 1960s and early 1970s. Second, the party could not accommodate the nationalist feelings of both Palestinians and Jews. Nonetheless, the Communist Party and later its youth wing managed to maintain a constant and firm framework where Palestinians and Jews together resisted the growing Zionist takeover of Palestine, all in the name of an internationalist ideology.

The 1948 War changed the demographic makeup of Palestine. The Palestinians, most of them ethnically cleansed during the war, became a minority in a Jewish state. The Palestinian Communists, members of the NLL, lost their base of power within the Palestinian working class, most of whom became refugees in the neighboring Arab states. Loyal to the Soviet Union, the Palestinian Communists had supported the UN Partition Plan and objected to the Arab states' invasion of Palestine. For that stand, they were persecuted in the territories under the Arab armies' control. They fared no better at the hands of the new Israeli authorities. The IDF did not distinguish between Palestinian political leanings and arrested Palestinian Communists, at times re-arresting those who had been detained by the Arab armies. Its newspaper shut down by the British, its power base dispersed, branded as traitors by the Palestinians, and suspected by the Israelis of subversion, the NLL sought to reunite with the Jewish Communists. The Jewish Communists who took part in the Israeli war effort were now willing to restore the binational makeup of the party.

The October 1948 reunification of the Palestinian and Jewish Communists was couched in the language of international Marxism-Leninism. The speakers at the festive Central Committee meeting marking the event all devoted their remarks to Western imperialism. The *Kol Ha'am* issue on the day of the union featured verbal attacks against imperialism using similar Marxist internationalist language. In an editorial named "On the Agenda," the union of Jewish and Palestinian Communists is compared to the Zimmerwald Congress held in Switzerland in 1915 by the antiwar Socialists, and the 1948 War is blamed on the British and American imperialists, as well as Arab reaction. The act of unification is celebrated as a manifestation of international working-class unity, not a simple political act but part "of a joint struggle against imperialism."[13] The present bloodshed is said to be contrary to the interest of Israelis and Palestinians.

Despite the continued use of Marxist terminology to describe the relations between Palestinians and Jews, the 1948 War changed this discourse. The first element to be added was advocacy on behalf of the Palestinian minority. The Communists in Palestine had been involved in advocating Palestinian rights since 1924. In the 1930s the party had objected to the attempt by the Zionist movement to push Palestinians out of the labor market under the slogan of "Avoda Ivrit" (Hebrew Labor). Yet until 1948 this advocacy had been on behalf of a majority of the country's inhabitants, albeit one struggling against an increasingly powerful minority. The Palestinians left in Israel after the Nakba were reduced to the status of a humiliated minority ruled by a military government. While the Jewish Communists justified the 1948 War as an anti-imperialist war of independence, they denounced the treatment of the Palestinians left under Israeli rule. Already in the early stages of the 1948 War, in a pamphlet published in the wake of the Jewish occupation of Haifa and the exodus of its Palestinian population, the party's Central Committee warned that the "mass departure of tens of thousands of Arabs from Haifa was meant as an incitement by British agents in the Middle East to provoke the Arabs in Eretz-Israel and the neighboring countries against the Jews."[14] The victorious Jewish side was encouraged to make peace with those Palestinians who desired it and win over the Palestinians left in the Jewish state. Again anti-imperialist internationalist language is used, but this time it inadvertently masks the hard reality of ethnic cleansing. The Jewish Communists invoked anti-imperialism to justify their support for the founding of Israel, enabling them not to engage fully with the Palestinian calamity. Thus, the call for an Arab-Jewish alliance against American imperialism served to lessen the Israeli blame for the fate of the Palestinians. Saying that does not discount the civil bravery of the Jewish Communists, who even in the midst of Israeli victory continued to fight for the democratic values that had been proclaimed upon the founding of Israel.

This advocacy of Palestinian rights also featured in the speeches made at the unity conference in Haifa. Resorting to the language of democratic civil rights, in her opening speech Vilenska vowed, in the name of all true Israeli patriots, "to fight so the new state will wipe away every manifestation of discrimination from its boundaries, and will be a home and motherland to all its citizens regardless of race, nationality, and faith."[15] Although Mikunis blamed the Palestinian leadership for the disaster that had befallen its people, he did not shy away from condemning the Israeli government's "antidemocratic policy against Israeli-Arabs . . . meaning the large-scale robbery, looting, and destruction of Arab property performed by thousands of soldiers and civilians without intervention; the liquidation of entire villages by demolishing their houses for no military purpose; the mass arbitrary arrests and deportations beyond the front lines; the ghettos for Arabs in the cities and the discriminations against them."[16]

The 1950s and early 1960s were marked by an intense public struggle by MAKI and Banki for the rights of Palestinian citizens in Israel. The Jewish

Communists' main aim was to end the military government imposed on the Palestinians after the 1948 War, and toward that end they sustained a persistent campaign against the persecution of Palestinians and discrimination against them. Seeking to attract audiences outside MAKI and Banki, and abiding by the rules of the Israeli political democratic system they were part of, the Jewish Communists phrased their appeals for Arab-Jewish fraternity in the language of civil rights. In that sense, the Communists struggled to instill democratic values within the Israeli democracy. At the same time, they also used class language and appealed to Jewish morality and historical sensibilities after the Holocaust.

Democratic sensibilities were appealed to in handbills describing the arbitrary arrests of Palestinians and disruption of their activities. A 1955 handbill of the Israeli Young Communist League tells the story of Reziek Abdu, a twenty-year-old from Nazareth, who was arrested, not placed on trial at first, and remained incarcerated even after a court found him not guilty. The handbill sharply criticizes the use of the British Emergency Laws in order to suppress Palestinian political activity. It warns of a process of infiltration of Fascism into Israel, stating: "Just as freedom cannot be divided, so too democracy cannot. Start with the Arabs and you'll end with the Jews. Start with the Communists and you'll end with MAPAM and Ahdut HaAvoda."[17]

In a January 1956 memo sent by the party's Central Committee to the Committee for Military Government appointed by the prime minster, the Communists clarified their stand. First describing in detail the methods of the military government, the memo goes on to refute the official logic justifying it on security grounds and to assert that the real reason for it was a "desire to expel the Arab population from Israel . . . [and] create favorable conditions for the Jewish magnates to rob the property of the Arab population and economically exploit the Arab population more easily."[18] The concepts used are those of democratic sensibility, as the document speaks in the name of an Israeli democratic patriot outraged by the government's treatment of its Palestinian citizens. Notably, an allusion is made to the recent Jewish history of oppression, Israeli racists being compared to the early twentieth-century Tsarist anti-Semitic gangs called the Black Hundreds.

One of the high points of the Communist struggle on behalf of the Palestinians came at the time of the Kafr Qasim massacre in 1956. The massacre was initially disclosed to the public by Tawfik Toubi in a Knesset speech, of which tens of thousands of copies were disseminated by Banki members across the country. A wall poster from a year later calls for a public rally in commemoration of the massacre. The massacre was used by the Communists to highlight other wrongs done to the Palestinians. A handbill of the Israeli Young Communist League entitled (in allusion to the biblical story of Cain and Abel) "The Blood Cries Out from the Ground" condemns the government's failure to investigate a series of Palestinian children's deaths from handling discarded ammunition. The document also denounces the arrest of fourteen activists in Nazareth. These events all took place against the backdrop of the Kafr Qasim trial. The handbill ends with a call to the Jewish youth in Israel to stop "the oppression, humiliation, and abusive policy of the Ben-Gurion government toward the Israeli-Arabs, which trample upon Israeli morals and the humanistic tradition of the Jewish people."[19]

The May Day clash in 1958 in Nazareth between Palestinian demonstrators and the Israeli police was another notable event in the Communist struggle for Palestinians' rights. The mass arrests and widespread repression that followed it were strongly condemned by the Jewish Communists, again using the language of democratic rights and Jewish morality in the struggle against the military government.

A wall poster from May 1958 tries to debunk the official version of the events in Nazareth, quoting supportive testimony of *Ha'aretz* reporter Shabtai Teveth and the poet Natan Alterman. It ends with an appeal to Jewish collective memory and national pride: "Jews! Will you sit quietly while the persecution of the Arabs continues? Will the Jewish people who came out of the ghetto—agree to a ghetto for the Arabs? The detainees must be returned to their families! The military government that shames our national honor must be abolished! Jew, speak up!"[20]

What should we make of the clear turn to Jewish empathy in these documents? First, the Jewish Communists undoubtedly used the basic elements of the evolving discourse in Israel around the Holocaust and Jewish history. Second, using this discourse was a powerful rhetorical weapon in the hands of the Jewish Communists, which made the plight of Palestinians understandable to Jews, still imbued with the memories of the Holocaust, and provoked many Jews to action to prevent similar actions by their own government. Third, the Jewish Communists themselves had come to identify with the Jewish historical narrative. However, this was far from just a rhetorical propaganda tool, as the Jewish Communists authentically identified with the Jewish sensitivities they used in order to end the military government and the discrimination against Palestinians.

The advocacy on behalf of Palestinians continued well into the late 1950s and the early 1960s. A 1962 handbill that calls for a meeting of Jewish and Palestinian youth asserts that "the campaign to end the military government is getting wider and stronger than ever."[21] By that point the Communists, using language that was shared by a wide range of Israelis, had managed to mobilize parties from the Left and Right to agitate for the abolition of the military government. Did the language shaped by the Jewish Communists since the 1920s, which was expressed in handbills, posters, and other propaganda tools, have any impact on historical reality? By 1966 the military government was annulled. When the Knesset voted to abolish the military government in 1963, even Herut supported the motion, using arguments based in liberal democratic principles. Indeed, the use of the language of civil rights for the Palestinian citizens of Israel by Herut indicates that this language, long present in MAKI's platform, shaped the political discourse around the military government, facilitating the wide public mobilization that enabled its abolishment. In contrast, the Marxist-Leninist anti-imperialist terms that the Jewish Communists used to describe their relations with their Palestinian comrades did not have currency beyond MAKI and Banki and were not used in non-Communist public channels.

The Symbolism of Arab-Jewish Fraternity

The earliest symbol expressive of the Jewish Communists' comprehension of the Palestinian Other can be found in a 1937 pamphlet, which shows two arms clasped in a handshake across the background of a map of Palestine.[22] The handshake clearly symbolizes mutual agreement and friendship. It is also a Communist symbol, signifying the coming together of two opposing sides, as for example in the symbol of the German Socialist Unity Party, which represented the coming together of Social Democrats and Communists. The map of Palestine represents the local element. This early symbol is a precursor of the symbolic language used by MAKI and Banki to represent Arab-Jewish fraternity, language consisting of both local elements and the symbols of international Communism. More than a decade later, in an article in the party organ, the handshake motif reappears as the symbol of the joining together of the Palestinian and Jewish Communists, this time beneath the distinctly Communist symbols of the Hammer and Sickle and the Red Star. The captions, in

Arabic and Hebrew, provide the local context: "The Unification of the Jewish and Arab Communists."[23]

The foremost symbol of Arab-Jewish fraternity from the 1950s to the mid-1960s was the Arab-Jewish duo, an image consisting of figures of an Arab and a Jew shaking hands or standing shoulder to shoulder. Its roots lie in Soviet Socialist Realism, one example of which is Vera Mokinah's statue (1936) *The Industrial Worker and the Kolkhoz Worker*.[24] The statue juxtaposes two opposites, city and country, industry and agriculture, man and woman, uniting them under the symbol of the Hammer and Sickle. The Jewish Communist model adapted the same motif to the local Israeli landscape, depicting the Palestinian either dressed in traditional Palestinian peasant clothing or marked by just a keffiyeh, and the Jewish figure dressed in European style. The image of the Palestinian and the background against which it is portrayed might be construed as paternalistic and Orientalist. However, this image of the traditional keffiyeh-clad Palestinian was to become part of Palestinian national iconography. For example, a 1980 PLO (Palestinian Liberation Organization) poster issued in Lebanon for Land Day depicts a Palestinian peasant wearing a traditional keffiyeh holding a pickaxe; the background is a terraced village representing the landscape of rural Palestine.[25] Although a direct influence is hard to establish, it is possible that some Communist images were shared by Palestinian nationalism and Communism.

A May Day issue of *Kol Ha'am* features an image of two workers, one of them Jewish and the other Palestinian. The Jew is wearing a beret typical of Jewish workers in the early years of Jewish immigration to Palestine, the Palestinian the traditional keffiyeh. Above the two figures a white dove is flying over a background of fields and industrial buildings. The Dove was a recurring symbol in the context of Arab-Jewish fraternity.

The Dove was widely used in the Eastern European People's Democracies and adopted from the Soviet symbolic vocabulary. It is also connected to biblical narrative, with connotations of peace, safety, and tranquility. Throughout the 1950s, it often appears in combination with the previous two elements, the symbols of international Communism and the Arab-Jewish duo.

In a wall poster announcing Banki's national peace camp in 1951, the background consists of two flags, one blue and the other red. The blue flag is adorned with a Peace Dove holding an olive branch, the Red Flag with the Israeli national flag signifying the local, the Hammer and Sickle, the Red Star, and two olive branches. Another Communist motif in the poster is a rising sun, its beams penetrating the red sky. The center of the picture is occupied by three figures. Two, one of them female, are manifestly Jewish, and the third is a Palestinian wearing a keffiyeh.[26]

A photograph taken in Ramla in 1951 provides another take on the motif of the Arab-Jewish duo. It shows two men, one a Palestinian wearing a keffiyeh, the other a Jew dressed in European style. The two are photographed from below, blowing trumpets, two Red Flags waving above them.[27] The influence of Soviet artistic motifs is evident in the heroic stance of the two figures, which is reminiscent of A. Rodchenko's Socialist-Realist photograph (1930) of *The Pioneer—The Trumpeter.*

Figure 6.1. Palestinian and Jewish Banki members, Acra 1951.

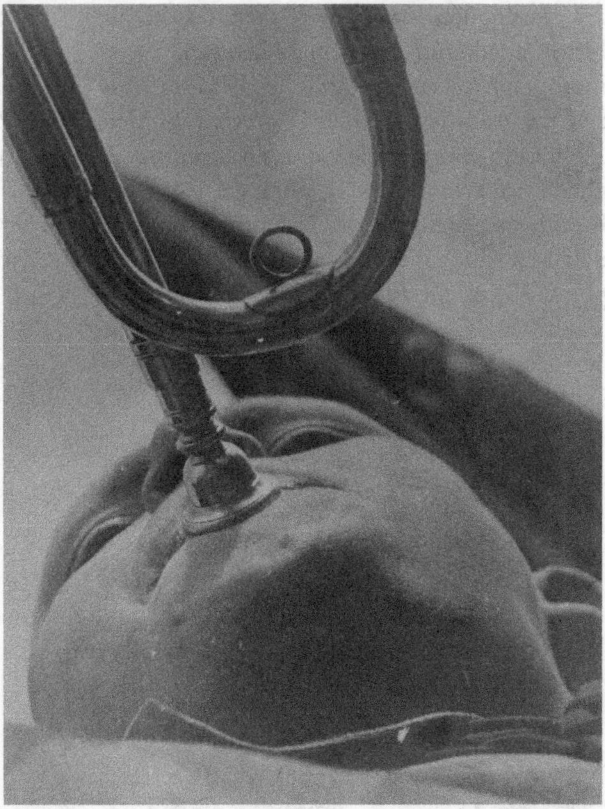

Figure 6.2. *The Pioneer—The Trumpeter*, 1930.

The fusion of Communism and local Arab-Jewish internationalism is perhaps best illustrated by a 1953 postcard that was distributed for the Bucharest Festival of Students and Youth. It shows a Palestinian figure and a Jewish figure, contrasted by their dress. The Jewish youth is holding the national flag. Below them appear idealized scenes of settlements with water towers, tents, and palm trees. The Arab-Jewish duo is stretching out their hands over a globe to a group of youths dressed in clothes representing the world's continents. Behind them wave flags adorned with the Peace Dove and the symbol of the WFDY, and banners with the words "Peace" and "Friendship." Arab-Jewish fraternity had become an integral part of Communist internationalism.[28]

The Jewish Communists mostly neglected to speak to their Palestinian comrades in Arabic; however, they conversed culturally with their Palestinian comrades in the language of Marxist internationalism. To advocate the case of the oppressed Palestinian minority in Israel to wider audiences, they used the language of Jewish historical sensibilities. However, to the Jewish Communists, especially in Banki, the understanding of Palestinians was an important part of their educational work. In an instructors' brochure created in the aftermath of the 1956 War, in January 1957, the young Jewish Communists were encouraged to learn about and discuss the Palestinian people. Like many of Banki's instructors' brochures, it is constructed in the form of a *Masechet*.

The cover of the brochure, entitled "We and Our Neighbors," shows an Arab wearing a keffiyeh standing next to a Jew dressed in European style. They are holding each other's shoulders and shaking hands, symbolizing the unity of Arabs and Jews. The background consists of a Jewish settlement and an Orientalist rendition of a Bedouin desert dwelling. The brochure itself is made up of three stories dealing with Palestinian-Jewish relations from the pre-1948 period to the then-current struggle against the military government. Each story is followed by points for a discussion after it has been read. The brochure ends with a discussion about the future road to peace.

The aim of the brochure was not only "to provide deep and convincing explanations of the reasons for the conflict and the way to peacefully resolve it," but also "to root out from children's hearts the fear, hate, and nationalistic arrogance toward the Arab people and nurture in their hearts friendship, trust, and the desire for peace," all to be achieved by studying the history and current affairs of the Palestinians. In recounting the history of the clash between Palestinians and Jews in pre-1948 Palestine, the brochure reverts to the language of the early Jewish Communists in the 1920s and 1930s. It asserts that Palestinian-Jewish relations in the pre-1948 era had been friendly. The conflict was not fueled by the peoples themselves, but by the British that set the two sides against each other. As the two oppressed peoples' struggle for freedom intensified, a solution had been offered in the form of the UN Partition Plan. The outbreak of the 1948 War is described, again in anti-imperialist terms, as an attack "by the Arab states encouraged by the British to end Palestinian and Jewish independence."

As regards the massive ethnic cleansing of Palestinians during the war, imperialism and the Israeli government are the culprits. "Who caused most of Israel's Arabs to flee or be deported from the country during the war?" the brochure asks, and in answer it lays the blame squarely on "the English and the Arab rulers who incited them to flee and leave the country, and also the government of Israel that was interested in their departure."[29] The assumptions that lay behind the Jewish Communists' narrative of the 1948 War reflected the way it was perceived in the official Israeli narrative, placing the blame on the Palestinian side and its rulers for inciting the flight of the Palestinians, on the Jewish Communists' ideological tendencies—namely, anti-imperialism, particularly British imperialism—and on the Israeli government. It is clear that by supporting the Israeli side in the war, the Jewish Communists failed to fully recognize the ethnic-cleansing nature of Zionist policies and practices during the war. They subsumed the colonial logic of Zionism, manifested in the displacement of the Palestinians, to a larger narrative of anti-imperialism and Arab cooperation with it. However, despite its obvious flaws, the Jewish Communist narrative subverted the Israeli narrative of the Nakba. The Jewish Communists rightly observed that most Palestinians had not taken part in the battles. They recognized the dismal results of driving out the Palestinians, recognizing it as an obstacle to reconciliation. In those respects, the Jewish Communists' portrayal of the war was not the prevailing one.

The third discussion deals with the military government. Here, in an internal document that was not intended for public consumption, Banki members use the language of appeal to Jewish sensibility. The military government is called a ghetto, and the policy toward the Palestinian citizenry of Israel described as "oppression, terror,"[30] its contribution to Israel's security being refuted. The last discussion is concerned with peace, citing the conditions that would enable peace, the end of military government, and a "severing of the connections with the enslavers and oppressors hated by the peoples of the Middle East."[31]

The brochure is meant not just to educate the young Communists about the history and geography of their Palestinian neighbors, but to indoctrinate them with the party line, and thus the text relies heavily on the anti-imperialist interpretation of the recent history of the Middle East. The Zionist-Palestinian conflict is presented to the Banki members as part of a great historical drama, the struggle between imperialism and anti-imperialism, driven by outside forces. This portrayal was indeed rooted in the Middle Eastern history of the 1950s and 1960s when the Big Powers still tried to exert control, as was the case in 1956 and in the Algerian war of independence. According to the brochure, the Palestinians had entirely lost their power of agency, becoming only heroic collective figures in the meta-historical struggle between imperialism and anti-imperialism. Much as Banki's perception of Palestinians was positive and motivated by a true desire to understand the lives and politics of Palestinians, as well as to bridge the gap between the conflicting sides, they never delved deeply into the effects the 1948 War had on Palestinian identity and nationalism.

Arab-Jewish Ritual

A 1962 Banki document states that "the big national festivals of Jewish and Arab youth have become a fine tradition; they demonstrate the desire for fraternity and peace."[32] Arab-Jewish fraternity was manifested, then, not only in the political struggle against the military government, but in ritual as well. Starting in the late 1940s in the aftermath of the 1948 War, Jews and Palestinians engaged in events intended to bond together both peoples.

The first documented mass ritual concerning Palestinians and Jews was the unification ceremony in Haifa on October 22, 1948. The ceremony itself was not elaborate, consisting of speeches that were delivered to applause from the audience. The May theater was bedecked with Red Flags; on either side of the stage stood the Israeli national flag and Red Flags. Between portraits of Lenin and Stalin stood the symbol of the convention, "a friendly handshake of brave hands—a symbol of friendly fraternity, the Hammer and Sickle."[33] The unification ceremony did not give rise to any ritualistic tradition among the Jewish and Palestinian Communists, despite its importance in the party's collective memory.

The first Arab-Jewish youth festival took place in 1949 on Mount Carmel overlooking the Jewish-Arab city of Haifa. It lasted for five days and included sports events and exhibitions on such themes as Banki's history, the achievements of the USSR, and the fallen of the 1948 War. The high point of the festival was a joint march of Palestinian and Jewish youths, the biggest in the country to that date.[34]

The next well-documented festival celebrating Arab-Jewish fraternity was held in April 1955 in Tel Aviv, against the background of escalating border skirmishes between Israel and its neighbors that led to the 1956 Sinai War. It was an elaborate enterprise whose aim was to promote the idea of Arab-Jewish fraternity.[35] The event required extensive preparations. A series of artistic balls were held in Palestinian and Jewish towns, including choirs, dance troupes, singing and dancing, and local festivals that included sports events and artistic performances. The preparations included public meetings at workplaces and schools where the idea of the festival was explained. Organizers and Jewish youth also traveled to Nazareth and Palestinian villages, and bags emblazoned with the festival symbol were distributed. The mass nature of the event is evident from the likely exaggerated but still telling numbers: around twelve thousand participants in the pre-festival balls and another twenty thousand that received the bags.

The festival began on Monday, April 4, 1955, when the participants, Jews and Palestinians, congregated in Tel Aviv. A rally was held in the evening, to which torch relays came from the four corners of the country. The next day was dedicated to movies and an afternoon ball, consisting of artistic performances and songs by the party's choirs. In the evening the festival participants sailed on the Yarkon River and held a bonfire party on its banks. The last day of the festival started with sports events followed by a symposium entitled Culture in the Service of Peace. The festival ended with a march to Independence Park.[36]

Two photos of the marches conducted during the festival attest to what had become the conventions of Jewish Communist representation of Arab-Jewish fraternity. The first shows a group of two young men and two women standing in front of banners. The men are wearing keffiyehs, and the women are garbed in European clothes. One man is holding a Peace Dove in one hand and the symbol of the festival in the other. The symbol consists of two profiled figureheads, one a Palestinian wearing a keffiyeh, the other a Jew. A second photo shows young men and women marching past watching bystanders. The group in the foreground consists of four young Palestinians, three of them dressed in traditional peasant clothing; the fourth is dressed in the Banki uniform and playing a flute. Behind them, a group of Jewish girls are holding up a banner.[37]

The rituals that enshrined Arab-Jewish fraternity in MAKI and Banki were meant to bond together Palestinians and Jews. The symbolism of Communist Arab-Jewish fraternity was filled with representations of bonding. The Arab-Jewish figures so prevalent in it were often depicted shoulder to shoulder, holding each other's shoulders, or shaking hands.

The group bonding of Palestinians and Jews is clearly evident in a wall poster produced for the 1955 festival, which shows a group of Palestinian and Jewish youths of mixed gender. The Palestinians are identified by their keffiyehs and head coverings. All are standing in a tight group, bonded together as one.[38] Another poster produced for May Day 1954 features three figures, two men and a woman. The two men reiterate the motif of the oft-seen Arab-Jewish duo, one of them bareheaded, the other wearing a keffiyeh. In allusion to proletarian internationalism, all three figures are carrying work tools in their hands. Above them a banner in Hebrew and

Arabic proclaims, "Long Live May Day 1954," a red Hammer and Sickle flag waving beside it.[39] These posters show how the Jewish Communists codified the communitas of Palestinians and Jews: Jews and Palestinians were bonded together despite their external differences. This communitas also originated from the bond between workers, as codified in terms of proletarian internationalism.

The rituals that were performed and the language used to describe them also express Jewish-Arab communitas. The immediate communitas formed between Palestinians and Jews at the April 1955 festival is given enthusiastic expression: "Together we marched; together we sang; together we laughed joked, found joy in our youth; our arms came together in dance and our legs danced jointly at the same pace; looks of joy and enthusiasm infused with brotherhood were exchanged."[40] The ritual activity that took place during the festival was also meant to create communitas between the Jewish and Palestinian participants, the bonfire and regatta on the river serving as good examples, or in the words of *Kol Hano'ar*: "With the flow of the Yarkon, the tunes of our Arab-Jewish songs and the echo answered back in tunes that blended together."[41]

Communitas arises from a state of liminality between and betwixt the various strata of the social hierarchy. Suitable conditions for such were created in the rituals surrounding Communist Arab-Jewish fraternity. The sites of the festivals in 1949 and 1955, Mount Carmel and the Yarkon River, respectively, placed the participants at the liminal margins of the urban centers and outside the social order they embodied and represented. The participants' status within Israel's social structure was also liminal. The Jewish Banki members were marginalized in Jewish-Israeli society, suspected and despised as the left-wing "Other." The Palestinian members of Banki were alienated from Israeli society as the Palestinian "Other," presumed to be connected to the enemy beyond the territorial borders of the state. This meeting of the marginalized was meant to alleviate the continued tension between Palestinians and Jews within Israel and with the Arab peoples in the region.

A rare photo from the 1949 Arab-Jewish Friendship Festival shows MAKI secretary general Shmuel Mikunis seated among a group of Palestinian and Jewish youths. To the unknowing onlooker, the participants may look the same. One boy is playing a flute. Others are dressed in the Banki uniform. One girl who is looking straight at the camera is wearing a keffiyeh. In many ways this is what the Jewish members of MAKI and Banki tried to create: a bond between Jews and Palestinians that would transcend the national identities of Palestinians and Jewish Israelis.[42]

Figure 6.3. Arab-Jewish Youth Festival, 1949.

The Jewish Communist and the Palestinian Other

The Jewish Communists' image of the Palestinians was in essence a positive one. Since the 1920s they had recruited, worked, and socialized with Palestinians in a way that was exceptional among both communities in Palestine. In stark contrast to Socialist-Zionist culture, which very quickly abandoned Socialist internationalist claims and developed a workers' culture and institutions for Jews only, the Jewish Communists remained loyal to proletarian internationalism. It was through those ideological lenses that they formed their understanding of Palestinians.

In Marxist-Leninist terms, the Jewish Communists perceived the Palestinians as the direct victims of Zionist colonization and British imperialism, and as those destined to undertake the revolutionary mission the Jewish working class could not perform. They also fervently believed that Jews and Palestinians had common interests, as workers, that far exceeded their national identities. In their view, only British imperialism and Zionism—as an expression of Jewish bourgeoisie profitmaking, thus dispossessing the Palestinians—were responsible for the conflict between Palestinians and Jews. From these basic tenets, it followed that the Palestinians were partners in a revolutionary, anti-imperialist, and anti-Zionist struggle. Until 1948 this mainly was the way the Jewish Communists perceived the Palestinians.

After 1948 this view was augmented by intensive advocacy for Palestinians within the Jewish state. The PKP had campaigned, from the 1920s, against the wrongs committed by Zionist settlers against Palestinians. After 1948, with the Palestinians now a persecuted minority, the Jewish Communists defended them, engaging in a struggle for civil democratic rights. In this struggle, which also reflected the growing sensitivity of the Jewish Communists to their own Jewish identity, they used the language of democratic rights and appealed to the Jewish collective memory of persecution. In that sense, in one of the most universalistic aspects of their identity as an Arab-Jewish fraternity, the Jewish Communists acted as Jews.

In the novel *A Locked Room*, a young Palestinian Communist becomes disillusioned with the party's stand on Palestinians. In an argument with his local branch secretary, which practically brings his membership in the party to an end, he says: "The Arabs in Israel are not Blacks who want equal status with the white man!" He accuses the party of "disregarding the national aspect; the Arabs in Israel are part of a people that were driven out of their land, whose lands were stolen, so that they became a people of refugees."[43]

This literary depiction reflects how the Communists misunderstood the Palestinian tragedy and the way it shaped modern Palestinian nationalism. As in the 1920s and 1930s, the Jewish Communists were blind to the power of Jewish and Palestinian nationalism over Palestinians and Jews alike. Trained in gazing at Palestinians through the lenses of Marxist-Leninist ideology, they could not completely fathom the impact of the Nakba on the Palestinians. Instead of confronting the issue head-on, they blamed Western imperialism for the plight of the Palestinians. The role played by the inept elites of both the Israelis and the Palestinians in precipitating the Nakba was only subordinate to the narrative of divisive imperialism, which pitted Jews and Palestinians against each other. The Palestinian calamity was discounted even in Banki's Jewish branches. One of the senior instructors of the Tel Aviv branch admits that its meaning was not discussed, even after visits to the destroyed Palestinian villages still seen in the Israeli landscape of the 1950s and early 1960s.[44] This myopic view of Palestinian nationalism skewed the Jewish Communists' perception of Palestinians. The Palestinians were the objects of empathy regarding their oppression as unequal citizens, seen as partners in the anti-imperialist struggle and to any agreement on the fate of the country, with their own national identity. But as for that identity having been shaped by the national trauma of deportation and loss of homeland, it was not part of the Jewish Communists' perception of the Palestinian Other.

Nonetheless, the Jewish Communist discourse of Arab-Jewish fraternity was not completely blind to the Palestinian experience of loss. The best example of that sensitivity is found not in political principles and statements, but in the realm of poetic expression. During the 1950s and early 1960s, Alexander Penn ran the literary section of *Kol Ha'am*. Besides his duties as a literary editor, he continued a practice that he had begun in the 1930s in the Histadrut organ *Davar*, writing a poetic column in reaction to the issues of the day under the pseudonym Yodh Het. At times, Penn chose to publish certain poems—apparently those he deemed politically important, like his great poem of the 1930s, "Against"—under his own name.

In a poem named "The Shame," Penn reacted to a case of police brutality against a Palestinian. The poem starts with an appeal to Jewish collective memory, "since the people's memory / in the thick of its history will be kept."[45] It then moves on to a more explicit invocation of Jewish history's recent trauma, portraying the restrictions imposed on Palestinians' movement as "the boundaries of the hangar of the ghetto."[46] Culminating in the thinly veiled verse "it is much known from Israel! It parallels history! We will not remind its near past, / crying out of smoldering walls . . . / To its name the nation's body, / will shudder in ashes it will run / An affront of its grieving heart / The years stand with their blood."[47] The poem expresses sensitivity to the Palestinians' plight, using Jewish history as its moral center. The portrayal of the Palestinian Other through the lens of Jewish sensitivity in the poem—as well as in other Jewish Communist texts—is indicative of the Jewish Communists' growing compassion toward their own identity. Poignantly, the Jewish Communists perceived the Palestinian Other in their own cultural terms. That may be attributed to their inability to recognize Palestinian political agency outside the anti-imperialist narrative. It might also be attributed to an attempt to comprehend the Palestinian Other in positive cultural terms that would be familiar to the Jewish Communists, as well as to others outside the party and Banki. It also points to the cultural differences between the Palestinian and Jewish Communists that were evident before 1948 and continued into the post-1948, ostensibly unified MAKI. The cultural misunderstanding was expressed in the political sphere. When MAKI, ever loyal to the USSR, in 1958 supported the Iraqi nationalist leader Abd al-Karim Qasim, who was backed by the Iraqi Communist Party and the Eastern Bloc, against the highly popular Nasser, Palestinians, who like the rest of the Arab world were infuriated by that move, dealt MAKI a heavy electoral loss in the 1959 election, reducing its Knesset representation from six members to three.

In contrast to this example stand three short poems under the collective name of "A People's Songs," published in the summer of 1958. The first poem, "Plundered Village," describes a destroyed Palestinian village where "on the bent fence / to the exploded of sighs of the house / as flags of calamity / silent in their blackness two *abaya*s hang." The poem goes on to condemn "the burner / Stand and inherent! / on the living, in shod trample / the plowman passes / in the rubbed strangers' field." It ends with a biblical reference: "a voice is vociferously sounding / it is not Rachel lamenting / land, land / it is Hagar mourning her sons!"[48] In the third poem, "Mother," Penn turns to the Palestinian experience of loss and exile, appropriating the poetic self of the mother who is standing on the main road, "refusing to be consoled," watching as "on the main road the flower was plucked / the daughter was expelled."[49] The mother and daughter metaphor is used to convey the Palestinian people's loss of their land. Penn does not give poetic form to the imperialist explanation. In the short middle poem of the cycle, named simply "Who?," he presents a series of poignant questions: "who said to the well block/ the one that came with a stone on its edge/ that deliberately strangled who is it?" His answer is at the same time explicit "the face of my brother who oppresses me I will remember." Hinting to the Jews that their relation with Palestinians was codified by the Communists as a brotherly one and inclusive, "the hate the son of my father it is the hate."[50] Penn's alternative response to the Palestinian tragedy, subverting the Zionist narrative of the 1948 War and the narrative of his own party, remained confined to the realm of poetry.

The Jewish Communists who participated in the 1948 War could not fully engage with the Palestinian tragedy. When the party absorbed the Left Men, many of them veterans of the war, the initial approach was reinforced. Thus, as in the 1930s, the Jewish Communists were unable to understand Palestinian nationalism. This blind spot alienated the Palestinian members, whose foundational experience was one of displacement and loss, connecting them to their brethren across the border. It was only in the 1970s, after the split and the 1967 War, when Rakah drew closer to the PLO, that a different understanding of Palestinian nationalism emerged.

Conclusion

The narrative of this book has portrayed the way a Jewish-Israeli identity could be formed outside the well-known mechanisms of identity formation in Israel. It has been shown here that outside the cultural spaces of agricultural schools, Zionist youth movements, the Histadrut, and the kibbutzim, an "Other" Israeli identity could be formed. Furthermore, this identity was shaped by a group of Eastern European and sabra Jews at the margins of Israeli politics and political culture. Through a series of cultural practices, the Jewish Communists in Palestine/Israel created from the early 1920s to the mid-1960s their own cultural space. It enabled them—through ritual, symbol, and mythmaking—to articulate their own Communist Jewish-Israeli identity.

This identity—which took shape in the Israeli Communist subculture—utilized Soviet, left-wing European, Jewish traditional, and Israeli local elements as metaphorical building blocks. An analysis of the different fragments of that identity yields a picture of the Jewish Communist in MAKI and Banki as a progressive Jew, an anti-Zionist Israeli patriot lacking a working-class identity but identifying deeply with workers, a militant pseudo-religious believer in the USSR with a positive yet myopic view of Palestinians.

Unpacking these different elements of Jewish-Israeli Communist identity uncovers the ritualistic, symbolic, and mythological levels of Communist identity. Zionism reshaped the Jewish traditional calendar along Zionist nationalist lines. The Jewish Communists picked and chose what they deemed to be progressive from Jewish tradition in order to create their own renditions of the Jewish holidays. Mainly Passover and Hanukkah—favored for their narratives of struggle against oppression—were reworked to accommodate class and Marxist contents and used as educational tools to shape a Jewish progressive Communist. MAKI and Banki used Socialist-Zionist cultural practices, according a class element to the narrative of Hanukkah and—by some accounts—rewriting the Passover Haggadah. Already recurrent in the culture of MAKI and Banki, the diffusion of Zionist elements into Communist subculture and identity—unsettling the balance between Jewish nationalist and Communist elements—was accelerated by the arrival of the "Left Men" to the party. This movement toward a more Israeli (i.e., Zionist) left exacerbated the tensions within the party, contributing to its 1965 split. This process is most evident in the attempt to move the initiation of new Banki members from May Day to Hanukkah, a move that shocked the party's old guard with its more internationalist Communist cultural preferences.

At the core of the Jewish-Israeli Communist identity stood anti-Zionism. From its formative stages, Communism in Palestine/Israel preferred Socialism over Zionism—including its self-proclaimed Socialist strands. However, components of Jewish nationalism detached from Zionism did diffuse into the Jewish-Israeli Communist identity. This development is very much in evidence in the way the Jewish Communists commemorated the Holocaust and the way they celebrated Israeli independence. The memory of the Holocaust—which hit the Jewish Communists hard, as it did many in the Yishuv—was deliberately sidelined during Israel's formative years. The active commemoration became mainly a preoccupation of the Zionist Left, centered on the Jewish armed resistance to the Nazi annihilation; the Jewish Communists tried to highlight their part in these events. Once again their cultural practices were intertwined with those of Socialist-Zionism. However, the Jewish-Israeli Communist memory of genocide in Europe was not without its distinct characterizations. The Jewish Communists emphasized the cooperation between Jews and non-Jews and the avenging role of the Red Army. They also emphasized the gap between the Jewish fighters, whom they associated with progressive left-wing forces, and the Judenräte, whom they viewed as a manifestation of the Jewish middle class. This narrow-minded discourse about the Holocaust masked a more nuanced view of the events in Europe that did take in the other victims and other forms of resistance. In the 1960s, however, as the view of the Holocaust started to change in Israeli society as a whole, so did the Communist view.

The Communist Party's role in the 1948 War entangled the party in a series of contradictions. The Jewish Communists supported a Jewish state and took part in the Israeli war effort, in contradiction to the party's anti-Zionism and its long-standing objection to a state for Jews only in

Palestine. In order to alleviate this ideological tension, MAKI and Banki rooted their support for Israeli independence in an anti-imperialist myth, placing emphasis more on the independence of the state and loyalty to it than on its Zionist context. Thus the Jewish Communists viewed the 1948 War as part of a global struggle against Western imperialism, a war in which the Israeli side represented a progressive force opposing the lackeys of British imperialism—the Arab states and Palestinian reaction. With that in mind, MAKI and Banki developed a cult around the Communists that had fallen in the party's struggle against the British, culminating in the cult around party secretary Eliyahu (Alyosha) Gozansky. They also took part in the public independence celebrations in the streets.

The way the Jewish Communists commemorated the Holocaust and understood their role in the events that led to the creation of Israel had a profound impact on their identity. From the juxtaposition of the celebration of Jewish armed resistance in Nazi-occupied Europe, with the anti-imperialist narrative of Israeli independence, Jewish Communists emerge as non-Zionist Israeli patriots. Through their understanding of the turbulent events of the twentieth century they found an alternative way into Jewish nationalism. It was a form of Jewish identity that, while not reliant on the Zionist Eretz-Israel, remained rooted in Socialist-Zionist practices and biases. It was more lenient—within ideological constraints—in its attitude toward the role played by non-Jews (mainly Poles) in the Holocaust and paid deference to the part the Soviets took in the war. However, despite its internationalist aspects, it was at its core a Jewish identity. As Israelis, the Jewish Communists developed a form of identity that enabled them, not unlike sections of Haredi society, to profess a limited loyalty to the state, defending its independence from imperialism while negating its Zionist ideological core.

May Day was undoubtedly the most important holiday in the Communist calendar. While the Jewish Communists were marginalized within the Zionist labor movement and working class, culturally they developed an extensive symbolic and ceremonial system around workers' militancy. The yearly May Day parade, which began as a Communist counter-ritual with the marchers bursting into the public sphere from the margins of underground existence, became a regimented Soviet-style march. Using a symbolic language that combined elements of local Israeli, Soviet, and radical European provenance, Banki created a political spectacle that presented a marching utopia of a Socialist Israel.

In contrast to the identity formation that marked other elements of the Communist subculture—for example, support of Israeli independence, commemoration of the Holocaust, and the blind glorification of and loyalty to the USSR—the Jewish Communists never developed a working-class identity. For a number of objective reasons that prevented MAKI and Banki from developing a large working-class following, the Jewish Communists developed only a somewhat abstract identification with workers. This lack of positive identity formation meant that the Jewish Communists never managed to fully understand the creation of a Mizrahi Jewish working class in post-1948 Israel. Consequently, the Communists never managed to recruit any substantial number of workers against the ethnically segmented capitalist order. Instead, MAKI and Banki diverted their energies mainly to the national conflict and the USSR—leaving the working class aside.

The Soviet Union loomed large in Jewish Communist consciousness. Perceiving it from the 1920s on as the fulfilment of a utopian dream, MAKI and Banki celebrated its two foundational events: the October Revolution and World War II. Both were celebrated on a cosmological pseudo-religious scale. Under the symbol of the joint Israeli and Soviet flags, the Jewish Communists celebrated the Soviet victory on May 9th in a mass rite. The rite featured Soviet symbolism at the site of a Zionist monument, as the Communists and the philo-Soviet community with them moved from the solemn to the carnivalesque.

The October Revolution was celebrated by the Jewish Communists as the start of a new era in human history. The day of the revolution was the occasion upon which the Jewish Communists celebrated the Socialist construction of the USSR, portraying the revolutionary events in 1917 Russia as the uprising of the underclasses led by the Bolshevik Party—all couched in the symbolism of the Soviet state. Like other Marxist revolutionaries, the Jewish Communists viewed the 1917 Revolution as part of a long lineage of rebels and revolutionaries stretching back to antiquity. Such episodes as the Paris Commune, the 1934 Vina Uprising, and the Spanish Civil War were used to inculcate the lesson that the Russian Revolution was the only right way to effect radical social change in party and youth members.

The Soviet holidays did not make the Jewish Communists a variant Israeli version of Soviet identity. Instead it made them believers. The Communist discourse about the USSR was couched in the language of a pseudo-religious faith. From the cosmological description of the 1917 Revolution as hailing a new era in human history to the celebration of the prowess of the Soviet armed forces during World War II, the Soviet Union was the temple in which the Jewish Communists offered their secular prayers. They were also in many ways blind believers; any criticism of the obvious flaws of the Soviet edifice—its imperial rule, the continued repression, and the Stalinist mass murders—was relegated to the realm of unholy anti-Soviet propaganda. Since the Soviet Union was perceived as the paragon of revolutionary virtue and the gatekeeper for who could claim to be a Communist, this blind view of the USSR lay at the core of the Jewish Communists' identity as Communists. Without its ideological approval, they could not see themselves as Communists.

The relations between Jewish and Arab Communists were complicated and sensitive. A core tenet of Communism in Palestine/Israel was Arab-Jewish joint action. The Jewish Communists advocated a struggle by the Palestinian and Jewish lower classes against Zionism and imperialism. On that premise, the Jewish Communists gazed upon their Palestinian comrades within three discursive frameworks. The first cast them as part of the joint anti-imperialist struggle, phrased in the ideological terms of Marxism-Leninism. The second was civil rights advocacy on behalf of the Palestinian citizens of Israel—who lived under military government. The third featured the use of Jewish traumatic collective memory as a way to garner public support for MAKI and Banki's struggle against the military government. There is no doubt that the Jewish Communists created a space that was more open and egalitarian to Palestinians. The evidence points to a joint life of political struggle and simple human relations with good intentions on the part of Arabs and Jews alike. This unique way of life was consecrated in the youth festivals and symbolic language that visualized Arab-Jewish fraternity. However, the Jewish Communists' understanding of the Palestinian Other was stereotypical and myopic. As positively as the Jewish Communists gazed upon Palestinians, they could not afford them real national agency and could not fully fathom the way the Nakba shaped the national identity of Palestinians.

The Jewish Communists' understanding of Palestinians was not part of their identity formation. There was no real way they could bridge the ethno-national divide. However, one part of the identity of the members of MAKI and Banki did come to the fore in dealing with their Palestinian comrades—the Jewish element. As they condemned the way the Israeli government treated its own citizens, the Jewish Communists used the memory of Jewish victimhood as a way to appeal to the Jewish majority. However, it was not just political expediency that lay behind this political cultural move—rather, it was a manifestation of the deepest layers of Jewish-Israeli Communist identity.

This has been the story of the rise and fall of the Israeli-Jewish Communist identity and the subculture within which it was formed. Having evolved from the 1920s in a process of diffusion of elements from Europe and from Palestine/Israel, it met its downfall due to the increased presence of a Zionist Israeli component in the identity of MAKI and notably Banki members. As the cultural transformation project of the Left Men gathered pace, the Communist internationalist and anti-Zionist parts of the Jewish Communist identity eroded. At the end of this process the Jewish Communists became just another version of Zionists, and then they were no more.

What insights can we garner from the historical narrative unfolded in this book? There are two, one more general and the other more specific to the Israeli case. Nationalism is often perceived as the product of an elite effort to nationalize the masses. This book shows that this assertion is only partly true and that a national culture can be produced bottom-up by nonelite groups. It also elucidates the fact that national identity can be multifaceted and differ from the one sanctioned by the established nationalist movements. The book also shows that nationalism can originate from the left even without a national liberation struggle, as was the case in China and Vietnam, but in a settler colonial situation.

Zionism is commonly perceived as the hegemonic form of Jewish nationalism in Palestine/Israel. This book has shown that beyond the Zionist hegemony and within local Israeli environments a non-Zionist national identity—not based on pre-Zionist Judaism—can be formed. Above all, the complex narrative of Jewish-Israeli Communist identity and subculture shows that there are ways to Israeliness that are progressive and inclusive, in contrast to the exclusionary framing of Jewish-Israeli Zionist identity in Palestine/Israel ever since the late nineteenth century.

Notes

Introduction

1. Between the time of Moshe Sneh's split from MAPAM (United Workers' Party) in 1952 and his followers' assimilation into MAKI in 1954, he formed the Socialist Left Party, or in short, the Left. Those who followed him to MAKI were thus dubbed the "Left Men."

2. Martin Ebon, "Communist Tactics in Palestine," *The Middle East Journal* 2 (1948): 255–69. The article gives a brief history of the party from the 1920s to 1943 and describes its tactics in 1948. The party is seen mainly as a tool of Soviet foreign policy.

3. For the Zionist historians, see Walter Laqueur's book, *Communism and Nationalism in the Middle East* (New York: Frederick A. Praeger, 1956), and, under the Israeli pseudonym *MPS-PKP-MKI*, Nachman List, "Gilguley Hakomunizem Be'artsot Arav Vebe'erets-Isra'el" [The Metamorphosis of Communism in the Arab States and Eretz-Israel], *Molad* 2, no. 9 (1969): 297–309, and "Tsadaḳ Haḳominṭern [Alef]" [The Comintern Was Right A.], *Keshet* 5, no. B (1963): 132–48, "Tsadaḳ Haḳominṭern [Daled]" [The Comintern Was Right D.], *Keshet* 6, no. D (1964): 103–17, "Tsadaḳ Haḳominṭern [Hey]" [The Comintern Was Right E.], *Keshet* 7, no. C (1965): 80–93; Yehuda Slozski, "Mimapsa Beve'idat Hayesod Shel Ha'Histadrut" [MPSA in the Founding Convention of the Histadrut], *Asufot* 14 (1970): 133–62, and "Mimapsa Ad Yaḳap [Peḳepe]" [From MPS to YKP (PKP)], *Asufot* 16 (1972): 3–18; Jacob Hen-Tov, *Communism and Zionism in Palestine: The Comintern and the Political Unrest in the 1920s* (Cambridge: Schenkman, 1974); Shmuel Dothan, "The Jewish Section of the Palestine Communist Party, 1937–1939," in *Zionism: Studies in the History of the Zionist Movement and of the Jewish Community in Palestine*, ed. Daniel Carpi and Gedalia Yogev, 243–62 (Tel Aviv: Massada, 1975), and *Adumim: Hamiflaga Haḳomunistit Be'erets-Isra'el* [Reds: The Communist Party in Eretz-Israel] (Kfar Sava: Shvana Hasofer, 1991); Yehoshua Porat, "Mahapkhanut Veṭerorizem Bemediniyut Hamiflaga Haḳomunixṭit

Hafalestinait (Pekape), 1929–1939" [Revolution and Terrorism in the Policy of the Palestine Communist Party (PKP), 1929–1939], *The New East* 18 (1968): 255–67, and "Haliga Leshiḥrur Le'umi (Atsabat Et-Taḥrir El-Vaṭani): Tḳumata, Mahuta Vehitparḳuta (1943–1948) [The National Liberation League: Its Rise, Its Essence and Fall (1943–1948)], *The New East* 14 (1968): 354–66; Eli Reches, "Jews and Arabs in the Israeli Communist Party," in *Ethnicity, Pluralism and the State in the Middle East*, ed. Milton J. Esman and Itamar Rabinovich, 121–38 (Ithaca: Cornell University Press, 1988), "Leshe'elat Hayaḥasim beyn Yehudim Ve'arvim Bemaki" [On the Question of the Relation between Arabs and Jews in MKI], in *State Government and International Relationships*, ed. Gabriel Shaper, 67–95 (Jerusalem: Bialik Institute, 1998), and *Ha'aravi Be'Isra'el: beyn Ḳomunizem Lele'umiyut Arvit* [The Arab Minority in Israel: Between Communism and Arab Nationalism] (Tel Aviv: Hakibbutz Hameuchad, 1993); Sondra Rubenstein, *The Communist Movement in Palestine and Israel, 1919–1984* (Boulder: Westview Press, 1985). All these historians share the same basic outlook on Communism.

4. For Palestinian historiography, see Bashear Suliman, "The Arab East in Communist Theory and Political Practice, 1918–1928," PhD diss., University of London, 1976; Musa Budeiri, *The Palestine Communist Party 1919–1948: Arab and Jew in the Struggle for Internationalism* (London: Ithaca Press, 1979); Maher Al-Sheriff's and Shamih Samara's works were written in Arabic, and their views as well as the views of all the Palestinian historians dealing with the subject can be found in Eli Reches, "Yehudim Ve'arvim Bapekape—Sugiya Bahisṭoryografya hafalasttinit-Arvit Bat-Zmanenu" [Arabs and Jews in the PKP—An Issue in Contemporary Arab-Palestinian Historiography], in *Zionism: A Literary Collection of the History of the Zionist Movement and the Jewish Yishuv*, ed. Matitiyahu Mintz, 175–86 (Tel Aviv: Hakibbutz Hameuchad, 1990).

5. For a cultural history of Communism in Palestine, see Joel Beinin, *Was the Red Flag Flying There? Marxist Politics and the Arab-Israeli Conflict in Egypt and Israel, 1948–1965* (Berkeley: University of California Press, 1990); Zachary Lockman, *Comrades and Enemies: Arab and Jewish Workers in Palestine, 1906–1948* (Berkeley: University of California Press, 1995); and Ilana Kaufman, *Arab National Communism in the Jewish State* (Jacksonville: University Press of Florida, 1997). The latest addition to the scholarly research of Communism in Israel is the documentary collection by Leon Zahavi, *Leḥud O Beyaḥad: Yehudim Ve'aravim Bemismakhey Haḳomintern 1919–1943* [Apart or Together: Jews and Arabs in Palestine according to Documents of the Comintern 1919–1943]. Jerusalem: Keter, 2005.

6. Jacob Markovizky, *Ḥultsa Levana Aniva Aduma* [White Shirt and Red Tie] (Tel Aviv: Hakibbutz Hameuchad, 2003), 13. All translations here and throughout, unless noted, are mine.

7. Markovizky, *Ḥultsa Levana Aniva Aduma*, 181. "Model of a youth movement that will conform its educational contents, and would see itself loyal to the state."

8. Markovizky, *Ḥultsa Levana Aniva Aduma*, 181.

9. Markovizky, *Ḥultsa Levana Aniva Aduma*, 21.

10. Slozski, "Mimapsa Beve'idat Hayesod Shel Ha'Histadrut," 135.

11. James Steppenbacker, "The Palestine Communist Party from 1919–1939: A Study of the Subaltern Centers of Power in Mandate Palestine," MA thesis, Ohio State University, 2009, 8.

12. Steppenbacker, "The Palestine Communist Party from 1919–1939," 149.

13. For a detailed account of the 1921 events, see Shmuel Dothan, *Adumim: Hamiflaga Haḳomunistit Be'erets-Isra'el* [Reds: The Communist Party in Eretz-Israel] (Kfar Sava: Shvana Hasofer, 1991), 67–70.

14. G. Z. Israeli, *Maps-Peḳape-Maḳi: Hahisṭorya shel Hamiflaga Haḳomunisṭit Be'Erets-Isra'el* [MPS-PKP-MKI: The History of the Communist Party in Eretz-Israel] (Tel Aviv: Am Oved, 1953), 17.

15. Dothan, *Adumim*, 63.

16. Shai Nisan, "The Palestinian Communist Party, 1936–1939," MA seminar paper, Hebrew University of Jerusalem, 2014, 17.

17. For a vivid description of the founding fathers of Communism, most of whom died in the Stalinist gulags, see List, "Tsadaḳ Haḳominṭern [Hey]."

18. Nisan, "The Palestinian Communist Party," 19.

19. Nisan, "The Palestinian Communist Party," 22, and Avner Ben-Zaken, *Ḳomunizem Ke'imperyalizem Ṭarbuti: Haziḳa eyn Haḳomunizem Ha'erets-Isra'eli Laḳomunizem Ha'aravi 1919–1948* [Communism as Cultural Imperialism: The Affinities between Eretz-Israeli Communism and Arab Communism 1919–1948] (Tel Aviv: Resling, 2006), 89–92.

20. Dothan, *Adumim*, 101.

21. List, "Tsadaḳ Haḳominṭern (Daled)," 112.

22. List, "Tsadaḳ Haḳominṭern (Daled)," 112.

23. List, "Tsadaḳ Haḳominṭern (Daled)," 117.

24. List, "Tsadaḳ Haḳominṭern (Daled)," 114.

25. Zahavi, *Leḥud O Beyaḥad*, 174.

26. Voluntary Report No. 49, "Police, Prisons and Crime in Palestine during 1932," March 23, 1933. The National Archives (US), 867N.105/8, 8. Quoted in Nisan, "The Palestinian Communist Party," 31.

27. Ben-Zaken, *Ḳomunizem Ke'imperyalizem Ṭarbuti*, 112.

28. A few Jewish activists tried to set some buildings on fire at the Levant Fair taking place in Tel Aviv. These actions failed dismally and were stopped immediately by the party's leadership. For details see Dothan, *Adumim*, 238.

29. Dothan, *Adumim*, 324.

30. Lockman, *Comrades and Enemies*.

31. Abigail Jacobson, " 'The National Liberation League' 1943–1948: An Alternative Political Discourse within Palestinian Society," MA thesis, Tel Aviv University, 2000, 15.

32. Israeli, *Maps-Peḳape-Maḳi*, 180.

33. Dothan, *Adumim*, 354, and Markovizky, *Ḥultsa Levana Aniva Aduma*, 61.

34. For a detailed history of their activity in 1945–1948 see Dothan, *Adumim*, 451–92.

35. Jacobson, "The National Liberation League," 69.

36. Markovizky, *Ḥultsa Levana Aniva Aduma*, 48.

37. Markovizky, *Ḥultsa Levana Aniva Aduma*, 50.

38. Markovizky, *Ḥultsa Levana Aniva Aduma*, 50.

39. Markovizky, *Ḥultsa Levana Aniva Aduma*, 51, Berl Balti, *Bema'avak al Haḳiyum Hayehudi: Ledmuto shel Moshe Sneh* [The Struggle for Jewish Survival: A Portrait of Moshe Sneh] (Jerusalem: Y. Marcus, 1981), 60–62.

40. For a detailed portrayal of the events that led to the schism of MAKI, see Markovizky, *Ḥultsa Levana Aniva Aduma*, 55–56.

41. Markovizky, *Ḥultsa Levana Aniva Aduma*, 55–56.

42. Markovizky, *Ḥultsa Levana Aniva Aduma*, 11.

43. Markovizky, *Ḥultsa Levana Aniva Aduma*, 11.

44. Markovizky, *Ḥultsa Levana Aniva Aduma*, 11.

45. There is no doubt that the Communist Party was politically and ideologically obedient to the Soviet Union. The Communists followed Soviet directives at times detrimental to the party among Jewish and Palestinian voters. Yet the historical reality of the relations between the party and the USSR was more complex. The Communists, at times, acted independently. The most glaring example is the Jewish Communists' recognition of the national rights of Jews in Palestine, advocating from 1945 a national home for Jews in Palestine. Culturally, there was a great deal of adulation for Soviet and Russian culture. Banki members sang Russian and Soviet songs and admired Soviet cultural, scientific, and technological achievements. Yet all these manifestations of cultural deference were celebrated in Hebrew—meaning they were local. In fact, the admiration of Soviet culture was seen in parts of the Zionist left from the 1930s to the 1950s, making the Communists part of a wider cultural trend. In all their adulation of Soviet culture, MAKI and Banki members did not become an Israeli version of *Homo Sovieticus*. They spoke Hebrew, singing and dancing to the tune of Israeli songs. They were conscious of typical Israeli cultural elements and wished to take part in them. They were Israelis.

46. The Jewish Communists shared many of the cultural and institutional traits of the Yishuv's evolving society. One typical example is party leader Eliyahu (Alyosha) Gozansky (1914–1948). He attended Mikve Israel Agricultural School, where he converted to Communism (see Tamar Gozansky, ed., *Ḳum Hitna'era! Eliyahu (Elyosha) Gojanski—Ktavav Ve'alav* [Arise, Ye Workers from Your Slumber: Life and Collected Works of Eliyahu (Alyosha) Gozansky] [Haifa: Pardes, 2009]). This institution, along with the Zionist youth movements, was the Yishuv's equivalent of British public schools, where the future leaders of Israel

were nurtured. See Oz Almog, *Hatsabar—Dyuḳan* [The Sabra—A Profile] (Tel Aviv: Am Oved, 1997). Gozansky's conversion to Communism shows to what extent the Jewish Communists were at odds with the society around them, while at the same time participating in the institutions of that society. The closeness of many Communists to the just-forming Israeli society and at the same time their remoteness from it is evident in the words of Nessia Shafran: "The Communists did not object to the Zionist project because of Jewish religious belief in the coming of the messiah . . . the Communists challenged Zionism for reasons taken from the same notions and values, which were common to most of the Eretz-Israeli *Yishuv*, and mainly to its leading elite." Nessia Shafran, *Shalom Lekha Ḳomunizm* [Farewell Communism] (Tel Aviv: Hakibbutz Hameuchad, 1983. I argue that this ambiguous status of the Communists lay at the base of the harsh reaction to them, chiefly in the 1950s.

47. The cultural interaction between Jews and Palestinians in the Communist Party in the years 1919–1948 is brilliantly illustrated by Avner Ben-Zaken's pioneering work. His argument is similar to the argument in this work that European frameworks of thought were transferred from a European to a non-European setting. He argues that Marxism, European by origin, was brought to the Near East by East European Jews and then transmitted to small groups of Palestinians. However, I do not accept his paradigm of "Cultural Imperialism," since Jewish Communists viewed Marxism as holding the potential for liberation and as not completely blind to local conditions.

48. Moshe Shamir, *Bemo Yadav: Pirkey Eliḳ* [With His Own Hands: Elik's Story] (Tel Aviv: Siffriath Poalim, 1965), 11.

49. The negation of the exile was a basic principle of Zionist ideology; it was to be found in "the foundation of all currents of Zionist thought." Rina Peled, *"Ha'adam Haḥadash" shel Hamahapekha Hatsyonit: Hashomer Hatsa'ir Veshorashav Ha'Erope'im* ["The New Man" of the Zionist Revolution: Hashomer Haza'ir and Its European Roots] (Tel Aviv: Am Oved, 2002), 27. The "remaking" project of the Zionist movement extended not just to the departure from Europe but also to the reinvention of the Jew himself. Indeed, the "new Jew" of the Zionist revolution was to have a Jewish culture, but this was to be reworked as distinct from Jewish tradition—Jewish by form but Zionist by content. Far from being a cliché, the history of Zionist holidays detailed in this book provides ample evidence for this complex cultural move.

Chapter 1. Basic Concepts and Political Ritual

1. Baruch Kimmerling, *Mehagrim, Mityashvim, Yelidim: Hamedina Vehaḥevra Be' Isra'el—beyn Ribuy Tarbuyot Lemilḥemot Tarbut* [Immigrants,

Settlers, Natives: The Israeli State and Society between Cultural Pluralism and Cultural Wars] (Tel Aviv: Am Oved, 2004), 169.

2. Moshe Czudnowski and Jacob Landau, *The Israeli Communist Party and the Elections for the Fifth Knesset, 1961* (Stanford: Hoover Institution on War, Revolution and Peace, 1965), 20.

3. See Johan Franzén, "Communism versus Zionism: The Comintern, Yishuvism, and the Palestine Communist Party," *Journal of Palestine Studies* 36, no. 2 (2007): 6–24; and Lea Miron, *Kokhav Adom Bedegel Kakhol-Lavan: Yaḥasa shel Hatnu'a Haḳomunisṭit Be'erets Latsiyonut Velamifal Hatsiyoni Betḳufat Hayeshuv ve'im Ḳom Hamedina* [A Red Star in the Israeli Flag] (Jerusalem: Magnes, 2011).

4. "Lamiflaga Haḳomunisṭit Hapaleśṭina'it 10.23.30" [To the Palestine Communist Party 10.23.30] in, Zahavi, *Leḥud O Beyaḥad*, 236.

5. Samuel Mikunis, *Besa'ar Tḳufot 1943–1969* [In the Storms of Our Times: Selected Articles and Speeches, 1943–1969] (Tel Aviv: Israeli Communist Party Central Committee, 1969), 388.

6. The characterization of Ahdut HaAvoda as right-wing is comparative to the radical groups that formed to its left, from which the Communist Party emerged. Sternhell, for example, shows how, in a gradual process, Ahdut HaAvoda negated the radical Socialist component of its ideology, enabling the 1930 unification with Hapo'el Hatza'ir. See Zeev Sternhell, *Binyan Uma O Tiḳun Ḥevra* [Nation-Building or a New Society?] (Tel Aviv: Am Oved, 1995).

7. Sternhell, *Binyan Uma*.

8. It should be noted that Sternhell's arguments were the subject of intense critical debate. Zionist scholars attacked both the research and the theory underlining *Binyan Uma O Tiḳun Ḥevra*. They argued that his historical portrayal is motivated by an Old Left purist view, one that gave little account for nationalism and its role even in Socialist movements. Another argument found flaws in Sternhell's methodology, arguing that he did not adequately survey the primary sources on which he based his research. Another take in that vein was aimed at his misrepresentation of historical facts. Most notable was the attempt of the Histadrut to impose an egalitarian pay scale according to family size. Sternhell argued that there was no serious attempt on the side of the Zionist Labour Movement to implement this measure. His criticizers argued the opposite. Generally the Zionist critics of Sternhell find it hard to depart from perceived notions and common wisdom that viewed Labour-Zionism as harmonization of progressive Socialism and nationalism. See Arieh Yaari, "Without Alternative: Examining Zeev Sternhell's Presumptions," *Iyunim Betḳumat Israel* 6 (1996): 586–91; Yosef Gorny, "The Historical Reality of Constructive Socialism," *Cathedra* 79 (1996): 182–91; Yitszhak Greenberg, "The Standard Family Wage—Ideology, Illusion and Realism," *Cathedra* 79 (1996): 192–98; and Anita Shapira, "Sternhell's Complaint," in *Yehudim Ḥadashim Yehudim Yeshanim* [New Jews Old Jews], ed. Anita

Shapira (Tel Aviv: Am Oved, 1997), 298–317. On his part Sternhell answered Gorny and Greenberg in article that vigorously reasserted his main arguments. See Zeev Sternhell, "Zionist Historiography between Myth and Reality," *Cathedra* 80 (1996): 209–24. Critics of Sternhell were not confined to Zionist scholars. Michael Shalev remarks that "Zeev Sternhell's important book poses a radical challenge to conservative approach to the legacy of the Zionist Labour Movement." Michael Shalev, "Time for Theory," *Theory and Criticism* 8 (1996): 231. However, he qualifies his endorsement of the book, saying "that in many ways including Sternhell's approach towards the intentions of 'big people' as the main instigators of history, Sternhell faithfully replicates the conservative school" (235). He also stated that in his inability to include economic and social factors and the relations with Palestinians in his analyses he copies "the same understanding of the Socialist element of the Zionist Labour Movement . . . the aspiration for equality among Jews instead of the ideal of transnational proletarian solidarity" (238). The choice I made—to use the heterodox work of this historian—speaks to the fundamental nature of the history presented in this book. The history of the Communist Party in Palestine/Israel is the history of anti-Zionist heterodoxy that argued the incompatibility of nationalism and Socialism, fact that did not go unnoticed by Sternhell's more sensitive and temperate critic Michael Shalev. He acknowledges that "the stance of the radical left was always that the Socialist pretensions of the Zionist Labour Movement were nothing more than false impression, no more than a means to achieve the real national goals. This was the base for the Communists parting with the *Histadrut* community after War World I" (232). Therefore the history presented does not wish to uphold "common wisdom" but to understand—not identify or agree with necessarily—the voices that mainstream Israeli historiography chose to sideline.

9. "The Ideology of the Kibbutz Ha'Artzi, Established by *Hashomer Hatza'ir*," Meḳorot (Origins), Booklet 5, 156–58, in Peled, *"Ha'adam Haḥadash,"* 53.

10. Meir Avizohar, *Ide'alim Ḥevratiyim Vele'umiyim Vehishtaḳfutam Be'olama shel Mapay: Mifleget Po'aley Erets-Isra'el Vebilti-Miflagtiyim 1930–1942* [National and Social Ideals as Reflected in MAPAI: The Israeli Labor Party 1930–1942] (Tel Aviv: Am Oved, 1990), 50. Avizohar's claims that a class society did not emerge in Palestine are disproved by the works of the Israeli sociologist Amir Ben-Porat. See Amir Ben-Porat, *Heykhan haburganim hahem? Toldot haburganut ha'isra'elit* [The Bourgeoisie: The History of the Israeli Bourgeoisie] (Jerusalem: Magnes Press, 1999); and Amir Ben-Porat, *Keytsad na'asta isra'el kapitalistit* [How Israel Became a Capitalist Society] (Haifa: Pardes, 2011).

11. Slozski, "Mimapsa Beve'idat Hayesod Shel Ha'Histadrut," 133–162.

12. *Unser Emet*, pamphlet quoted in Slozski, "Mimapsa Beve'idat Hayesod Shel Ha'Histadrut," 157.

13. "The Communist Movement," in Israeli, *Maps-Peḳape-Maḳi*, 27.

14. "Haḳongres Hashvi'i shel Hamiflaga Haḳomunisṭit Hapaleśṭina'it, Detsember 1930" [The Seventh Congress of the Palestinian Communist Party, December 1930], in Zahavi, *Leḥud O Beyaḥad*, 259.

15. "Haliga Le'havana Arvit-Yehudit, 'Ha'emet,' Ogust 1940" [The League for Arab-Jewish Understanding, 'Ha'emet,' August 1940], Lavon Institute for Labour Movement Research, IV-445-2 (Tel Aviv, Israel).

16. "At the End of World War Two," in Mikunis, *Besa'ar Tḳufot*, 44.

17. "Beyom Hashana shel Hahistadrut" [On the Anniversary of the Histadrut], in Mikunis, *Besa'ar Tḳufot*, 218.

18. Edut Bemishpaṭt Ḳol Ha'am Ben-Guryon [Testimony in the Kol Ha'am—Ben-Gurion Trial], in Mikunis, *Besa'ar Tḳufot*, 118.

19. Communism in Palestine/Israel inherited early Bolshevism's polemics against Jewish nationalism, especially against those of the nationalist Marxist Bund. Indeed Soviet ideology and practice denied any kind of Jewish national expression in the Soviet Union. See Joseph Stalin, *Marxism and the National Question* (Moscow: Foreign Languages, 1945).

20. Stalin, *Marxism and the National Question*, 11.

21. Moshe Sneh (1909–1972) was an Israeli politician and thinker. He started his political career as a liberal Zionist in Poland. After arriving in Palestine in 1940, he was one of the key figures in the leadership of the Yishuv, mainly in the Haganah. At this period he started to lean to the left and led the left wing of MAPAM. He broke away from it in 1952, joining MAKI in 1954. In 1965 he played a key role in the split-up of MAKI and led the Jewish MAKI until his death in 1972.

22. Moshe Sneh, *Sikumim Bashe'ela Haleumit: Le'or Hamarksizem-Leninizem* [On the National Question: Conclusions in the Light of Marxism-Leninism] (Tel Aviv: Left Socialist Party, 1954), 8.

23. Sneh, *Sikumim Bashe'ela Haleumit*, 13.

24. Sneh, *Sikumim Bashe'ela Haleumit*, 62.

25. Sneh, *Sikumim Bashe'ela Haleumit*, 72.

26. Sneh, *Sikumim Bashe'ela Haleumit*, 85.

27. Sneh, *Sikumim Bashe'ela Haleumit*, 116.

28. Sneh, *Sikumim Bashe'ela Haleumit*, 133.

29. Sneh, *Sikumim Bashe'ela Haleumit*, 76.

30. Sneh, *Sikumim Bashe'ela Haleumit*, 144.

31. Sneh is not unique in developing such argumentation and it is often repeated by various party leaders like MAKI general secretary Shmuel Mikunis. See "Will MAPAM Stop Its Degeneration?," *Zu Haderech—Organ of the Communist Party of Israel on Problems of Theory and Practice*, June 1953.

32. For a short history of the Bund, see Jack Jacobs, ed., *Jewish Politics in Eastern Europe: The Bund at 100* (New York: New York University Press, 2001); and *Bunda'im*, a film directed by Eran Torbiner, Tel Aviv, 2011.

33. Jacobs, "Creating a Bundist Counter-Culture: Morgenstern and the Significance of Cultural Hegemony," in *Jewish Politics in Eastern Europe*, 60.

34. For the anti-Zionist politics of the Polish Bund as well as its Marxism and place in the world Socialist movement, see Abraham Brumberg, "The Bund History of Schism," in Jacobs, *Jewish Politics in Eastern Europe*, 81–90; and Mario Kessler, "The Bund and the Labour and Socialist International," in Jacobs, *Jewish Politics in Eastern Europe*, 183–97.

35. For the contribution of the Bund to interwar Yiddish culture, see Nathan Cohen, "The Bund's Contribution to the Yiddish Culture in Poland between the Two World Wars," in Jacobs, *Jewish Politics in Eastern Europe*, 112–30.

36. Ya'ad Biran, "Be'erets-Isra'el Asher al Havisla" [In Eretz-Israel That Is on the Vistula], *Davḳa: Erets Yidish Vetarbuta* [Davka: The Land of Yiddish and Its Culture] 7 (2010): 15.

37. Richard Stites, "The Origins of Soviet Ritual Style: Symbol and Festival in the Russian Revolution," in *Symbols of Power: The Aesthetics of Political Legitimation in the Soviet Union and Eastern Europe*, ed. Claes Arvidsoon and Lars Erik Blomqvist (Stockholm: Almqvist & Bissell International, 1987), 24.

38. James Von Geldern, *Bolshevik Festivals, 1917–1920* (Berkeley: University of California Press, 1993), 40.

39. Von Geldern, *Bolshevik Festivals*, 85.

40. Stites, "The Origins of Soviet Ritual Style," 33.

41. Stites, "The Origins of Soviet Ritual Style," 34.

42. NEP: Russian for New Economic Plan. This economic policy loosened the grip of the Soviet state on the economy by allowing the market to rebuild the war-ravaged country. The party enabled the peasants to sell foodstuffs to the cities and revived some private ownership in the cities. The state only kept control at the command heights of the economy. This new move hailed a temporary return to normalcy and an easing of the radical tension of the revolution and of the civil war eras.

43. Rosalinde Sartori, "Stalinism and Carnival: Organization and Aesthetics of Political Holidays," in *The Culture of the Stalin Period*, ed. Hans Günther (New York: St. Martin's Press, 1990), 54.

44. Christel Lane, *The Rites of Rulers: Ritual in Industrial Society—the Soviet Case* (Cambridge: Cambridge University Press, 1981), 141.

45. Eric Weitz, *Creating German Communism 1890–1990: From Popular Protests to Socialist State* (Princeton: Princeton University Press, 1997), 242.

46. Alan Nothnagle, *Building the East German Myth: Historical Mythology and Youth Propaganda in the German Democratic Republic, 1945–1989* (Ann Arbor: University of Michigan Press, 1999), 40.

47. Josie McLellan, *Antifascism and Memory in East Germany: Remembering the International Brigades 1945–1989* (Oxford: Clarendon Press, 2004), 88.

48. Zionism was definitely not an anti-Semitic movement. However, the Zionist negation of exile and the attempt to create a "new Jew" showed the

internalization of some anti-Jewish stereotypes. For instance, when discussing the sabra, the archetype of the new native Jew, Oz Almog points to the fact that Jews envied non-Jews. For the early Zionists, the gentile was both admired and resented for his unassuming rootedness in his land, a quality the Zionists felt was missing in the exilic Jew. One aspect of this envy "was the disavowal of the exilic Jew, to the point of his demonization (at times, paradoxically, in an anti-Semitic manner)." Almog, *Hatsabar—Dyuḳan*, 128.

49. Almog, *Hatsabar—Dyuḳan*.

Chapter 2. The Creation of a Jewish Progressive Tradition

1. Moshe Sneh, "Erkhey Haḳidma Ve'hashalom Bamasoret Vebatarbut Hayehudit: Al Toda'a Yehudit" [The Values of Progress and Peace in Jewish Tradition and Culture: On Jewish Consciousness], *Kol Ha'am*, January 6, 1959.

2. Sneh, "Erkhey Haḳidma Ve'hashalom Bamasoret Vebatarbut Hayehudit," *Kol Ha'am*, January 6, 1959.

3. Shafran, *Shalom Lekha Ḳomunizm*, 139.

4. Palestinian Young Communist League, *Hamufti Matityahu Vemered Ha'ikarim Hagadol Lifney Alpa'im Shana: Sipur Le'Hanuka* [The Mufti Matityahu and the Great Peasants Uprising Two Thousand Years Ago: A Story for Hanukkah], Lavon Institute for Labour Movement Research, IV-445-2.

5. Palestinian Young Communist League, *Hamufti Matityahu*, 7.

6. "Ḥaim Diskin Gibor Brit Hamo'atsot" [Haim Diskin Hero of the Soviet Union], *Kol Hano'ar*, January 1943.

7. "Ḥanuka" [Hanukkah], *Kol Hano'ar*, January 1943.

8. The wide gap in the documentation about Hanukkah is explained by the unavailability of primary documents. Not many documents concerned with the party's subculture were produced in the underground years. More attention to the cultural aspects of the life of the party, and as a result more documents, started to appear after legalization.

9. "Ḥanuka," *Kol Hano'ar*, January 1943.

10. "Ḥanuka," *Kol Hano'ar*, January 1943.

11. "Ḥanuka," *Kol Hano'ar*, January 1943.

12. "Lebney Hamakabim" [To the Sons of the Maccabees], *Kol Hano'ar*, December 1947.

13. "Lebney Hamakabim," *Kol Hano'ar*, December 1947.

14. "Lebney Hamakabim," *Kol Hano'ar*, December 1947.

15. "Ḥanuka—Lemi Shayakh Hayom Haze?" [Hanukkah—Whose Day Is It?], *Kol Hano'ar*, November 20, 1956.

16. "Ḥanuka—Lemi Shayakh Hayom Haze?," *Kol Hano'ar*, November 20, 1956.

17. "Ḥanuka—Alon Lamadrikh, November 1955" [Hanukkah—Instructor's Brochure, November 1955], Yad Tabenkin Archives, File #1.

18. "Ḥanuka—Aloņ Lamadrikh, November 1955," Yad Tabenkin Archives, File #1.

19. "Ḥanuka—Alon Lamadrikh, November 1956" [Hanukkah—Instructors' Brochure, November 1956], Yad Tabenkin Archives, File #2.

20. "Ḥanuka—Alon Lamadrikh, November 1956," Yad Tabenkin Archives, File #2.

21. Shoshana Shmuely, interview by author, Tel Aviv, Israel, February 22, 2009.

22. "Mazkirut Bney Amal Behakhana Avur Ḥanuka" [Secretariat of the Junior Level Banki in Preparation for Hanukkah], Yad Tabenkin Archives, File #3.

23. The Cultural Section of the Central Committee of the Israeli Young Communist League, "Ḥanuka Ḥag Ha'orot Ḥag Haḥerut, November 1963" [Hanukkah the Holiday of Lights, the Holiday of Freedom, November 1963], Yad Tabenkin Archives, File #5.

24. The Cultural Section of the Central Committee of the Israeli Young Communist League, "Ḥanuka Ḥag Ha'orot Ḥag Haḥerut, November 1963," Yad Tabenkin Archives, File #5.

25. Shafran, *Shalom Lekha Ḳomunizm*, 103.

26. In an interview fifty years and more after the fact, Yoram Gozansky still vividly remembered Penn's performances and described them as a once-in-a-lifetime experience; Yoram Gozansky, interview by author, Tel Aviv, Israel, February 23, 2009.

27. The Cultural Section of the Central Committee of the Israeli Young Communist League, "Ḥanuka Ḥag Ha'orot Ḥag Haḥerut, November 1963," Yad Tabenkin Archives, File #5.

28. Tamar Gozansky, interview by author, Tel Aviv, Israel, February 21, 2009. Yoram Gozansky, interview by author, Tel Aviv, Israel, February 23, 2009.

29. Carmit Gai, *Masa Leyad-Ḥana* [Back to Yad-Hannah] (Tel Aviv: Am Oved, 1992), 258.

30. The portrayal of the rites in Tel Aviv and Yad Hana is based on interviews with Zafrira Kelorman and Yoram Gozansky. See Zafrira Kelorman, interview by author, November 6, 2005. Yoram Gozansky, interview by author, Tel Aviv, Israel, February 23, 2009.

31. The Cultural Section of the Central Committee of the Israeli Young Communist League, "Ḥanuka Ḥag Ha'orot Ḥag Haḥerut, November 1963," Yad Tabenkin Archives, File #5.

32. Victor Turner, *The Ritual Process: Structure and Anti-Structure* (Ithaca: Cornell University Press, 1969). Communitas was later standardized by Turner in his analysis of Christian pilgrimage rituals. He defined it as "a relational quality of full unmitigated communication, even communion, between definite and determinate identities, which arises spontaneously in all kinds of groups, situations,

and circumstances." Victor Turner and Edith Turner, *Image and Pilgrimage in Christian Culture Anthropological Perspectives* (New York: Columbia University Press, 1978), 250. He clearly connected the concept to the qualities of "lowliness, sacredness, homogeneity and comradeship" (250).

33. The ritual language of the Jewish Communists and the elements from which it is constructed are derived from concepts developed in Clifford Geertz, "Centers, Kings, and Charisma: Reflections on the Symbolics of Power," in *Local Knowledge*, ed. Clifford Geertz (New York: Basic Books, 1983). Geertz argues that the line between the symbolic of power and power itself is in many cases blurred. Symbolic power emanating from centers of power affects and reflects reality as perceived and idealized by wielders of power and those affected by it. As case studies for his theory, Geertz adduces three historical events: Queen Elizabeth I's Royal Progress on January 14, 1559, entering London a day before her coronation; the medieval court of Java's king, Hayam Wuruk; and Mulay Hasan of Morocco (121–26).

34. Yair Tzaban remembered in an interview the shock his decision caused old party member Pnina Fainhauz, to the point that she needed him personally to calm her, without much success; Yair Tzaban, interview by author, Tel Aviv, Israel, February 12, 2009.

35. "Méavdot Leḥerut," *Kol Hano'ar*, 1943.

36. "Pesaḥ Ḥag Haḥerut" [Passover the Holiday of Freedom], *Kol Ha'am*, April 13, 1949.

37. "El Hano'ar Ḥag Hapesaḥ" [To the Youth Passover], *Kol Ha'am*, March 19, 1956: "The holiday has two aspects: the first a holiday of liberty, the second a spring holiday."

38. Yuval Dror, "Tnu'ot Hano'ar Be'veit Hasefer" [Youth Movements in the School], in *Tnu'ot Hano'ar 1920–1960* [Youth Movements 1920–1960], ed. Mordechai Naor (Jerusalem: Ben-Zvi Institute, 1989), 161: "Those movements were influenced by two basic models of European movements: the German youth movement ('the Free'), which was much closer to the Eretz-Israel workers' movements; and the English Scouts, which is identified as a 'youth movement for the youth.'"

39. "Hagadat Pesaḥ Begirsa Hamatima Leshe'ifot Hapo'alim Vekol Tomḥey Hashalom" [Passover Haggadah in a Version Suited to the Aspirations of Workers and All Supporters of Peace], *Kol Ha'am*, April 15, 1957.

40. Nissim Calderon, interview by author, March 3, 2009.

41. Symbol will be used in the context of this research as defined by Victor Turner. Turner, "Symbols in Ndembu Ritual," in *The Forest of Symbols: Aspects of Ndembu Ritual*, ed. Victor Turner (Ithaca: Cornell University Press, 1967), 19–47, defines symbol as the basic unit of ritual. The ritual act clusters around one dominant symbol, which reflects the values and norms of a given society.

42. The secularization and the penetration into Jewish society of modern ideologies like Socialism and the Jewish Enlightenment of the nineteenth century made secularized Jews unable to perform the rituals connected to the old religious belief systems. See Clifford Geertz, "Ritual and Social Change: A Javanese Example," *American Anthropologist* 59 (1957): 32–54.

Chapter 3. Holocaust, Independence, and Remembrance in Israeli Communist Commemoration

1. Eliyahu Gojanski, *Grodna* [Grodno] (Tel Aviv: Israeli Communist Party, 1979), 25.

2. Gojanski, *Grodna*, 31.

3. Gojanski, *Grodna*, 32.

4. "Dam taḥat dam!" [Blood for Blood!], Lavon Institute for Labour Movement Research, IV-445-2.

5. "Mikhtav Poliṭi Mispar Shalosh, 12 Le'April 1946" [Political Letter Number 3, 12 April 1946], Yad Tabenkin Archives, File #20.

6. Yechiam Weitz, "The Political Dimensions of Holocaust Memory in Israel during the 1950s," in *The Shaping of Israeli Identity: Myth, Memory and Trauma*, ed. Robert Wistrich and David Ohana (London: Frank Cass, 1995), 130.

7. See "Psaḳ Hadin" [The Verdict], Israeli State Archives, File Series 30.0.50, Jerusalem, Israel.

8. See, for example, "The Masses of the People Expressed Their Protest against the Criminal Negotiation with the Bonn Neo-Nazi Government," *Kol Ha'am*, January 6, 1952. On the same page, a headline quoted party secretary Shmuel Mikunis as saying at a rally in Haifa "that those who vote for the negotiation with the neo-Nazis will enter the people's blacklist."

9. "Lezeḥer Mordey Geto Varsha" [In Memory of Warsaw Ghetto Rebels], *Kol Hano'ar*, April 1951.

10. "Hagiborim" [The Heroes], *Kol Ha'am*, May 5, 1959.

11. "Lema'an Ha'emet Hahisṭorit" [For the Historical Truth], *Kol Ha'am*, May 3, 1959.

12. Yair Tzaban, interview by author, Tel Aviv, Israel, February 12, 2009.

13. "Moreshet Mordey Geto Varsha" [The Legacy of the Warsaw Ghetto Rebels], *Kol Ha'am*, April 19, 1956.

14. The ANFO was established on the twelfth anniversary of the uprising in 1955. It was made up of representatives of Jewish soldiers from the Allied armies, the Spanish Civil War, and the anti-Nazi underground. The organization was headed by Avraham Berman, then a MAKI Knesset Member, and was controlled by party members. The Communist nature of the organization was also

evident in its founding resolutions, which called on all Israeli citizens "to mobilize for the holy struggle against the revival of the Nazi Wehrmacht." The Founding Resolutions of the Anti-Nazi Fighters Organization in Israel, *Kol Ha'am*, April 19, 1955. The ANFO was involved in a wide range of activities: agitating against West Germany and Israeli polices, sponsoring memorial rites commemorating the Warsaw uprising and exhibits dealing with the Holocaust, holding meetings to explain such issues as the Eichmann trial, demonstrations, and sending delegates to memorial services in Eastern Europe.

15. "Haloḥamim Ha'anti Natsim Yemalu et Shvuatam" [The Anti-Nazi Fighters Will Fulfill Their Vow], *Kol Ha'am*, March 4, 1955.

16. "Nitsoley Hasho'a Hitaḥedu" [Holocaust Survivors Unite], *Kol Ha'am*, January 21, 1956.

17. "El Hano'ar. 11 Shanim Le'aḥar Mered Geto Varsha" [To the Youth. 11 Years after the Warsaw Ghetto Uprising], *Kol Ha'am*, April 29, 1954.

18. Roni Stauber, *Haleḳaḥ Lador: Sho'a Vegvura Bamaḥshava Hatsiburit Baret Beshnot Haḥamishim* [Lessons for This Generation: Holocaust and Heroism in Israeli Public Discourse in the 1950s] (Jerusalem: Yad Ben-Zvi Press, 2000), 7.

19. Stauber, *Haleḳaḥ Lador*, 14–33.

20. Stauber, *Haleḳaḥ Lador*, 2.

21. "Jews' Philosophical and Theological Responses to the Holocaust," Yad Vashem Information Center, https://www.yadvashem.org/odot_pdf/Microsoft%20Word%20-%201831.pdf, accessed December 23, 2018.

22. "Jews' Philosophical and Theological Responses to the Holocaust," Yad Vashem Information Center, https://www.yadvashem.org/odot_pdf/Microsoft%20Word%20-%201831.pdf, accessed December 23, 2018.

23. "Mishpaṭ Aykhman" [The Eichmann Trial], *Kol Ha'am*, June 1, 1962.

24. "Pniya Tsiburit shel Irgun Haloḥamim Ha'anti Natsim" [Public Appeal of the Anti-Nazi Fighters Organization], *Kol Ha'am*, April 19, 1960.

25. "Melukhlakhey Bergen-Belzen" [The Bergen-Belsen Dirty Ones], *Kol Ha'am*, April 24, 1960; "Haparpar" [The Butterfly], *Kol Ha'am*, April 24, 1960.

26. Avraham Berman, "Edut" [Testimony], *Kol Ha'am*, May 4, 1961.

27. "Mered Geto Varsha, Alon Lamadrikh, Merts 1963" [The Warsaw Ghetto Uprising, Instructors' Brochure, March 1963], Lavon Institute for Labour Movement Research, IV-85-104-7.

28. "Mered Geto Varsha, Alon Lamadrikh, Merts 1963," Lavon Institute for Labour Movement Research, IV-85-104-7.

29. "Lepo'aley Palesṭina" [To the Workers of Palestine], in Zahavi, *Leḥud O Beyaḥad*, 42.

30. "Tazkir Pnimi Ḥatum al Yedey Haboza'im" [An Internal Memo Signed by Abozaim], in Zahavi, *Leḥud O Beyaḥad*, 43.

31. "Tazkir Pnimi Ḥatum al Yedey Haboza'im" [An Internal Memo Signed by Abozaim], in Zahavi, *Leḥud O Beyaḥad*, 43.

32. "Haḥlaṭa Benoge'a Lashe'ela Hale'umit Veha'emda Hapoliṭit Ha'akhshavit" [Resolution Regarding the National Question and the Current Political Stand], in Zahavi, *Leḥud O Beyaḥad*, 259.

33. "No'ar" [Youth], Yad Tabenkin Archives, Files #17, 18.

34. "No'ar Hitgayes! 1948, Tel Aviv" [Youth Enlist! 1948, Tel Aviv], Yad Tabenkin Archives.

35. Communist support for the state and the war effort was not just verbal. Party members enlisted in the Haganah and the IDF, as described in an interview with Eliyahu (Alyosha) Gozansky to a reporter in Poland: "The great majority of the party members fight in the ranks of the Haganah . . . four out of five members of the Young Communist League were wounded in the battlefield." "Hakol Lema'an Haḥazit! Hakol Lema'an Hanitsaḥon" [All for the Front! All for Victory!], *Kol Ha'am*, August 20, 1948. The party leaders used their connections in the new regimes in Eastern Europe to facilitate the procurement of arms and manpower for the Israeli war effort. The first feelers by the party started as early as 1947. Eliyahu Gozansky, who was a member of the Party Secretariat, and Ruth Lubitz were sent to "Bulgaria and other Socialist countries to feel the pulse regarding the possibilities of helping Mapilim [illegal immigrants to Palestine—ALB]." "Pe'ilut Hamiflaga Haḳomunisṭit shel Erets-Isra'el Legiyus Ezra Poliṭit Vetsva'it Lemilḥemet Ha'atsma'ut, Edut Shmu'el Mikunis" [The Activity of the Eretz-Israel Communist Party to Mobilize Political and Military Aid for the Independence War], Shmuel Mikunis Testimony, Lavon Institute for Labour Movement Research, IV-85-47. Another initial contact was made by a Communist youth delegation that participated in building a railroad in Yugoslavia. During the war, both before and after the proclamation establishing Israel, the party was active in sending arms and men from Eastern Europe. For example, in February 1948 Mikunis sent four hundred volunteers from Yugoslavia, and in Poland he was authorized by Gomułka to send recruits to an officers' school. After May 1948 he arranged for Jewish volunteers to be sent from Czechoslovakia to Israel and secured the purchase of heavy mortars by the Yugoslavs for Israel. The anti-imperialist discourse is apparent even in Mikunis's remarks; reporting on his talks with Slánský, he says he convinced him to support the Yishuv "because it is an anti-imperialist need to resolve an important issue in the Middle East that has become a focus of bloodshed . . . that there is a comprehensive strategy to drive out British imperialism from the region" (IV-85-47). Apart from their political and military aid, the Jewish Communists recruited their subculture's resources for the war effort, sending the party's choir to cheer the soldiers at the front. "Hahofa'a shel Maḳhelat 'Ron' Bamaḥane Hatsva'i" [The Performance of the 'Ron' Choir in the Army Camp], *Kol Ha'am*, April 2, 1948; and "Maḳhelat Hapo'alim 'Ron' " ['Ron' Workers Choir], *Kol Ha'am*, November 30, 1948.

36. "Isra'el beyn Ha'umot" [Israel among the Nations], *Kol Ha'am*, April 25, 1948.

37. "Milḥemet Ha'atsma'ut" [The War of Independence], Yad Tabenkin Archives, File #2.

38. Shoshana Shmuely, interview by author, Tel Aviv, Israel, February 22, 2009. The Left Men also named the youth section of their party after him.

39. "Yitsḥaḳ Śade Ha'ish" [Yitzhak Sadeh the Man], *Kol Ha'am*, September 19, 1952; and "Shalosh Shanim me'az Moto shel Yitsḥaḳ Śade" [Three Years since the Death of Yitzhak Sadeh], *Kol Ha'am*, August 22, 1955.

40. On the polemics that the two Communist leaders conducted against the Bund, see V. I. Lenin, *One Step Forward Two Steps Back: The Crisis in Our Party* (Moscow: Progress, 1978); and Stalin, *Marxism and the National Question*.

41. For a description of the Communist underground in Tel Aviv of the 1920s in which Yael Garson took an active part, see: Leah Trachtman-Falhan, *MiTel Aviv Lemoskva: Zikhronot Yaldut* [From Tel Aviv to Moscow: Childhood Memoirs] (Tel Aviv: Saar and the author, 1989).

42. "Yael Garson" [Yael Garson], *Kol Hano'ar*, February 4, 1942. For the children's strike, see Leah Trachtman-Falhan's memoirs.

43. "Yael Garson," *Kol Hano'ar*, February 4, 1942.

44. After the establishment of Israel, Siyoma Mernonynski's death was the subject of an investigative committee convened at MAKI's insistence. The committee, the first of its kind in the State of Israel, found that Mernonynski had been beaten to death by the Jewish CID detectives who interrogated him, "since he was not willing to reveal information about himself and his actions." "Masḳanot Va'adat Haḥaḳira Le'inyan Retsiḥato shel Siyoma Mernonynski" [The Conclusions of the Investigative Committee in the Matter of Siyoma Mernonynski's Murder], *Kol Ha'am*, September 4, 1949. Mernonynski's death sowed confusion among his murderers and they disposed of his body. The officers involved, now in the service of the Israeli police, closed ranks and would not admit their guilt, so no criminal charges could be brought against them; however, the committee recommended "to the management of the service employing them to seriously consider whether they are worthy to stay in service in light of the committee's conclusions" ("Masḳanot Va'adat Haḥaḳira Le'inyan"). The officers involved were fired but later reinstated, rising to high ranks in the Israeli police.

45. "Siyoma Mernonynski" [Siyoma Mernonynski], *Kol Ha'am*, August 1941.

46. "Zikhro Yihiye La'ad!" [His Memory Will Live Forever!], *Kol Ha'am*, July 6, 1951.

47. "Ruḥo Ḥaya Imanu, Tiye Imanu La'ad" [His Spirit Lives among Us, Will Live among Us Forever], *Kol Ha'am*, July 7, 1961.

48. "Eliyahu Gojanski" [Eliyahu Gozansky], *Kol Ha'am*, December 26, 1948.

49. "Dorot shel Ḳomunisṭim Yilmedu et Ma'aśav" [Generations of Communists Will Study His Deeds], *Kol Ha'am*, December 31, 1948.

50. "Dorot shel Ḳomunisṭim Yilmedu et Ma'aśav," *Kol Ha'am*, December 31, 1948.

51. "Hamonim Livu et Haḥaver Eliyahu Gojanski Lemenuḥat Olamim" [Multitudes Accompanied Comrade Eliyahu Gozansky to His Eternal Rest], *Kol Ha'am*, February 14, 1948.

52. *Kol Ha'am*, October 24, 1949.

53. T. Gozansky, *Ḳum Hitna'era!*, 428.

54. T. Gozansky, *Ḳum Hitna'era!*, 428.

55. T. Gozansky, *Ḳum Hitna'era!*, 429.

56. T. Gozansky, *Ḳum Hitna'era!*, 431.

57. T. Gozansky, *Ḳum Hitna'era!*, 428.

58. Shafran, *Shalom Lekha Ḳomunizm*, 91.

59. For the way the SED adopted German nationalism, see Nothnagle, *Building the East German Myth*.

60. Nissim Calderon, interview by author, Tel Aviv, Israel, March 3, 2009.

61. *Kol Ha'am*, October 28, 1948. Quoted in Ben-Zaken, *Ḳomunizm Ke'imperyalizm Ṭarbuti*, 180.

62. Maoz Azaryahu, *Pulḥaney Medina: Ḥagigot Ha'atsma'ut Vehantsaḥat Hanoflim Be'Isra'el* [State Cults: Celebrating Independence and Commemorating the Fallen in Israel 1948–1956] (Beer Sheva: Ben-Gurion University Press, 1995), 220.

63. Ron Barkai, *Kmo Seret Mitsri* [Like an Egyptian Movie] (Tel Aviv: Xargol, 2001), 193.

64. Nissim Calderon, interview by author, Tel Aviv, Israel, March 3, 2009.

65. Dani Peter-Petrziel, *Lev Betsad Śmol: al Ḥinukh Veḥevra* [Heart on the Left: On Education and Society] (Tel Aviv: Tcherikover, 2000), 78.

66. Peter-Petrziel, *Lev Betsad Śmol*, 79.

67. Peter-Petrziel, *Lev Betsad Śmol*, 79.

Chapter 4. Workers' Utopia and Reality in Israeli Commonism

1. Slozski, "Mimapsa Beve'idat Hayesod Shel Ha'Histadrut," 149.

2. Dothan, *Adumim*, 82.

3. An interview with David De Vries, "Why Did the Diamond Workers Strike So Often during World War Two?," in *Ḳum Hitna'era!*, ed. T. Gozansky, 35–42; and David De Vries, *Diamonds and War: State, Capital and Labor in British-Ruled Palestine* (Oxford: Berghahn Books, 2010).

4. Interview with David De Vries, "Why Did the Diamond Workers Strike So Often during World War Two?," 20.

5. Interview with David De Vries, "Why Did the Diamond Workers Strike So Often during World War Two?," 165.

6. Shafran, *Shalom Lekha Ḳomunizm*, 25.

7. Shafran, *Shalom Lekha Ḳomunizm*, 63.

8. Rachel Sharabi, "Tiksey Ḥag Ha'eḥad Bemay Ba'aśor Harishon Lamedina: Miḥag Seḳṭoryali Leḥag Mamlakhti" [May Day Rituals in the First Decade of Israel: From a Sectoral Holiday to a State Holiday], *Megamot* 44, no. 1 (2005): 108.

9. Nachman List, "Tsadaḳ Haḳominṭern [Alef]" [The Comintern Was Right A], *Keshet* 5-B Booklet B (1963): 147.

10. Bullas Farah, *Mehashilton Ha'othmani Lamedina Ha'ivrit: Sipur Ḥayav she Ḳomunist Vepaṭriyoṭ Palastini 1910–1991* [From Ottoman Rule to the Hebrew State: The Life Story of a Communist and Palestinian Patriot 1910–1991], trans. Udi Adiv (Haifa: 2009), 22.

11. "Hava'ad Hamerkazi shel Hamiflaga Haḳomunisṭit Be'erets-Isra'el, Berlin, April 1923" [The Central Committee of the Communist Party in Eretz-Israel, Berlin, April 1923], Lavon Institute for Labour Movement Research, IV-445-2.

12. May Day Manifesto of MPSA distributed in Jaffa, 1921, in Suliman Bashear, "The Arab East in Communist Theory and Political Practice, 1918–1928," PhD diss., Birbeck College, University of London, 1976.

13. T. Gozansky, *Ḳum Hitna'era!*, 142.

14. "Lano'ar Ha'oved shel Palesṭina! Ha'eḥad Be'May 1929!" [To the Working Youth of Palestine! May Day 1929!], Lavon Institute for Labour Movement Research, IV-445-208.

15. Avraham Myling, "Kaḥ Haya Alyusha" [So Was Alyosha], in *Ḳum Hitna'era! Eliyahu (Elyosha) Gojanski—Ktavav Ve'alav* [Arise, Ye Workers from Your Slumber: Life and Collected Works of Eliyahu (Alyosha) Gozansky] (Haifa: Pardes, 2009), 401.

16. "Lehishtatfut Beḥag Ha'eḥad Be'May" [For Participation in May Day Holiday], *Kol Ha'am*, April 10, 1946.

17. "Hamitsad shel Hamiflaga Haḳomunisṭit Be'Tel Aviv Likhvod Ha'eḥad Be'May" [The Communist Party March in Tel Aviv in Honor of May Day], *Kol Ha'am*, May 16, 1946.

18. "Hamitsad shel Hamiflaga Haḳomunisṭit Be'Tel Aviv Likhvod Ha'eḥad Be'May," *Kol Ha'am*, May 16, 1946.

19. "Sisma'ot Hamiflaga Haḳomunisṭit Hapaleśtina'it La'eḥad Be'May" [The Slogans of the Palestinian Communist Party for May Day], *Kol Ha'am*, April 26, 1946.

20. Sharabi, "Tiksey Ḥag Ha'eḥad Bemay Ba'aśor Harishon Lamedina," 115.

21. In photographs of the May Day demonstrations in 1959 and 1961 in Tel Aviv and Jerusalem, the older party members are seen marching holding banners in their hands in a loosely coordinated column or in groups. *Ma'araḥot ma'avak beyn shtey véidot, 1957–1961* [The Campaigns of Struggle between Two Conferences, 1957–1961], The Israeli Communist Party, 1961.

22. "May Day—The International Workers Day," author's archives.

23. For Yoska Valershtiean's personal history, see "Ani Ma'ashim et Adolf Ayḥman" [I Accuse Adolf Eichmann], *Kol Ha'am*, February 9, 1961; Yoska Valershtiean, interview by author, Tel Aviv, Israel, November 14, 2005.

24. Yoska Valershtiean, interview by author, Tel Aviv, Israel, November 14, 2005.

25. Daliya Vintrob and Manheam Vintrob, interview by author, Tel Aviv, Israel, May 29, 2005.

26. *Kol Hano'ar*, May–June 1960.

27. Markovizky, *Ḥultsa Levana Aniva Aduma*, 145.

28. The description of the incidents in Haifa and Tel Aviv is based on interviews with Zafrira Kelorman and Yoram and Tamar Gozansky. See Zafrira Kelorman, interview by author, Tel Aviv, Israel, November 6, 2005; Tamar Gozansky, interview by author, Tel Aviv, Israel, February 21, 2009; Yoram Gozansky, interview by author, Tel Aviv, Israel, February 22, 2009.

29. The term "dominant symbol" was defined by Victor and Edith Turner in *Image and Pilgrimage in Christian Culture* as "presiding over the whole procedure, sometimes over particular phases. Their meaning is highly constant and consistent throughout the symbolic system" (245).

30. May Day 1958 where two distinct rows of flags, the Red Flag and the national flag, respectively, can be seen. The photo is located in the personal archives of Yoram Gozansky.

31. A photo of Banki members dressed in keffiyehs, holding aloft the symbol of the movement, alongside Jewish Communist Party members of mixed gender. *Ma'araḥot ma'avak beyn shtey vé'idot, 1957–1961.*

32. Yoska Valershtiean, interview by author, Tel Aviv, Israel, November 14, 2005.

33. A Palestinian member of Banki is depicted in May Day 1959 wearing the Banki uniform and a keffiyeh, marching with the Red Flag in hand together with female Banki members. There is nothing traditional or exotic in his appearance, and other than the headscarf he is wearing European clothing. The garment is only used to proclaim his nationality. Yad Tabenkin Archives, File #18/2.

34. The photograph is located in the personal archives of Yoram Gozansky.

35. "Teḥi Ha'eḥad Be'May—Yom Hasolidariyut Habeynle'umit shel Hapo'alim Vehano'ar" [Long Live May Day—International Solidarity Day of the Workers and the Youth].

36. "No'ar! Ne'arim Vene'arot!" [Youths! Young Men Young Women!], Yad Tabenkin Archives, File #2.

37. "Ḥomer Lemesibot Eḥad Be'May Ve'arvey Ḳvutsot" [May Day Material for Parties and Group Evenings], Yad Tabenkin Archives, File #4.

38. "Ḥomer Lemesibot Eḥad Be'May Ve'arvey Ḳvutsot," Yad Tabenkin Archives, File #4.

39. "Maḥleḳet Ḥinukh Vetarbut: Ḥomer Lemesibot Eḥad Be'May" [The Department of Education and Culture: Material for May Day Parties], Yad Tabenkin Archives, File #4.

40. Alon Bney Amal, "Ha'eḥad Be'May 1962" [Bney Amal brochure, May Day 1962], Yad Tabenkin Archives, File #25.

41. Shafran, *Shalom Lekha Ḳomunizm*, 55–68.

42. Gai, *Masa Leyad-Ḥana*, 219.

43. Shafran, *Shalom Lekha Ḳomunizm*, 114.

44. Nissim Calderon, interview by author, Tel Aviv, Israel, March 3, 2009; Yoram Gozansky, interview by author, Tel Aviv, Israel, February 22, 2009.

45. Gai, *Masa Leyad-Ḥana*, 219.

46. Yair Tzaban, interview by author, Tel Aviv, Israel, February 12, 2009.

Chapter 5. Revolution and the Soviet Union among Israeli Communists

1. Zahavi, *Leḥud O Beyaḥad*, 51.

2. Zahavi, *Leḥud O Beyaḥad*, 399.

3. The term "philo-Soviet community" represents circles of people who for various reasons were sympathetic toward the Soviet Union without being MAKI members. It is a more flexible and less biased concept than the Cold War notions of fellow travelers or sympathizers. The philo-Soviet community changed after World War II. At first it included Socialist Zionists that identified with the Soviet war effort as well as Communists and even whole parties that supported the USSR, namely, MAPAM. From the mid-1950s, as the Socialist Zionists lost their illusions about the Soviet Union, it included people closer to MAKI. Nonetheless, it still included many unaffiliated leftists that were not party members.

4. "Tokhnit La'avoda Bano'ar, Detsember 1941" [A Plan for Activity among the Youth, December 1941], Yad Tabenkin Archives, File #3.

5. Ruth Lubitz, *Ḳoroteha shel Yedidut* [History of a Friendship] (Tel Aviv: Movement of Friendship Israel-USSR, 1984), 19.

6. The posters are from the Lavon Institute for Labour Movement Research, IV-519.

7. Banki and MAKI poster collection, "Im Ata Rotse Lishmoa" [If You Want to Hear], Yad Tabenkin Archives, File #17-18.

8. Porat, "Mahapkhanut Veṭerorizm Bemediniyut Hamiflaga Haḳomunisṭit Hafalestinait (Pekepe), 1929–1939," 255.

9. "Hatsava Ha'adom Baḳrav!" [The Red Army in Battle!], *Kol Ha'am*, August 1941.

10. "Hatsava Ha'adom Baḳrav!," *Kol Ha'am*, August 1941.

11. "Hadam Zo'ek min Ha'adama!" [The Blood Calls for Revenge!], *Kol Hano'ar*, October 1942.

12. "Milḥemet Hashiḥrur" [The War of Liberation], Lavon Institute for Labour Movement Research, IV-445-2.

13. "Matnat Hano'ar Latsava Ha'adom" [The Youths' Gift to the Red Army], Lavon Institute for Labour Movement Research, IV-445-2.

14. Lavon Institute for Labour Movement Research, IV-104-85-7.

15. "Ba'anu Le'Berlin im Ḥerev Bikhdey La'aḳor et ze La'ad Mi'Berlin" [We Came to Berlin by Sword in Order to Root It Out Forever from Berlin], *Kol Hano'ar*, May 1955.

16. "Have'ida Hale'umit shel Liga Vi" [National Conference of V League], *Davar*, July 13, 1945.

17. "Niṭa Ya'ar Hatsava Hasovyeti" [The 'Soviet Army Forest' Was Planted], *Davar*, June 23, 1945.

18. Photograph of the monument, *Kol Ha'am*, June 26, 1950.

19. "5,000 Anashim Nishba'im Lehagen al Hashalom" [5,000 People Swear to Defend Peace], *Kol Ha'am*, May 10, 1952.

20. In a photograph from the ceremony, Ḥaya Kadmon is seen reading her poetry on the main stage and a choir singing accompanied by a violin. *The Campaigns of Struggle between Two Conferences, 1957–1961* and Yad Tabenkin Archives, File #17-2.

21. "Alafim Hefginu Beya'ar Hatsava Hasovyeti" [Thousands Demonstrated in the Soviet Army Forest], *Kol Ha'am*, May 15, 1955.

22. Victor and Edith Turner, in *Image and Pilgrimage in Christian Culture*, describe the ritual pilgrimage process as forming a normative communitas: "Religious systems and pilgrimage systems are exemplars of normative communitas, each originating in a non-utilitarian experience of brotherhood and fellowship, which the participating group attempts to preserve, in and by its religious, moral and legal codes, and its religious and civil ceremonies" (135). The pilgrimage to the Red Army Forest exhibits the same characteristics, but in a secular system. As will be shown, the Communist pilgrimage created these feelings of sameness and brotherhood in order to reinforce Communist norms, in this case loyalty to the Soviet Union.

23. "Im Oley Haregel Leya'ar Hatsava Hasovyeti" [With the Pilgrims to the Soviet Army Forest], *Kol Ha'am*, May 13, 1955.

24. "Im Oley Haregel Leya'ar Hatsava Hasovyeti," *Kol Ha'am*, May 13, 1955.

25. "Aḥdut Lema'an Hanitsaḥon" [Unity for Victory], Yad Tabenkin Archives; Tamar Gozansky Tamar and Angelika Timm, eds., *Be'ad Haneged! Hamiflaga Haḳomunisṭit Ha'Isra'elit 1919–2009* [Against the Mainstream: The Communist Party of Israel (CPI) 1919–2009] (Tel Aviv: Rosa Luxemburg Foundation, 2009), 75; and "Congres Hayedidut Ha'Isra'elit Sovyeṭit" [The Israel-Soviet Union Friendship Congress], Yad Tabenkin Archives, File # 17-8. The joined flags symbol was so prevalent that it appeared on badges: "Teḥi Yedidut Isra'el Brit Hamo'atsot" [Long Live Israel-Soviet Union Friendship], Yad Tabenkin Archives.

26. *Bema'arakhot Hama'avaḳ beyn Ve'ida Leve'ida May 1952–May 1957* [The Campaigns of Struggle between Conference and Conference, May 1952–May 1957]. An invitation to a show on the fortieth anniversary of the revolution, where the monument is seen decorated with the two flags and the Red Star in an olive woodcut.

27. Dothan, *Adumim*, 48.

28. "Kol Asher Huśag al Yedey Mahapekhat Oḳṭober" [All That Was Achieved by the October Revolution], Lavon Institute for Labour Movement Research, File IV-445-2.

29. "Teḥi Hashvi'i Be'November, Yom Mahapekhat Oḳṭober Hasotsyalisṭit Hagdola" [Long Live the 7th of November, the Day of the Great October Socialist Revolution!], Lavon Institute for Labour Movement Research, IV-445-2.

30. "Teḥi Hashvi'i Be'November, Yom Mahapekhat Oḳṭober Hasotsyalisṭit Hagdola," Lavon Institute for Labour Movement Research, IV-445-2.

31. "Haḳomuna Haparisa'it" [The Paris Commune], Yad Tabenkin Archives, File #25.

32. "Mered Vina" [The Vienna Uprising], Yad Tabenkin Archives, File #25.

33. For a description of Milman, see Mordechay Avi-Shaul, *Mefaḳed Ivri Besfarad Haloḥemet: Ḳapitan Mordekhai Milman* [Mark Milman: Jewish Captain in Fighting Spain] (Tel Aviv: Author, 1945); "Spain," Yad Tabenkin Archives, File #3.

34. *averim Mesaprim al Jimy* [Friends Tell about Jimmy] (Jerusalem: Ariel, 1999).

35. Avi-Shaul, *Mefaḳed Ivri Besfarad Haloḥemet*, 10.

36. Avi-Shaul, *Mefaḳed Ivri Besfarad Haloḥemet*, 23.

37. "Shvi'i Be'November—Yom Hamahapekha Hagdola" [7 November—The Day of the Great Revolution], Yad Tabenkin Archives, File #3.

38. "Hanośe: Brit Hamo'atsot" [The Subject: The Soviet Union], Yad Tabenkin Archives, File #19.

39. "45 Shanim me'az Mahapekhat Oḳṭober" [45 Years since the October Revolution], Yad Tabenkin Archives.

40. "Oḳṭober 1917 Hamahapekha Hasotsyalisṭit Harishona" [October 1917 the First Socialist Revolution], Yad Tabenkin Archives.

41. Yair Tzaban admits that his doubts about the USSR began in the early 1960s, as the reality he had seen on his visits to the USSR did not accord with the more utopian and enthusiastic outlook of his younger days. Yair Tzaban, interview by author, Tel Aviv, Israel, February 12, 2009.

42. "Teḥi Hashvi'i Be'November Vehamoledet Hasotsyalisṭit Besakana!" [Long Live November 7th and the Socialist Motherland Is in Danger!], Lavon Institute for Labour Movement Research, IV-425-26, Tel Aviv, Israel.

43. Gozansky and Timm, *Be'ad Haneged!*, 77.

44. Gozansky and Timm, *Be'ad Haneged!*, 76.

45. Gozansky and Timm, *Be'ad Haneged!*, 79.

46. Nissim Calderon, interview by author, Tel Aviv, Israel, March 3, 2009.

47. Yoram Gozansky, interview by author, Tel Aviv, Israel, February 23, 2009.

48. Yair Tzaban, interview by author, Tel Aviv, Israel, February 12, 2009. Shoshana Shmuely, interview by author, Tel Aviv, Israel, February 22, 2009.

49. Shafran, *Farewell Communism*, 179.

Chapter 6. Arab-Jewish Fraternity: Language, Perception, Symbol, and Ritual

1. The term "ethnic cleansing" is well rooted in the historical works of Israel's revisionist historians. Both Benny Morris and Ilan Pappe argue that the idea of "transfer" of the Palestinian population outside of the Jewish state was embedded in Zionist ideology and practice. With the exception of MAPAM, transfer ideology was discussed among "the Jewish mainstream of the late 1930s and 1940s." Benny Morris, *Leydata shel Be'ayat Hapliṭim Hafalesṭinim 1947–1949* [The Birth of the Palestinian Refugee Problem, 1947–1949] (Tel Aviv: Am Oved, 1991), 44. Men like David Ben-Gurion, Yosef Weitz, and others were the ones who set the ideological principles that would evolve into the de-Arabization of Palestine. MAPAM may have objected to some acts of removal of Palestinians. However, that did not prevent kibbutzim affiliated with the party to take over lands of depopulated Palestinian villages; neither did they raise a strong voice of protest against the unfolding ethnic cleansing. Morris sets his portrayal in the context of the Yishuv's military needs, situating the de-Arabization of Palestine as part of a war and describing the deportations inspired by Yishuv's war masterplan, Plan D (*Dalet*). This plan, the formal plan drafted by the heads of the Haganah, was meant to be implemented after the withdrawal of the British forces from Palestine on May 15, 1948, but in actuality it was put into action in April 1948 (92–94). For Morris, the plan was driven primarily by military considerations, namely, the clearing of possible invasion routes by the Arab Armies to Palestine of a possibly hostile population. However—according to Morris—the plan was used by the Haganah and later the IDF field commanders as ideological-operational reasoning for mass deportations. The need not to leave a garrison in the villages that the Jewish forces occupied was translated into the removal of their inhabitants. However, the Jewish side's actions, mainly after 1948, were more deliberately aimed at clearing the territories the Haganah had occupied from their Palestinian population. Pappe, in contrast to Morris, sees it as a plain and simple blueprint for ethnic cleansing, built upon earlier contingency plans drafted by David Ben-Gurion and his associates since late 1946. Ilan Pappe, *The Ethnic Cleansing of Palestine* (London: Oneworld, 2006), 28. He is unequivocal in his depiction of the 1948 War as a classic case of ethnic cleansing, on a par with recent cases such as 1990s Yugoslavia. Pappe charts a straight line from Zionism's transfer ideology to its fulfillment during the war. The use of "ethnic cleansing"—admittedly a controversial concept—arises from the fundamental difference between the two scholars. Morris's account of the history of the 1948 War originates from a "realistic" understanding of the Zionist-Palestinian conflict. This approach brings to the fore geopolitical and military motivations as the prime movers of the historical process. Pappe pictures the historical process of 1947–1949 from a different point of view. He argues for a historiography that

analyzes its facts from a moralistic standpoint. For him the injustices brought upon the Palestinian people can be analyzed in the context of the term "ethnic cleansing," as developed in the post–World War II era. Both interpretations have, in my opinion, merit and are based on sound archival research and historical analysis. That being said, I am more inclined to Pappe's approach. History is not just the tale of diplomats, generals, and leaders making grand decisions—it is a morality play where we search for lessons that will inform us in creating a better future.

2. Markovizky, *Ḥultsa Levana Aniva Aduma*, 93.

3. Yair Tzaban, interview by author, Tel Aviv, Israel, February 12, 2009.

4. Yoram Gozansky, interview by author, Tel Aviv, Israel, February 23, 2009.

5. "Haproṭoḳol shel Pgishat Hava'ad Hapo'el shel Haḳominṭern 21.9.1920" [The Protocol of the Meeting of the Comintern Executive Committee 21.9.1920], in Zahavi, *Leḥud O Beyaḥad*, 26.

6. "Lepo'aley Paleśṭina" [To the Workers of Palestine], in Zahavi, *Leḥud O Beyaḥad*, 42.

7. Dothan, *Adumim*, 98.

8. "Havana beyn Ha'amim" [Understanding between the Peoples], Lavon Institute for Labour Movement Research, IV-445-2.

9. "Po'aley Kol Ha'olam Hitaḥedu" [Workers of All Lands Unite], Lavon Institute for Labour Movement Research, IV-445-2.

10. "The League for Arab-Jewish Understanding 'Hamet' August 1940."

11. "Tafḳid Hamiflaga Vehano'ar Haḳomunisṭi Barekhov Hafalaśṭini" [The Role of the Party and Communist Youth in the Palestinian Public], Lavon Institute for Labour Movement Research, IV-445-2.

12. Bullas Farah, in *From the Ottoman Rule to the Hebrew State*, described the new recruits to the party after 1936 as follows: "The comrades that came from the national movement with no fixed worldview and no clear ideology were only revolutionary patriots. It was not possible to see in them the social facet and they were not interested in social problems. Most of them came from the middle class. . . . They had only heard about Marxist ideology and the Soviet Union, but knew nothing about Marxism and the social, political, and social structure of the Soviet Union" (68). Budeiri, in *The Palestine Communist Party 1919–1948*, described the members of the Palestinian intelligentsia that were attracted to the party in the war years as "disillusioned with the traditional leaders and . . . drawn not so much by the party's advocacy of communism, but by its support of the Arab independence struggle, its modernity and methods of organization" and by "the identification of the party with the Soviet Union whose growing prowess in the war was attracting enthusiastic admirers among the educated youth" (97).

13. "Al Ha'ajenda, im Ha'iḥud" [On the Agenda, with the Unification], *Kol Ha'am*, October 22, 1948.

14. “Lamaginim! Lano’ar! Lehamoney Hayeshuv!” [To the Defenders! To the Youth! To the Masses of the Yishuv!], *Kol Ha’am*, April 26, 1948.

15. “Ve’idat Ha’iḥud Ha’internatsyonalisṭit shel Hamiflaga Haḳomunisṭit Ha’Isra’elit, Heyfa, 22.10.48” [The Internationalist Unification Convention of the Israeli Communist Party, Haifa, 22.10.48], “Ne’um Ptiḥa” [Opening Speech], *Kol Ha’am*, October 24, 1948.

16. “Ve’idat Ha’iḥud Ha’internatsyonalisṭi shel Hamiflaga Haḳomunisṭit Ha’Israelit, Heyfa, 22.10.48” [The Internationalist Unification Convention of the Israeli Communist Party, Haifa, 22.10.48], “Haderekh Lanitsaḥon” [The Road to Victory], *Kol Ha’am*, October 24, 1948.

17. “Brit Hano’ar Haḳomunisṭi Ha’Isra’eli, 13 Le’Yuni 1955” [The Israeli Young Communist League, June 13, 1955], Yad Tabenkin Archives.

18. “Tazkir Lava’ada shel Hamimshal Hatsva’i—Baṭlu et Hamimshal Hatsva’i! Mugash al Yedey Hava’ad Hamerkazi shel Hamiflaga Haḳomunisṭit Ha’Isra’elit, Yano’ar 1956” [Memo to the Committee for Military Government—Abolish the Military Government! Presented by the Central Committee of the Israeli Communist Party, January 1956], Yad Tabenkin Archives, File #20.

19. “Hadam Zo’eḳ min Ha’adama, 17 Be’November, 1957” [The Blood Cries Out from the Ground, November 17, 1957], Yad Tabenkin Archives.

20. “Ha’emet al Netseret, Tel Aviv, May 1958” [The Truth about Nazareth, Tel Aviv, May 1958], Yad Tabenkin Archives, File #17-18.

21. “Pniya Tsiburit Letalmidey Hatikhonim” [Public Appeal to the Secondary Students], Yad Tabenkin Archives.

22. “Lehavana bein Ha’amim” [“Understanding between the Peoples”], Lavon Institute for Labour Movement Research, IV-445-2.

23. “Al Ha’ajenda, im Ha’iḥud” [On the Agenda, with the Unification], *Kol Ha’am*, October 22, 1948.

24. Tami Michaeli, ed., *Ta’amula Veḥazon: Omanut Sovieṭit Ve’Isra’elit 1930–1955* [Propaganda and Vision: Soviet and Israeli Art 1930–1955] (Jerusalem: Israel Museum, 1997), 4.

25. Zeina Maasri, *Off the Wall: Political Posters of the Lebanese Civil War* (New York: I. B. Tauris, 2009).

26. “Hikonu Lefesṭival Hashalom Hale’umi shel Banki al Har Hakarmel, 28 Be’Sepṭember, 1951–2 Le’Oḳṭober 1951” [Be Ready for Banki’s National Peace Camp on Mount Carmel, September 28, 1951–October 2, 1951], Yad Tabenkin Archives.

27. Photograph from the archives of Yoram Gozansky, February 23, 2009.

28. Yad Tabenkin Archives, File #17-8.

29. “Alon Lamadrikh, Anu Veshkhenenu Ha’am Ha’aravi Ha’erets-Isra’eli” [Instructors’ Brochure, We and Our Neighbors the Arab Eretz-Israeli People], Yad Tabenkin Archives, File #24.

30. "Alon Lamadrikh, Anu Veshkhenenu Ha'am Ha'aravi Ha'erets-Isra'eli," Yad Tabenkin Archives, File #24.

31. "Alon Lamadrikh, Anu Veshkhenenu Ha'am Ha'aravi Ha'erets-Isra'eli," Yad Tabenkin Archives, File #24.

32. "Hafesṭival Hale'umi shel No'ar Yehudi Ve'arvi, Heyfa, 6–7 Be'Yuli 1962" [National Festival of Jewish and Arab Youth, Haifa, July 6–7, 1962], Yad Tabenkin Archives.

33. "Nosda Ha'aḥdut Ha'internatsyonalisṭit shel Hamiflaga Haḳomunisṭit Ha'Isra'elit" [The International Unity of the Israeli Communist Party Founded], *Kol Ha'am*, October 24, 1948.

34. Leah Babko, interview by author, Tel Aviv, Israel, February 12, 2009.

35. "Fesṭival Hayedidut" [The Festival of Friendship], Yad Tabenkin Archives, File #1.

36. "Fesṭival Hano'ar Hayehudi-Arvi" [The Jewish-Arab Youth Festival], *Kol Hano'ar*, April 1955.

37. *The Campaigns of Struggle between Conference and Conference, May 1952–May 1957.*

38. Gozansky and Timm, *Be'ad Haneged!*, 64.

39. Gozansky and Timm, *Be'ad Haneged!*, 66.

40. "Fesṭival Hano'ar Hayehudi-Arvi," *Kol Hano'ar*, April 1955.

41. "Fesṭival Hano'ar Hayehudi-Arvi," *Kol Hano'ar*, April 1955.

42. Gozansky and Timm, *Be'ad Haneged!*, 8.

43. Shimon Ballas, *Ḥeder Na'ul* [A Locked Room] (Tel Aviv: Zmora, Bitan, Modan, 1980), 123.

44. Dani Peter-Petrziel, interview by author, Tel Aviv, Israel, February 15, 2009.

45. "Yud Ḥet, Habusha" [Yodh Het, The Shame], *Kol Ha'am*, December 25, 1953.

46. "Yud Ḥet, Habusha," *Kol Ha'am*, December 25, 1953.

47. "Yud Ḥet, Habusha," *Kol Ha'am*, December 25, 1953.

48. Alexander Penn, "Hakfar Haḥarev" [Plundered Village], *Kol Ha'am*, August 15, 1958.

49. Alexander Penn, "Ima" [Mother], *Kol Ha'am*, August 15, 1958.

50. Alexander Penn, "Mi?" [Who?], *Kol Ha'am*, August 15, 1958.

Bibliography

Archives

Three archives hold most of the primary sources used in this book:

1. Yad Tabenkin—The Research and Documentation Center of the Kibbutz Movement, Ramat Efal, Israel. All numbered files are from the MKI-Banki Division. Files that are not numbered were randomly bundled, unspecified and unmarked, in the archives.
2. Lavon Institute for Labour Movement Research, Tel Aviv, Israel.
3. Israeli State Archives, Jerusalem, Israel.

Newspapers

Kol Ha'am
Kol Hano'ar
Davar
Ha'aretz
Ma'ariv

Books and Articles

Algazy, Yosef. "Milḥemet Ha'ezraḥim Hasfaradit Be'rei Hayitonut Ha'ivrit Be'eretz-Isra'el/Palestina" [The Spanish Civil War in the Hebrew Press in Eretz-Israel/Palestine]. In *Hafashizem Lo Ya'avor: Milḥemet Ha'ezraḥim Besfarad 1936–1939* [Fascism Shall Not Pass: The Spanish Civil War, 1936–1939. Tel Aviv: Zmora-Bitan, 2000.

Almog, Oz. "Andarṭot Leḥalaley Milḥama Be'Isra'el: Nitu'aḥ Semyology" [Monuments to the Fallen in Israel: A Semiotic Analysis]. *Megamot* 2 (1992): 179–210.

———. *Hatsabar—Dyuḳan* [The Sabra—A Profile]. Tel Aviv: Am Oved, 1997.

Åman, Andres. "Symbols and Rituals in the People's Democracies during the Cold War." In *Symbols of Power: The Esthetics of Political Legitimation in the Soviet Union and Eastern Europe*, edited by Claes Arvidsson and Lars Erik Blomqvist, 43–60. Stockholm: Almqvist & Wiksell International, 1987.

Avi-Shaul, Mordechay. *Mefaḳed Ivri Besfarad Haloḥemet: Ḳapitan Mordekhai Milman* [Mark Milman: Jewish Captain in Fighting Spain]. Tel Aviv: Author, 1945.

Aviv, Isaac. *Mahapekha Vemahapekha Shekeneged Bisfarad: Harepubliḳa Hashniya Vemilḥemet Ha'ezraḥim (1931–1939)* [Revolution and Counterrevolution in Spain: The Second Republic and the Civil War (1931–1939)]. Tel Aviv: Ministry of Defense, 1991.

Avizohar, Meir. *Ide'alim Ḥevratiyim Vele'umiyim Vehishtakfutam Be'olama shel Mapay: Mifleget Po'aley Erets-Isra'el Vebilti-Miflagtiyim 1930–1942* [National and Social Ideals as Reflected in Mapai: The Israeli Labor Party 1930–1942]. Tel Aviv: Am Oved, 1990.

Azaryahu, Maoz. "Ha'andarṭa Ha'Isra'elit: Mitos Omanut Vepoliṭiḳa" [The Israeli Monument: Myth, Art, and Politics]. *Studio* 37 (1995): 24–25.

———. *Pulḥaney Medina: Ḥagigot Ha'atsma'ut Vehantsaḥat Hanoflim Be'Isra'el* [State Cults: Celebrating Independence and Commemorating the Fallen in Israel 1948–1956]. Beer Sheva: Ben-Gurion University Press, 1995.

Ballas, Shimon. *Beguf Rishon* [First-Person Singular]. Benei Berak: Hakibbutz Hameuchad, 2009.

———. *Ḥeder Na'ul* [A Locked Room]. Tel Aviv: Zmora, Bitan, Modan, 1980.

Balti, Berl. *Bema'avak al Haḳiyum Hayehudi: Ledmuto shel Moshe Sneh* [The Struggle for Jewish Survival: A Portrait of Moshe Sneh]. Jerusalem: Y. Marcus, 1981.

Barkai, Ron. *Kmo Seret Mitsri* [Like an Egyptian Movie]. Tel Aviv: Xargol, 2001.

Bashear, Suliman. "The Arab East in Communist Theory and Political Practice, 1918–1928." PhD diss., Birkbeck College, University of London, 1976.

Beevor, Anthony. *The Battle for Spain: the Spanish Civil War 1936–1939*. New York: Penguin Books, 2006.

Beinin, Joel. "The Palestine Communist Party 1919–1948." *Middle East Research and Information Project* 55 (1977): 3–17.

———. *Was the Red Flag Flying There? Marxist Politics and the Arab-Israeli Conflict in Egypt and Israel, 1948–1965*. Berkeley: University of California Press, 1990.

Ben-Ami, Shlomo. *Sfarad beyn diḳṭaṭura ledemoḳratya 1936–1977* [Spain: From Dictatorship to Democracy 1936–1977). Tel Aviv: Am Oved, 1990.

Ben-Amos, Avner. "Bama'agal Haroked VeHamezamer: Ṭexṭim Veḥagigot Paṭriyoṭim Beḥevra Ha'Isra'el it" [In the Singing and Dancing Circle: Patriotic Rituals and Celebrations in Israeli Society]. In *Paṭriyoṭizem: Ohavim Otakh Moledet* [Patriotism: Homeland Love], edited by Avner Ben-Amos and Daniel Bar-Tal, 275–316. Tel Aviv: Tel Aviv University Press, 2004.

Ben-Porat, Amir. *Heykhan haburganim hahem? Toldot haburganut ha'isra'elit* [The Bourgeoisie: The History of the Israeli Bourgeoisie]. Jerusalem: Magnes Press, 1999.

———. *Keytsad na'asta isra'el kapitalistit* [How Israel Became a Capitalist Society]. Haifa: Pardes, 2011.

Ben-Zaken, Avner. *Ḳomunizm Ke'imperyalizm Ṭarbuti: Haziḳa beyn Haḳomunizm Ha'erets-Isra'eli Laḳomunizm Ha'aravi, 1919–1948* [Communism as Cultural Imperialism: The Affinities between Eretz-Israeli Communism and Arab Communism, 1919–1948). Tel Aviv: Resling, 2006.

Berman, Adolf-Abraham. *Bamaḳom asher Ya'ad li Hagoral: Im Yehudey Varsha, 1939–1942* [In the Place Where Fate Placed Me: With Warsaw's Jews, 1939–1942). Tel Aviv: Hakibbutz Hameuchad, 1978.

———. *Miyemey Hamaḥteret* [The Days of Jewish Resistance]. Tel Aviv: Hamenora, 1971.

Biran, Ya'ad. "Be'erets-Isra'el Asher al Havisla" [In Eretz-Israel That Is on the Vistula]. *Davḳa: Eretz Yidish Vetarbuta* [Davḳa: The Land of Yiddish and Its Culture] 7 (2010): 14–16.

Borochov, Dov Ber. *Ktavim Nivḥarim Kerekh 1* [Selected Works, First Volume]. Tel Aviv: Am Oved, 1944.

———. *Ktavim Kerekh Rishon* [Works, Vol. 1]. Tel Aviv: Hakibbutz Hameuchad, 1955.

———. *Ktavim Kerekh Shlishi* [Works, Vol. 3]. Tel Aviv: Hakibbutz Hameuchad, 1966.

Botman, Selma. *The Rise of Egyptian Communism, 1939–1970*. Syracuse: Syracuse University Press, 1988.

Brown, Archie. *The Rise and Fall of Communism*. New York: Harper Collins, 2012.

Brumberg, Abraham. "The Bund History of Schism." In *Jewish Politics in Eastern Europe: The Bund at 100*, edited by Jack Jacobs, 183–97. New York: New York University Press, 2001.

Brzoza, Chanoch. *Drakhim Rishonot* [Early Roads]. Tel Aviv: Am Hassefer, 1965.

Budeiri, Musa. "The Palestine Communist Party, Its Arabisation and the Arab Jewish Conflict in Palestine, 1929–1948." PhD diss., London School of Economics, 1977.

———. *The Palestine Communist Party 1919–1948: Arab and Jew in the Struggle for Internationalism*. London: Ithaca Press, 1979.

———. "Reflections on a Silenced History: The PCP and Internationalism." *Jerusalem Quarterly* 49 (2009): 69–78.

Centner, Israel. *MiMadrid ad Berlin* [From Madrid to Berlin]. Tel Aviv: Malan, 1966.

Czudnowski, Moshe, and Jacob Landau. *The Israeli Communist Party and the Elections for the Fifth Knesset, 1961*. Stanford: Hoover Institution on War, Revolution and Peace, 1965.

Defronzo, James. *Revolutions and Revolutionary Movements*. Boulder: Westview Press, 2011.

Devlin Kevin. "Communism in Israel: Anatomy of a Split." *Survey* 62 (1967): 141–51.

Don-Yehiya, Eliezer. "Ḥag Masorti Vemitos Le'umi: Ḥag Ḥanuka Vemitos Hamakabim Batsiyonut, Bayeshuv Uvimdinat Isra'el" [Traditional Holiday and National Myth: Hanukkah and the Myth of the Maccabees in Zionism, the Yishuv, and the State of Israel]. In *Between Tradition and Modernism*, edited by Eliezer Don-Yehiya, 581–610. Jerusalem: Bar-Ilan University Press, 1995.

———. "Hanukkah and the Myth of the Maccabees in the Zionist Ideology and in Israeli Society." *Jewish Journal of Sociology* 34, no. 1 (1992): 5–23.

Dothan, Shmuel. *Adumim: Hamiflaga Haḳomunistit Be'erets-Isra'el* [Reds: The Communist Party in Eretz-Israel]. Kfar Sava: Shvana Hasofer, 1991.

———. "The Jewish Section of the Palestine Communist Party, 1937–1939." In *Zionism: Studies in the History of the Zionist Movement and of the Jewish Community in Palestine*, edited by Daniel Carpi and Gedalia Yogev, 243–62. Tel Aviv: Massada, 1975.

———. "Reshito shel Ḳomunizem Le'umi Yehudi Be'eretz-Isra'el" [The Beginning of Jewish National Communism in Eretz-Israel]. *Hatsiyonut* 2 (1971): 208–36.

Doyle, William. *The French Revolution—A Very Short History*. Oxford: Oxford University Press.

Dror, Yuval. "Tnu'ot Hano'ar Be'veit Hasefer" [Youth Movements in the School]. In *Tnu'ot Hano'ar, 1920–1960* [Youth Movements, 1920–1960], edited by Mordechai Naor, 159–71. Jerusalem: Ben-Zvi Institute, 1989.

Dubnov, Simon. *Divrey Yemey Am Olam* [World History of the Jewish People Vols. 1–12]. Tel Aviv: Dvir, 1939.

Ebon, Martin. "Communist Tactics in Palestine." *The Middle East Journal* 2 (1948): 255–69.

Edelstein, Meir. "Lapilug Bemaki Beshnat 1965" [On the Split in MKI in 1965]. *Ma'asaf* 5 (1983): 146–95.

———. "The 1965 Split in Maki and CPSU." *Soviet Jewish Affairs* 3, no. 4 (1973–1974): 23–38.

Eshel, Nimrod. *Shvitat Hayamayim* [The Seamen's Strike]. Tel Aviv: Am Oved, 1994.

Ettinger, Shmuel. *Toldot Am Isra'el: Kerekh Shlishi Ba'et Haḥadasha* [History of the Jewish People: Volume 3 Modern Times). Tel Aviv: Dvir, 1969.

Farah, Bullas. *Mehashilton Ha'othmani Lamedina Ha'ivrit: Sipur Ḥayav she Ḳomunist Vepaṭriyoṭ Palastini 1910–1991* [From the Ottoman Rule to the Hebrew State: The Life Story of a Communist and Palestinian Patriot 1910–1991). Translated by Udi Adiv. Haifa: Udi Adiv, 2009.

Fast, Howard. *Aḥay, Giborey Hatehila* [My Glorious Brothers]. Bnei Brak: Hakibbutz Hameuchad, 2009.

Floers, Alexander. "The Arab CPs and the Palestine Problem." *Khamsin* 6, no. 9 (1979–1981): 21–40.

———. "Recent Studies on the History of the PCP." *Khamsin* 6, no. 9 (1979–1981): 41–51.

Floyd, David. *Russia in Revolt: 1905—The First Crack in Tsarist Power*. London: Macdonald & Co., 1969.

Franzén, Johan. "Communism versus Zionism: The Comintern, Yishuvism, and the Palestine Communist Party." *Journal of Palestine Studies* 36, no. 2 (2007): 6–24.

———. *Red Star over Iraq: Iraqi Communism before Saddam*. London: Hurst & Company, 2011.

Gai, Carmit. *Masa Leyad-Ḥana* [Back to Yad-Hannah]. Tel Aviv: Am Oved, 1992.

Gat, Rephael. "Tnu'ot Hano'ar shel Eretz Isra'el Ha'ovedet 1930–1945—Derekh Hithavutan Vemeoravutan Hapoliṭit" [The Socialist Youth Movements in Palestine, 1930–1945: The Emergence of the Movements and their Political Involvement]. PhD diss., Tel Aviv University, 1974.

Geertz, Clifford. "Centers, Kings, and Charisma: Reflections on the Symbolics of Power." In *Local Knowledge: Further Essays in Interpretive Anthropology*, edited by Clifford Geertz, 121–46. New York: Basic Books, 1983.

———. *The Interpretation of Cultures*. New York: Basic Books, 1973.

———. "Ritual and Social Change: A Javanese Example." *American Anthropologist* 59 (1957): 32–54.

Gojanski, Eliyahu. *Bema'arakhot Hama'amad Veha'am: Kovets Ma'amarim Vene'umim* [In the Battles of Class and Nation: Selected Articles and Speeches]. Tel Aviv: Central Committee of the Communist Party of Israel, 1959.

———. *Grodna* [Grodno]. Tel Aviv: Israeli Communist Party, 1979.

Goldberg, Giora. "Adaptation to Competitive Politics: The Case of Israeli Communism." *Studies in Comparative Communism* 14, no. 4 (1981): 331–51.

Gonen, Binyamin. *Ḥayim Adumim: Taḥanot Beḥayey Ḳomunisṭ Isra'eli* [Life in Red: Memories of an Israeli Communist]. Haifa: Pardes, 2009.

Gornick, Vivian. *The Romance of American Communism*. New York: Basic Books, 1977.

Gorny, Yosef. "The Historical Reality of Constructive Socialism." *Cathedra* 79 (1996): 182–91.

Gorny, Yosef, Avi Bareli, and Yitzhak Greenberg, eds. *Maḥberet Avoda Le'irgun Ovdim: Leket Ma'amarim al Histadrut Ha'ovdim Beyemey Hayeshuv Vehamedina* [The Histadrut from a Workers' Society to Trade Union: Selected Essays on the Histadrut]. Beer-Sheva: Ben-Gurion University Press, 2000.

Gozansky, Tamar, ed. *Ḳum Hitna'era! Eliyahu (Elyosha) Gojanski—Ktavav Ve'alav* [Arise, Ye Workers from Your Slumber: Life and Collected Works of Eliyahu (Alyosha) Gozansky]. Haifa: Pardes, 2009.

Gozansky, Tamar, and Angelika Timm, eds. *Be'ad Haneged! Hamiflaga Haḳomunisṭit Ha'Isra'elit 1919–2009* [Against the Mainstream: The Communist Party of Israel (CPI) 1919–2009]. Tel Aviv: Rosa Luxemburg Foundation, 2009.

Greenberg, Yitszhak. "The Standard Family Wage—Ideology, Illusion and Realism." *Cathedra* 79 (1996): 192–98.

Greenstein, Ran. "Class, Nation and Political Organization: The Anti-Zionist Left in Israel/Palestine." *International Labor and Working-Class History* 75 (2009): 85–108.

———. "A Palestinian Revolutionary: Jabra Nicola and the Radical Left." *Jerusalem Quarterly* 46 (2009): 32–48.

———. "Socialist Anti-Zionism: A Chapter in the History of the Israeli Radical Left." *Socialist History* 35 (2009): 20–39.

———. *Zionism and Its Discontents: A Century of Radical Dissent in Israel/Palestine*. London: Pluto Press, 2014.

Greilsammer, Alain. "Communism in Israel: 13 Years after the Split." *Survey* 23, no. 3 (1978): 172–90.

Halperin, Hagit. *Tseva Haḥayim: Ḥayav Veyetsirato shel Alexander Pen* [The Color of Life: The Life and Works of Alexander Penn]. Tel Aviv: Hakibbutz Hameuchad, 2007.

Halperin, Yechiel. *Isra'el Vehaḳomunizem: Mahapekhat Am Gola* [Israel and Communism: Revolution of an Exiled People]. Tel Aviv: Eretz-Israel Workers Party, 1951.

Ḥamishim Shana Lamiflaga Haḳomunisṭit Ba'aretz [Fifty Years of the Communist Party in Palestine/Israel]. Tel Aviv: Central Committee of the Communist Party of Israel, 1970.

Handelman, Don. *Models and Mirrors*. New York: Berghahn Books, 1998.

Harel, Isser. *Rigul Sovyeṭi: Ḳomunizem Berets-Isra'el* [Soviet Espionage: Communism in Israel]. Tel Aviv: Edanim, 1987.

Hargreaves, J. D. "The Comintern and Anti-Colonialism: New Research Opportunities." *African Affairs* 92 (1993): 255–61.

Hen-Tov, Jacob. *Communism and Zionism in Palestine: The Comintern and the Political Unrest in the 1920s*. Cambridge: Schenkman, 1974.

Horne, Gerald. "The Red and the Black: The Communist Party and African-Americans in Historical Perspective." In *New Studies in the Politics and Culture of U.S. Communism*, edited by Michael E. Brown, Randy Martin, Frank Rosengarten, and George Snedeker, 199–260. New York: Monthly Review Press, 1992.

Israeli, G. Z. *Maps-Peḳape-Maḳi: Hahisṭorya shel Hamiflaga Haḳomunisṭit Be'Erets-Isra'el* [MPS-PKP-MKI: The History of the Communist Party in Eretz-Israel]. Tel Aviv: Am Oved, 1953.

Jackson, Gabriel. *The Spanish Republic and the Civil War 1931–1936*. Princeton: Princeton University Press, 1967.

Jacobs, Jack, ed. *Jewish Politics in Eastern Europe: The Bund at 100*. New York: New York University Press, 2001.

———. "Creating a Bundist Counter-Culture: Morgenstern and the Significance of Cultural Hegemony." In *Jewish Politics in Eastern Europe: The Bund at 100*, edited by Jack Jacobs, 59–68. New York: New York University Press, 2001.

Jacobson, Abigail. " 'The National Liberation League' 1943–1948: An Alternative Political Discourse within Palestinian Society." MA thesis, Tel-Aviv University, 2000.

Kadmon, Haya. *Mivḥar Shirim* [Selected Poems]. Tel Aviv: Tarbut L'aam, 1971.

Kahane, Reuven, and Tamar Rapoport. *Ne'urim Vehaḳod Habilti-Formali* [Youth and the Code of Informality]. Jerusalem: Bialik Institute, 2007.

Karpel, Dalia. "Bemosḳva Ḳar'u La Yamina" [In Moscow They Called Her Yemina]. *Haaretz*, December 7, 2004.

Katkov, George, and Harold Shukman. *Lenin's Path to Power: Bolshevism and the Destiny of Russia*. London: Macdonald St Giles House, 1971.

Katz, Jacob. *Et Laḥḳor Ve'et Lehitbonen: Masa Hisṭorit al Darko shel Beyt Isra'el Me'az Tse'eto Me'artso ve'ad Shuvo Eleha* [A Time for Inquiry, a Time for Reflection: A Historical Essay on Israel through the Ages]. Jerusalem: Merkaz Zalman Shazar, 1998.

Kaufman, Ilana. *Arab National Communism in the Jewish State*. Jacksonville: University Press of Florida, 1997.

Kautsky, Karl. *Mishnato Hakalkalit shel Ḳarl Marks* [Kommunistische Bewegungen im Mittelalter]. Tel Aviv: Hakibbutz Hameuchad, 1956.

———. *Tnu'ot Ḳomunistiyot Beyemey-Habeynayim* [Karl Marx Ökonomische Lehren Gemeinverständlich Dargestelit Und Erläutert]. Merhavia: Sifriat Poalim, 1949.

Keeran, Roger. *The Communist Party and the Auto Workers Unions*. Bloomington: Indiana University Press, 1980.

Kelidar, Abbas. "Aziz al-Haj: A Communist Radical." In *The Integration of Modern Iraq*, edited by Abbas Kelidar, 183–92. London: Croom Helm, 1979.

Kelley, Robin D. G. *Hammer and Hoe: Alabama Communists during the Great Depression*. Chapel Hill: University of North Carolina Press, 1990.

Kemp-Welch, Anthony, ed. *Stalinism in Poland, 1944–1945: Selected Papers from the Fifth World Congress of Central and East European Saudis, Warsaw, 1995*. London: Macmillan Press, 1999.

Kenez, Peter. *Cinema and Soviet Society 1917–1953*. New York: Cambridge University Press, 1992.

Kershaw, Ian. *Fateful Choices: Ten Decisions that Changed the World, 1940–1941*. New York: Penguin Books, 2007.

———. *Hitler: Hubris: 1889–1936*. London: W. W. Norton and Company, 1998.

———. *Hitler: Nemesis: 1936–1945*. London: W. W. Norton and Company, 2000.

————. *The "Hitler Myth": Image and Reality in the Third Reich*. New York: Oxford University Press, 1987.

————. *The Nazi Dictatorship: Problems and Perspectives of Interpretation*. London: Edward Arnold, 1985.

Kessler, Mario. "The Bund and the Labour and Socialist International." In *Jewish Politics in Eastern Europe: The Bund at 100*, edited by Jack Jacobs, 112–30. New York: New York University Press, 2001.

————. "The Comintern and Left Po'ale Zion, 1919–1922." In *Be'ad Haneged! Hamiflaga Haḳomuniṣṭit Ha'Isra'elit 1919–2009* [Against the Mainstream! The Communist Party of Israel (CPI) 1919–2009], edited by Tamar Gozansky, 13–20. Tel Aviv: Rosa Luxemburg Foundation, 2009.

Khalidi, Rashid. *Palestinian Identity: The Construction of Modern National Consciousness*. New York: Columbia University Press, 1997.

Khenin, Dov, and Dani Filc. "Shvitat Hayamayim" [The Sailors' Strike]. *Te'orya Uviḳoret* [Theory and Criticism] 12 (1999): 89–98.

Kimmerling, Baruch. *Mehagrim, Mityashvim, Yelidim: Hamedina Vehaḥevra Be' Isra'el—beyn Ribuy Tarbuyot Lemilḥemot Tarbut* [Immigrants, Settlers, Natives: The Israeli State and Society—between Cultural Pluralism and Cultural Wars]. Tel Aviv: Am Oved, 2004.

Kimmerling, Baruch, and Joel Migdal. *Palestinayim: Am Behivatsruto* [Palestinians: The Making of a People]. Jerusalem: Keter, 1999.

Klehr, Harvey. *The Heyday of American Communism: The Depression Decade*. New York: Basic Books, 1984.

Koestler, Arthur. *Afela Batsaharayim* [Darkness at Noon]. Or Yehuda: Kinneret, Zmora-Bitan, Dvir, 2011.

Lagruo, Pieter. "Victims of Genocide and National Memory: Belgium, France and the Netherlands 1945–65." In *The World War Two Reader*, edited by Gordon Martel, 383–421. New York: Routledge, 2004.

Lamm, Zvi. *Tnu'at Hano'ar Hatsiyonit Bemabat Le'achor* [The Zionist Youth Movements in Retrospect]. Tel Aviv: Sifriat Polim, 1991.

Lane, Christel. *The Rites of Rulers: Ritual in Industrial Society—the Soviet Case*. Cambridge: Cambridge University Press, 1981.

Laqueur, Walter. *Communism and Nationalism in the Middle East*. New York: Frederick A. Praeger, 1956.

Largo, Pieter. "Victims of Genocide and National Memory: Belgium, France and the Netherlands 1945–65." In *The World War Two Reader*, edited by Gordon Martel, 383–421. New York: Routledge, 2004.

Lazarus-Yafeh, Hava. *Ha'islam* [Islam]. Tel Aviv: Ministry of Defense, 1980.

————. *Od Śiḥot al Dat Ha'islam* [Religious Thought and Practice in Islam]. Tel Aviv: Ministry of Defense, 1985.

Lefebvre, Henri. *Marksizm* [Le Marxisme]. Tel Aviv: Resling, 2005.

Lenin, V. I. *A Great Beginning: Heroism of the Workers in the Rear "Communist Subbotniks."* Peking: Foreign Languages Press, 1977.

———. *On Proletarian Culture*. Moscow: Novosti Press Agency, 1969.

———. *A Speech in the Third Komsomol Congress*. Tel Aviv: Central Committee of the Israeli Young Communist League, 1958.

Levin, Ruth. *Hayesharim Hayu Ita: Sfarad 1936–1939* [The Righteous War with Spain 1936–1939]. Tel Aviv: Ofakim, 1987.

———. *Viduy Me'uḥar* [A Belated Confession]. Tel Aviv: Yaron Gulan, 1995.

Liebman, Charles, and Eliezer Don-Yehiya. *Civil Religion in Israel*. Berkeley: University of California Press, 1983.

List, Nachman. "Gilguley Haḳomunizm Be'artsot Arav Uve'erets-Isra'el" [The Metamorphosis of Communism in the Arab States and Eretz-Israel] *Molad* 2, no. 9 (1969): 297–309.

———. "Tsadaḳ Haḳominṭern [Alef]" [The Comintern Was Right (A)]. *Keshet* 5-B (1963): 132–48.

———. "Tsadaḳ Haḳominṭern [Daled]" [The Comintern Was Right (D)]. *Keshet* 6-D (1964): 103–17.

———. "Tsadaḳ Haḳominṭern [Hey]" [The Comintern Was Right (E)]. *Keshet* 7-C (1965): 80–93.

Lockman, Zachary. *Comrades and Enemies: Arab and Jewish Workers in Palestine, 1906–1948*. Berkeley: University of California Press, 1995.

Lubitz, Ruth. *Baḥarti Liḥyot Bema'avak* [I Chose a Life of Struggle]. Tel Aviv: Hasher, 1985.

———. *Ḳoroteha shel Yedidut* [History of a Friendship]. Tel Aviv: Movement of Friendship Israel–USSR, 1984.

Maasri, Zeina. *Off the Wall: Political Posters of the Lebanese Civil War*. New York: I. B. Tauris, 2009.

Margalit, Elkana. *Anatomya shel Śmol: Po'aley Tsiyon Śmol Be'erets-Isra'el (1919–1946)* [The Anatomy of the Left: The Left Po'aley Zion in Eretz-Israel (1919–1946)]. Tel Aviv: L. L. Peretz, 1976.

———. *Hashomer Hatsayir: Me'edat Ne'urim Lemarksizm Mahapkhani* [Hashomer Hatza'ir: From Youth Community to Revolutionary Marxism]. Tel Aviv: Hakibbutz Hameuchad, 1971.

Markovizky, Jacob. "Hamirdaf Haḥar 'Ha'aḥim Ha'adumim': Haboleshet Habriṭit Vehapekape (1921–1933)" [The Chase after the 'Red Brothers': The British Secret Police and the PKP (1921–1933)]. *Iyunim Bitkumat Israel* 12 (2002): 289–303.

———. *Ḥultsa Levana Aniva Aduma* [White Shirt and Red Tie]. Tel Aviv: Hakibbutz Hameuchad, 2003.

———. "Ḳonspiratsya Ḳomunisṭit o Siyu'a La'aḥim: Giyus Habrigada Hachekhslovaḳit, 1948–1949" [Communist Conspiracy or Aiding the Brothers: Recruitment of the Czech Brigade, 1948–1949]. *Iyunim Betḳumat Israel* 6 (1996): 190–201.

Matthews, Weldon C. *Confronting an Empire, Constructing a Nation: Arab Nationalists and Popular Politics in Mandate Palestine*. London: I. B. Tauris, 2006.

McDougall, Alan. *Youth Politics in East Germany: The Free German Youth Movement 1946–1968*. Oxford: Clarendon Press, 2004.

McLellan, Josie. *Antifascism and Memory in East Germany: Remembering the International Brigades 1945–1989*. Oxford: Clarendon Press, 2004.

Michael, Sami. *Ḥasut* [Refuge]. Tel Aviv: Am Oved, 1997.

———. *Ḥofen shel Arafel* [A Handful of Fog]. Tel Aviv: Am Oved, 1979.

Michaeli, Tami, ed. *Ta'amula Veḥazon: Omanut Sovieṭit Ve'Isra'elit 1930–1955* [Propaganda and Vision: Soviet and Israeli Art 1930–1955]. Jerusalem: Israel Museum, 1997.

Mikunis, Samuel. *Besa'ar Tḳufot 1943–1969* [In the Storms of Our Times: Selected Articles and Speeches, 1943–1969]. Tel Aviv: Israeli Communist Party Central Committee, 1969.

Miron, Lea. *Kokhav Adom Bedegel Kaḥol-Lavan: Yaḥasa shel Hatnu'a Haḳomunisṭit Be'erets Latsiyonut Velamifal Hatsiyoni Betḳufat Hayeshuv ve'im Ḳom Hamedina* [A Red Star in the Israeli Flag]. Jerusalem: Magnes, 2011.

Mishler, Paul. *Raising Reds: The Young Pioneers, Radical Summer Camps, and Communist Political Culture in the United States*. New York: Columbia University Press, 1999.

Morris, Benny. *Leydata shel Be'ayat Hapliṭim Hafalesṭinim 1947–1949* [The Birth of the Palestinian Refugee Problem 1947–1949]. Tel Aviv: Am Oved, 1991.

———. *Milḥamot Hagvul shel Isra'el, 1949–1956: Hahistanenut Ha'aravit, Pe'ulot Hagmul Vehasfira Le'aḥor Lemivtsa Ḳadesh* [Israel's Border Wars, 1949–1956: Arab Infiltration, Israeli Retaliation and the Countdown to the Suez War]. Tel Aviv: Am Oved, 1996.

Mosse, George. *Fallen Soldiers: Reshaping the Memory of the World Wars*. New York: Oxford University Press, 1990.

———. *The Nationalization of the Masses*. Ithaca: Cornell University Press, 1975.

Myling, Avraham. "Ko Haya Alyusha" [So Was Alyosha]. In *Ḳum Hitna'era! Eliyahu (Elyosha) Gojanski—Ktavav Ve'alav* [Arise, Ye Workers from Your Slumber: Life and Collected Works of Eliyahu (Alyosha) Gozansky], edited by Tamar Gozansky, 401–04. Haifa: Pardes, 2009.

Nahas, Dunia. *The Israeli Communist Party*. New York: St. Martin's Press, 1976.

Naimark, Norman. *The Russians in Germany: A History of the Soviet Zone of Occupation, 1945–1949*. Cambridge: Harvard University Press, 1995.

Naisman, Mark. *Communists in Harlem: During the Depression*. New York: Grove Press, 1983.

Naor, Mordechai, ed. *Tnuot Hano'ar 1920–1960* [The Youth Movements 1920–1960]. Jerusalem: Ben-Zvi Institute, 1989.

Nisan, Shai. "The Palestinian Communist Party, 1936–1939." MA seminar paper, Hebrew University of Jerusalem, 2014.

Nothnagle, Alan. *Building the East German Myth: Historical Mythology and Youth Propaganda in the German Democratic Republic, 1945–1989.* Ann Arbor: University of Michigan Press, 1999.

Ofrat, Gideon. *Adama, Adam, Dam: Mitos Haḥaluts Vepulḥan Ha'adama Bemaḥazot hahityashvut* [Earth, Man, Blood: The Myth of the Pioneer and the Ritual of Earth in Eretz-Israel Settlement Drama]. Tel Aviv: Tcherikover, 1980.

Overy, Richard. *Russia's War.* London: Penguin Books, 1997.

Pappe, Ilan. *The Ethnic Cleansing of Palestine.* London: Oneworld, 2006.

Peled, Rina. *'Ha'adam Haḥadash' shel Hamahapekha Hatsiyonit: Hashomer Hatsa'ir Veshorashav Ha'eropeim* ["The New Man" of the Zionist Revolution: Hashomer Hatza'ir and Its European Roots]. Tel Aviv: Am Oved, 2002.

Peter-Petrziel, Dani. *Lev Betsad Śmol: al Ḥinukh Veḥevra* [Heart on the Left: On Education and Society]. Tel Aviv: Tcherikover, 2000.

———. *Lev Betsad Śmol: Kerekh Sheni* [Heart on the Left: Part Two]. Haifa: Pardes, 2008.

Phuong, Xuan. "Vietnam: On Her Attraction to Vietnamese Communism." In *The Communist Experience in the Twentieth Century: A Global History through Sources,* edited by Glennys Young, 21–26. New York: Oxford University Press, 2012.

Piterberg, Gabriel. *The Returns of Zionism: Myth, Politics and Scholarship in Israel.* London: Verso, 2008.

Porat, Yehosua. "Haliga Leshiḥrur Le'umi [Atsabat Et-Taḥrir El-Vaṭani]: Tḳumata, Mahuta Vehitparḳuta (1943–1948) [The National Liberation League: Its Rise, Essence and Fall (1943–1948)], *New East Quarterly of the Israel Oriental Society* 14 (1968): 354–66.

———. "Mahapkhanut Veṭerorizm Bemediniyut Hamiflaga Haḳomunisṭit Hafalestinait (Pekepe), 1929–1939" [Revolution and Terrorism in the Policy of the Palestine Communist Party (PKP), 1929–1939]. *The New East Quarterly of the Israel Oriental Society* 18 (1968): 255–67.

Reches, Eli. *Ha'aravi Be'Isra'el: beyn Ḳomunizm Lele'umiyut Arvit* [The Arab Minority in Israel: Between Communism and Arab Nationalism]. Tel Aviv: Hakibbutz Hameuchad, 1993.

———."Jews and Arabs in the Israeli Communist Party." In *Ethnicity, Pluralism and the State in the Middle East,* edited by Milton J. Esman and Itamar Rabinovich, 121–38. Ithaca: Cornell University Press, 1988.

———. "Leshe'elat Hayaḥasim beyn Yehudim Ve'arvim Bemaki" [On the Question of the Relation between Arabs and Jews in MAKI]. In *State Government and International Relationships,* edited by Gabriel Shaper, 67–95. Jerusalem: Bialik Institute, 1998.

———. "Yehudim Ve'arvim Bapekape—Sugiya Bahisṭoryografya Hafalasṭinit-Arvit Bat-Zmanenu" [Arabs and Jews in the PKP—An Issue in Contemporary

Arab-Palestinian Historiography]. In *Zionism: A Literary Collection of the History of the Zionist Movement and the Jewish Yishuv*, edited by Matitiyahu Mintz, 175–86. Tel Aviv: Hakibbutz Hameuchad, 1990.

Rein, Raanan, ed. *Hafashizem Lo Ya'avor: Milḥemet Ha'ezraḥim Besfarad 1936–1939* [They Shall Not Pass: The Spanish Civil War 1936–1939]. Tel Aviv: Zmora-Bitan, 2000.

Rosenberg, Julius, and Ethel Rosenberg. *Mikhtavim Mibeyt-Hamavet* [Letters from the Death House]. Tel Aviv: Hakibbutz Hameuchad, 1953.

Rubenstein, Annette T. "The Cultural World of the Communist Party and African-Americans in Historical Perspective." In *New Studies in the Politics and Culture of U.S. Communism*, edited by Michael E. Brown, Randy Martin, Frank Rosengarten, and George Snedeker, 239–60. New York: Monthly Review Press, 1993.

Rubenstein, Sondra. *The Communist Movement in Palestine and Israel, 1919–1984*. Boulder: Westview Press, 1985.

Sadeh, Yitzhak. *MisAviv Lamedura* [Around the Campfire]. Tel Aviv: Hakibbutz Hameuchad, 1953.

Said, Edward. *Orientalism*. New York: Vintage Books, 1978.

———. *The Question of Palestine*. New York: Vintage Books, 1992.

Sandler, Shmuel. "Ben-Gurion's Attitude Towards the Soviet Union." *Jewish Journal of Sociology* 21, no. 2 (1979): 149–60.

Sartori, Rosalinde. "Stalinism and Carnival: Organization and Aesthetics of Political Holidays." In *The Culture of the Stalin Period*, edited by Hans Günther, 41–47. New York: St. Martin's Press, 1990.

Schatzker, Haim. "Tnu'at Hano'ar Hayehudit Begermanya beyn Hashanim 1900–1933" [The Jewish Youth Movement in Germany between the Years 1900–1933]. PhD diss., Hebrew University, 1969.

Schloss, Ruth. *Rut Shlos: Edut Meḳomit* [Ruth Schloss: Local Testimony]. Ein Harod: Ein Harod Museum of Art, 2006.

Segev, Tom. *Hamilyon Hashvi'i: Ha Yisra'elim Vehasho'a* [The Seventh Million: The Israelis and the Holocaust]. Jerusalem: Keter, 1991.

Service, Robert. *Comrades: Communism—A World History*. London: Pan Books, 2007.

Shafir, Gershon. *Land, Labor and the Origins of the Israeli-Palestinian Conflict 1882–1914*. Berkeley: University of California Press, 1989.

Shafran, Nessia. *Shalom Lekha Ḳomunizm* [Farewell Communism]. Tel Aviv: Hakibbutz Hameuchad, 1983.

Shamir, Moshe. *Bemo Yadav: Pirkey Eliḳ* [With His Own Hands: Elik's Story]. Tel Aviv: Siffriath Polalim, 1965.

———. *Melekh Baśar Vadam* [The King of Flesh and Blood]. Tel Aviv: Am Oved, 1983.

Shapira, Anita. "Hasmol Begdud Ha'avoda Vehapekape ad 1928" [The Left in the Labor Brigades and the P.K.P. until 1928]. *Hatsiyonut* 2 (1971): 148–68.

———. "Sternhell's Complaint." In *Yehudim Ḥadashim Yehudim Yeshanim* [New Jews Old Jews], edited by Anita Shapira, 298–317. Tel Aviv: Am Oved, 1997.

Shalev, Michael. "Time for Theory." *Theory and Criticism* 8 (1996): 225–37.

Shapiro, Yonathan. *Aḥdut-Haavoda Hahisṭorit: Atsmauto shel Irgun Poliṭi* [The Organization of Power]. Tel Aviv: Am Oved, 1975.

Sharabi, Rachel. "Tiksey Ḥag Ha'eḥad Bemay Ba'aśor Harishon Lamedina: Miḥag Seḳṭoryali Leḥag Mamlakhti" [May Day Rituals in the First Decade of Israel: From a Sectoral Holiday to a State Holiday]. *Megamot* 44, no. 1 (2005): 106–36.

Siam, Abu. "The First May Day in Palestine." In *Inprecor* [Marxist magazine of the Third International]. May 27, 1926.

Slann, Martin. "Ideology and Ethnicity in Israel's Two Communist Parties: The Conflict between Maki and Rakah." *Studies in Comparative Communism* 7, no. 4 (1974): 359–74.

Slozski, Yehuda. "Mimapsa Ad Yaḳap (Peḳepe)" [From MPS to YKP (PKP)]. *Asufot*, 16 (1972): 3–18.

———. "Mimapsa Beve'idat Hayesod Shel Ha'Histadrut" [MPSA in the Founding Convention of the Histadrut]. *Asufot* 14 (1970): 133–62.

Sneh, Moshe. *Sikumim Bashe'ela Haleumit: Le'or Hamrksizem-Leninizem* [On the National Question: Conclusions in the Light of Marxism-Leninism]. Tel Aviv: Left Socialist Party, 1954.

Somekh, Sasson. "Erev—Aruḥat Ere vim Alexander Pen" [Evening—Dinner with Alexander Penn]. *Haaretz*, January 8, 2007.

Spiegel, Yair. "Sokhnim shel 'Hamaḥlaḳa Leḥaḳirot Pliliyot' (CID) Bamiflaga Haḳomunisṭit Ha'eretz Isra'elit" [Agents of the Criminal Investigative Department (CID) in the Eretz-Israeli Communist Party]. *Iyunim Betkumat Isra'el* 12 (2002): 271–88.

Stalin, Joseph. *Marxism and the National Question*. Moscow: Foreign Languages, 1945.

Stauber, Roni. *Haleḳaḥ Lador: Sho'a Vegvura Bamaḥshava Hatsiburit Baret Beshnot Haḥamishim* [Lessons for This Generation: Holocaust and Heroism in Israeli Public Discourse in the 1950s]. Jerusalem: Yad Ben-Zvi Press, 2000.

Steppenbacker, James. "The Palestine Communist Party from 1919–1939: A Study of the Subaltern Centers of Power in Mandate Palestine." MA thesis, Ohio State University, 2009.

Sternhell, Zeev. *Binyan Uma O Tiḳun Ḥevra?* [Nation-Building or a New Society?]. Tel Aviv: Am Oved, 1995.

———. "Zionist Historiography between Myth and Reality." *Cathedra* 80 (1996): 209–24.

Stites, Richard. "The Origins of Soviet Ritual Style: Symbol and Festival in the Russian Revolution." In *Symbols of Power: The Esthetics of Political Legitimation in the Soviet Union and Eastern Europe*, edited by Claes Arvidsson and Lars Erik Blomqvist, 23–42. Stockholm: Almqvist & Bissell International, 1987.

———. *Revolutionary Dreams: Utopian Vision and Experimental Life in the Russian Revolution*. New York: Oxford University Press, 1989.

Tamari, Slaim. "Najati Sidqui (1905–79): The Enigmatic Jerusalem Bolshevik." *Journal of Palestine Studies* 32, no. 2 (2003): 79–94.

Thomas, Hugh. *The Spanish Civil War*. Middlesex: Penguin Books, 1986.

Toubi, Taufik. *Bedarko* [In His Way]. Haifa: Raya, 2012.

Touma, Emile. *Hatnu'a Hale'umit Hafalasṭinit Veha'olam Ha'arvi* [The Palestinian National Movement and the Arab World]. Tel Aviv: Mifras Books, 1990.

Trachtman-Falhan, Leah. *MiTel Aviv Lemoskva (Zikhronot Yaldut)* [From Tel Aviv to Moscow (Childhood Memoirs)]. Tel Aviv: Saar and Author, 1989.

Trepper, Leopold. *Hatizmoret Ha'aduma Sheli: Zikhronotav shel Rosh Hatizmoret Ha'aduma* [My Red Orchestra: The Memories of the Head of the Red Orchestra]. Jerusalem: Edanim, 1975.

Turner, Victor. *The Ritual Process: Structure and Anti-Structure*. Ithaca: Cornell University Press, 1969.

———. "Symbols in the Ndembu Ritual." In *The Forest of Symbols: Aspects of Ndembu Ritual*, edited by Victor Turner, 19–47. Ithaca: Cornell University Press, 1967.

Turner, Victor, and Edith Turner. *Image and Pilgrimage in Christian Culture: Anthropological Perspectives*. New York: Columbia University Press, 1978.

Tzor, Muki, and Yuval Danieli, eds. *Yotsim Beḥodesh Ha'Aviv: Pesaḥ Erets-Isra'eli Bahagadot min Haḳibuts* [The Kibbutz Haggadah: Israeli Pesach in the Kibbutz]. Jerusalem: Keter, 2004.

Tzur, Eli. "The Silent Pact: Anti-Communist Cooperation between the Jewish Leadership and the British Administration in Palestine." *Middle Eastern Studies* 35, no. 2 (1999): 103–31.

Vilenska, Esther. *Arakhim Vema'arakhot* [Value Concepts and Class Struggles]. Tel Aviv: Hedim, 1977.

———. *Ha'internatsyonal Hasotsyalisṭi Vehithavut Haḳominṭern* [The Socialist International and the Formation of the Comintern]. Tel Aviv: Am Oved, 1974.

———. *Hashe'ela Hale'umit: Bahalakha Vebama'aśe* [The National Question in Bolshevik Theory and Practice]. Tel Aviv: Hedim, 1977.

———. *Pirḳey Ḥa'im* [Chapters from My Life]. Tel Aviv: Keren, 1984.

Vilner, Meir. "Ḥamishim Shana Lamiflaga Haḳomunisṭit Ba'aretz" [50 Years of Our Communist Party Struggle]. In *50 Shana Lamiflaga Haḳomunisṭit Ba'aretz* [Fifty Years of the Communist Party in Palestine/Israel]. Tel Aviv: Central Committee Communist Party of Israel, 1970.

Von Geldern, James. *Bolshevik Festivals, 1917–1920*. Berkeley: University of California Press, 1993.

Weitz, Eric. *Creating German Communism 1890–1990: From Popular Protests to Socialist State*. Princeton: Princeton University Press, 1997.

Weitz, Yechiam. "Beheksher Politi: Hamemad Hapoliti shel Zikhron Hasho'a Beshnot Haḥamishim" [Political Context: The Political Dimension of Holocaust Memory in the 1950s]. *Iyunim Bitkumat Isra'el* 1 (1996): 271–87.

———. "Haḥok Le'aśiyat Din Banatsim Vebeozrehem Veyaḥasa shel Haḥevra Ha'Isra'elit Bishnot Haḥamishim Lasho'a Velenitsoleha" [The Law to Bring to Justice the Nazis and Their Collaborators and Israeli Society's Attitude toward the Holocaust and Survivors in the Fifties], *Cathedra* 82 (1996): 153–64.

———. "The Political Dimensions of Holocaust Memory in Israel during the 1950s." In *The Shaping of Israeli Identity: Myth, Memory and Trauma*, edited by Robert Wistrich and David Ohana, 129–45. London: Frank Cass, 1995.

Wilentz, Sean, ed. *Rites of Power: Symbolism, Ritual and Politics since the Middle Ages*. Philadelphia: University of Pennsylvania Press, 1985.

Yaari, Arieh. "Without Alternative: Examining Zeev Sternhell's Presumptions." *Iyunim Betkumat Israel* 6 (1996): 586–91.

Young, Glennys. *The Communist Experience in the Twentieth Century: A Global History through Sources*. New York: Oxford University Press, 2012.

Young, James E. "When a Day Remembers: A Performative History of *Yom ha-Shoah*." *History and Memory* 2 (1990): 54–75.

Zahavi, Leon. *Lehud O Beyahad: Yehudim Ve'aravim Bemismakhey Hakomintern 1919–1943* [Apart or Together: Jews and Arabs in Palestine according to Documents of the Comintern 1919–1943]. Jerusalem: Keter, 2005.

Zerubavel, Yael. *Recovered Roots: Collective Memory and the Making of Israeli National Tradition*. Chicago: University of Chicago Press, 1995.

Websites

Adiv, Udi. "Toldot Hapekape Bere'i Sifro shel Bullas Farah" [The History of the PKP as Reflected in Bullas Farah's Book]. *Hagada Hasmolit—The Left Bank: Critical Forum for Society and Culture*. http://hagada.org.il/2009/09/05. Accessed September 5, 2009.

Davidi, Efraim. "Gvulot Hazikaron: beyn Historya Lepolitika" [The Limits of Memory: Between History and Politics]. *Hagada Hasmolit—The Left Bank: Critical Forum for Society and Culture*. http://hagada.org.il/2009/10/14/. Accessed October 14, 2009.

Gonen, Binyamin. "Al Tafkido shel Emil Touma Behakamat Maki" [The Role of Emile Touma in Founding MKI]. *Hagada Hasmolit—The Left Bank: Critical*

Forum for Society and Culture. http://hagada.org.il/2009/09/09. Accessed September 9, 2009.

———. *Ktsat historiya lama'avak hanoḥeḥi ve'ha'atidi bahistadrut* [A Little History of the Present and Future Struggle at the Histadrut]. http://hagada.org.il/2006/12/04/. Accessed December 4, 2006.

———. "90 Shana Lahistadrut: Haḳomunisṭim Vehama'avakim Hama'amadi'im" [90 Years to the Histadrut: The Communists and Class Struggles]. *Hagada Hasmolit—The Left Bank: Critical Forum for Society and Culture*. http://hagada.org.il/2010/12/26. Accessed December 26, 2010.

Films

Madrid lifney Ḥanita [Madrid before Hanita]. Directed by Eran Torbiner. Israel, 2006. DVD.

Bunda'im [Bunda'im]. Directed by Eran Torbiner. Tel Aviv, Israel, 2011. DVD.

Haḳomunisṭim Ha'aḥronim [The Last Communists]. Directed by Eran Torbiner. Israeli Channel One. Israel, 2010. https://www.youtube.com/watch?v=3bE6uhKxmYU.

Index